Eccezion
Team #1 Chef
6/25

Chef John Bogan

Recipes From The Seasons Of My Life

Lake Geneva School of Cooking, LLC
727 Geneva Street
Lake Geneva, WI 53147
www.lakegenevaschoolofcooking.com

Copyright 2020 John Bogan

All rights reserved. No part of this publication may be reproduced or transmitted in any form or by any means, electronic or mechanical, including photocopying and recording, or by any information storage and retrieval system without written permission from the publisher.

Chef John Bogan: Recipes From The Seasons Of My Life
www.lakegenevaschoolofcooking.com

ISBN: 978-0-615-81293-9

Printed in United States

AUTHOR: Chef John Bogan
PROJECT DESIGN DIRECTOR: Mackenna Bogan
PHOTOGRAPHER: Ryan Bensheimer
OTHER PHOTOS PROVIDED BY: Holly Leitner
GRAPHIC DESIGN: Nei-Turner Media Group, Inc.
RECIPE TASTER: Kim Marks and the Prairie View Residents

ON THE COVER: Chef John Bogan at The Riviera, Lake Geneva, Wisconsin

Published by Nei-Turner Media Group, Inc.
400 Broad Street, Lake Geneva, WI 53147
ntmediagroup.com

Personal Dedication

I would like to personally dedicate this book to my father, Lawrence "Larry" Bogan, and the memory of my mother, Teresa.

Professional Dedication

I would like to professionally dedicate this book to the memory of Don "Hollywood" Smith and the Great Jean Banchet.

From left: Chef Don "Hollywood" Smith, the Great Chef Jean Banchet, and Chef John Bogan

From left: Briana Kaiulani Lee and Mackenna Anuhea Teresa

Contents

Personal Foreword   6

Professional Foreword   9

In Appreciation   11

Introduction   13

Signature Popovers   17

Spring   23

Hawaiian Ohana   53

Summer   73

Farm Fresh   103

Fall   121

Signature Sausage Making   149

Winter   165

Appendix   193

Index   208

Personal Foreword

Chef John brings people together and connects them in a very joyful way. There is always an aura of celebration and passion around him. He creates interest, excitement, and energy whether leading a cooking class, working with young chefs, catering an event, supporting a local charity, or just spending time in the kitchen with family and friends. Chef John is a natural mentor, instructor, and motivator.

I have been fortunate enough to experience these qualities since our chance meeting when Chef John Bogan was only known as "John" or "Buzz Bogan" to his friends. We were both culinary students at Johnson and Wales University in Providence, Rhode Island in the 1980s and we had just completed our first two years of classes, receiving our Associate's degrees in Culinary Arts. We each decided to return the following year to continue our education, working towards Bachelor's degrees in Food Service Management.

I had spread the word through my network of friends that I was looking for a roommate in Federal Hill, the "Little Italy" of Providence. We were days away from the school year starting when I got a call from John. We arranged to meet, and to my surprise, he arrived on his motorcycle, complete with a leather jacket and dark shades. This was his standard style before becoming known for his immaculately pressed chef's coat and tall white toque. Despite a bit of uncertainty, I agreed to live with him.

At first, I couldn't imagine John and I having anything in common other than culinary school. I was from Boston, Massachusetts, and grew up in a typical middle-class, Italian-American family where festive meals with "La Famiglia" included large platters of pasta and traditional Sicilian dishes. For me, food and family were very important and both were at the center of my everyday life and special occasions.

John was from a large Irish-American family and grew up in the rural farmlands of Upstate New York. The Bogan "Clan" grew all types of vegetables and raised farm animals. Although this was different from my childhood, it was a great benefit of living with John, as care packages of pickles, cheeses, and baked goods would arrive from his home. My favorite was always his mother's bread and butter pickles and local Herkimer cheddar cheese. As you can imagine, this was all very foreign for a twenty year old from the suburbs, who had only visited a farm during a grammar school field trip.

Despite all the differences, it wasn't long until we started to realize our connection. Our love for food, family, and celebrations was the common bond that made us friends and has kept us "family" for the past 40 years. Over the years, there have been many special moments and memories we have shared, including graduations, careers moves, weddings, births, baptisms, and the passing of family and friends. Of course, they all involved special meals coordinated and executed by the two of us working together, but always influenced by Chef John's infectious personality and "can do, make it happen" mindset. John has the ability to not let small worries get in the way of the big picture. He believes in working hard and taking time to share and enjoy life. This quality is the secret to his success and has served him, and those around him, well.

The first example of his success was our work together at the Trattoria D'Antuono, on Federal Hill. I was the cook of this new Italian restaurant when the opening chef unexpectedly left. The owners, Frank and Jean, asked me to take over and bring in a friend to help. That friend was, of course, John. With our young creativity, ambition, and commitment, the restaurant became a huge success. There were lines out the door, glowing reviews, local celebrities dining, and a long list of regulars. All of this caught the attention of our school and administration would often bring in guests to show off two of their students. Our signature dish at the Trattoria D'Antuono was the Pan Fried Calamari and that recipe is featured in this book.

Chef Mark Sapienza

After graduation, John and I both left Rhode Island to start our own careers. John started with a national restaurant group, and I went back to Massachusetts to work in Boston. As fate would have it, after John's training, he was assigned to one of the company's signature properties, The Top of the Hub in Boston. I was working at the Sheraton Hotel and Towers in the same complex. We found ourselves, once again, sharing an apartment and continuing our lifelong friendship. As time passed, our careers grew and we both moved on to new and exciting opportunities. John moved to Chicago, where he not only found success and recognition as an Executive Chef, but also met his wife, Jacque, and started a family. He has two beautiful daughters, Briana and Mackenna, and I am a proud Godfather to both.

I moved to Palm Beach, the first stop of positions along the East Coast and Europe where I continued my career in luxury hotels and eventually ended up back in Boston. Even with the distance between us, we remained close—visiting each other as often as possible and creating a large network of extended family and friends, or "Ohana" as John would say. His connection and love for the Hawaiian islands is showcased in several of his signature dishes, such as Jacque's Kona Crusted Chateaubriand or Shrimp Briana Kaiulani.

As you read this cookbook, remember the importance of family and friends. Enjoy cooking, eating, and sharing these recipes from the "Seasons" of Chef John's life. Don't let life's small challenges get in the way, celebrate, and welcome to one great Clan, La Famiglia, Ohana. —Chef Mark Sapienza.

Mark Sapienza's professional career as a culinary leader spans over 35 years in luxury hotels, including properties in Palm Beach, Florida; Montauk, and Westchester, New York; London, England; Hong Kong; and his hometown of Boston, Massachusetts. He was invited to participate in the "Best Hotel Chefs in America" dinner series presenting his talents at the James Beard House in New York City. Additionally, he has hosted two James Beard regional "Taste of America Dinners" coordinating with awarded celebrity chefs. He also served as Executive Chef for the French government presentation of the Legion of Honor award to Julia Child, working with her longtime friend Jacques Pepin. Chef Mark has been recognized for his charitable contributions, support for the sustainable practices, and the mentorship and promotion of the culinary arts. He is a member of the American Culinary Federation and Les Amis d'Escoffier Society.

Chef Russ Tronsen

Dominic Trumfio

Professional Foreword

In the spring of 2004, I first met Chef John at an American Culinary Federation–Geneva Lakes Chapter (ACF-GLC) end of year celebration at The French Country Inn. I was invited to attend as a guest along with two other Chef Members; Joe Rodriguez and David Ross. This event was where I forged a long lasting relationship and friendship with Chef John Bogan. For those that know Chef John, he is all about hospitality both professionally and personally. He instantly makes people feel welcome and treats them like he would treat a family member. At this event, he threw one heck of a celebration (more like a party) that got me hooked, and I signed up to become a member of the ACF-GLC that night.

Through becoming a member, I got to be a part of the culinary pulse in the Geneva Lakes area. Chef John, a staple in the area, has always been known to invest in the future of the profession. He takes young culinarians and teaches them the skills needed to be a professional culinarian. Through my relationship with the ACF-GLC, I had the honor to participate in several events hosted each year that supported the organization and many local charitable organizations. I was able to have my students participate in these events and work alongside these great local chefs. Many of my students have fond memories of working with Chef John because of his welcoming, energetic, and electric personality. Some enjoyed it so much that they eventually became employees at the Lake Geneva School of Cooking.

John has been a long-time supporter of the Badger High School ProStart Culinary Program. Whether he had students of mine working for him or not, he has been a loyal and dedicated supporter of the program. This leads us up to the formation of the Geneva Lakes Burger Throwdown.

Back in the winter of 2011, a group of four people sat down at the Lake Geneva School of Cooking one night and created something nobody could have ever anticipated it would become what it has today. The idea was brought to us by Todd Wilkins, who at the time was representing Consumers Meat Packing Company. He was looking to grow visibility with the brand in the Geneva Lakes Area. He wanted to host an event where chefs could create a custom burger for a throwdown and have people pay to attend and sample the burgers. Money raised would support the local Badger High School culinary program.

Chef John, Todd Baior, Todd Wilkins, and myself created the event and it instantly became a hit in the Geneva Lakes area. The event has sold out year after year, drawing over 1,000 guests annually. Chef John has been on the planning team since its inception and is the emcee and judges coordinator each year. We even named the People's Choice Trophy the "Bogan Cup" in honor of Chef John's commitment to the culinary scene and support of the future of this profession. We affectionately refer to it as our own version of the Stanley Cup. When not in possession of the current winner, the trophy sits front and center in the kitchen of the Lake Geneva School of Cooking, where Chef John uses it to promote our annual event. Each Spring before the event is held, we do the Bogan Cup Tour. Chef John has one of his staff, Chef Jake, escort the trophy around the area while wearing white gloves, and we visit the establishments of teams that will compete to create excitement for the event. This is another example of how Chef John builds camaraderie and strength within the culinary community.

In my 15-plus years of knowing Chef John, he has always been a person I admire for his professionalism and the way he treats all people. He treats his employees and guests like family from the moment you first meet him. He has hosted my students and staff in his school of cooking and they all leave with smiles on their faces and their stomachs more than satisfied. He even has dance parties with his guests at the conclusion of a night at the school of cooking—disco lights and all! As you partake in this very special cookbook, you will feel the love for his work and will hopefully feel a part of his culinary family too. —Russ Tronsen

Russ Tronsen, was the Badger High School Culinary ProStart Instructor (2001-2015) and ACF-GLC Chapter member. He built the culinary program at Badger High School, which over his tenure, was highly recognized and respected within the state and nation. Under his direction, the program won nine state culinary championships and two national titles; more than any other program in the State of Wisconsin. Tronsen credits the success, in part, from the support of the local culinary community and individuals such as Chef John Bogan.

Kim Marks

Chef Cloe Acup

Chef Chris Stefan

Chef John Grober

Chef Jake Pierce

In Appreciation

Cloe Acup
Lenny Baggeson
Ryan Bensheimer
Jacque Bogan
Briana Bogan
Mackenna Bogan
Wilhelm Bogan
Bill & Susan Bosworth
Jennifer Brassfield
Jay DeSanto
Bill & Carol Dick
Henry Dimiceli
Sean Dimiceli
Dr. Bob & Dianne Fasano
Pat, Beth & Tia Flanagan
John Grober
Eric Heinz
Kahi Kaonohi
Cindy & Corey Lehr
Kim Marks
Kim & Steve Minette
Bobby Moderow Jr.
Jerry Pawlak
Jake Pierce
Roche-Valusek Family
Mark Sapienza & Family
Chris Stefan
Charlie "The Boy" Smith
Russ Tronsen
Dominic & Marge Trumfio
Cathy Wilson

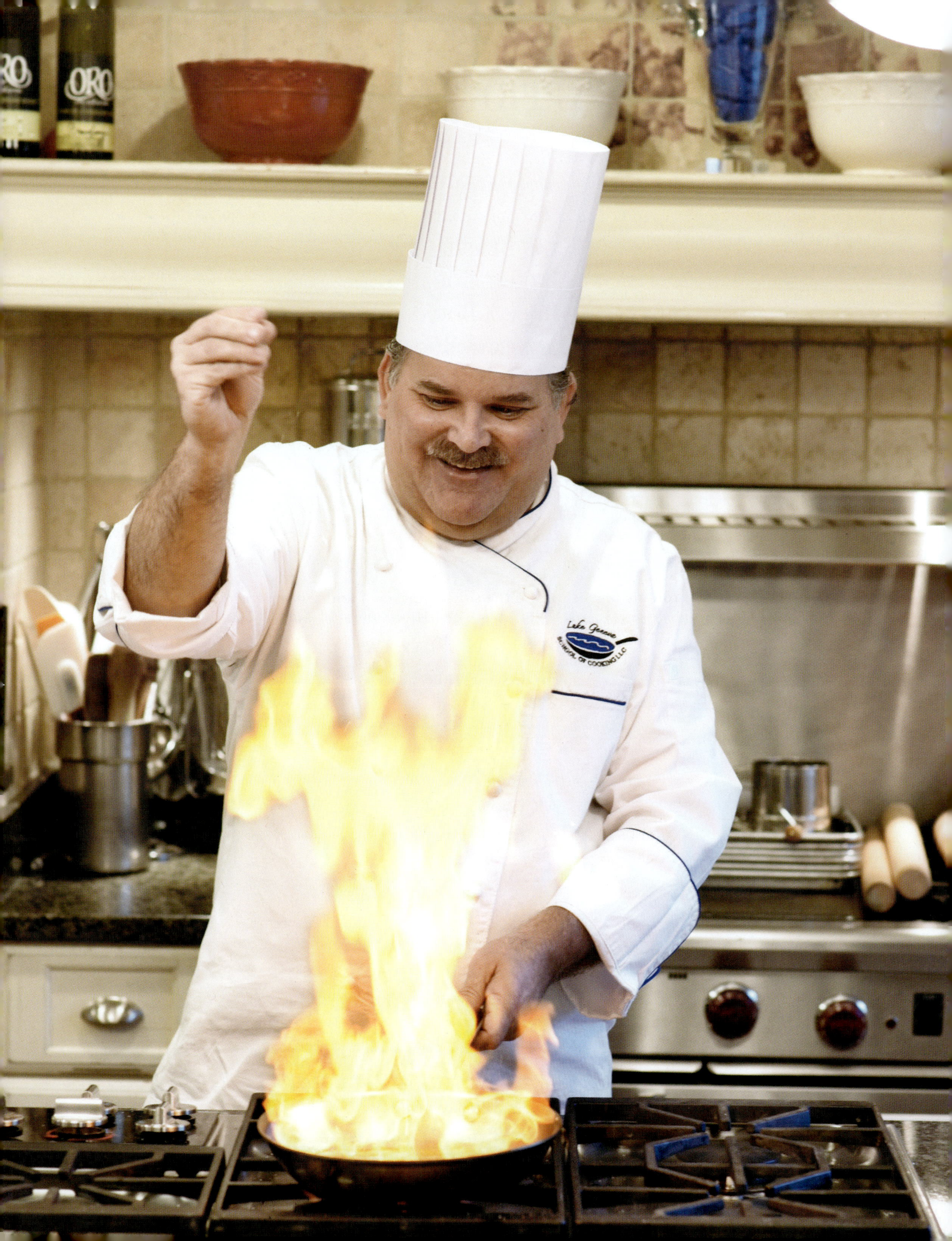
ORO
ORO
Lake Geneva
SCHOOL OF COOKING LLC

INTRODUCTION

Traditions and celebrations have always held the power to bring people together, no matter how far away we are. I hold traditions and celebrations close to my heart, and believe that family is the most important thing we have in life.

Food has always been an integral component of traditions and celebrations. Coming together over food is a tradition as old as time. I hope the recipes in this cookbook find their way into your own traditions and celebrations with you and your family.

My love for food started with my father, Larry. He is a true American father, with about five acres of property, dubbed the Bogan Ranch. Every year on Memorial Day weekend, we would plant our garden. Together we planted hundreds of tomato and broccoli plants, peapods, green beans, corn, squash, pumpkins, potatoes, asparagus, rhubarb, and more. We had a strict weekly weeding schedule and worked tirelessly for our harvest. We also raised our own pigs. One of my favorite memories of our pigs was when one sow, named Snow White, gave birth to 7 piglets. It was a very exciting time to be on the ranch. Another great memory of my childhood on the ranch was in 1977, when our maple trees produced 27 gallons of maple syrup. We simmered down the maple sap and used mason jars to preserve it. I still have one mason jar left from that year, and it is still perfectly clear and has a wonderful amber color. Even though this was a lot for a young boy, I admired my father's hard work and tending to the ranch became less work and more of a way of life.

Every summer I would roll my farm stand to the side of the road and sell the fresh vegetables my father and I grew. My family also raised Rhode Island Red Hens and collected the eggs. I created a delivery service for my neighbors where I would bike all around town delivering fresh corn on the cob and eggs, but I always made sure I was home by 5 p.m. for dinner. My mother, Teresa, a bonafide saint, would prepare our family dinners from our abundance of harvest from the ranch and beef that we would purchase from our neighbor's farm.

My grandmother, Tid, also loved cooking with our fresh farm produce. Every weekend we would have a Sunday family supper and she served baked ham, pot roast, many sides, and multiple pies. She would start preparing Sunday's dinner on Wednesday, and every one of her 9 kids and 35 grandchildren would show up for our supper tradition.

At the age of 12, I traveled to Spring Green, Wisconsin, for my summer vacation to work with my uncle, Chef Wilhem Bogan, at the Apple Hill Restaurant. My uncle lived in New Orleans, but came to Wisconsin during the summers to escape the southern heat. I worked 6 days a week, from 9 a.m. to 10 p.m., at the restaurant. As an all around prep cook, dishwasher, lunch cook, and dinner cook, I also made 50 loaves of bread and 4 apple pies each day. This was not a routine I was excited about at my young age. However, I noticed my uncle did not feel the same way. The busier the restaurant was, the happier he was, and at that moment I realized that I wanted to be the chef.

It was 1980 when I headed off the Bogan Ranch to attend Johnson and Wales University in Providence, Rhode Island. For me, cooking seemed to come naturally, and I wanted to further my culinary knowledge. During college, I would go to school from 9 a.m. - 3 p.m. After school, I would go to Federal Hill, the Italian neighborhood of Providence, and I would work the Garde Manger Station at Camille's Roman Gardens. When that shift was over, I would walk to the Brown University Campus to work at a bakery from 11 p.m. - 4 a.m. I would then sleep for 3 hours and get ready for class at 9 a.m.

It was in Federal Hill that I met this Sicilian guy—Mark Sapienza. Mark was working at a newly opened restaurant named Trattoria D'Antuono. After the head chef suddenly left, Frank and Jean D'Antuono, owners of the Trattoria, asked Mark to take over and to bring in a friend to help. They brought in the Irish guy. I left Camille's and Chef Mark and I put the Trattoria D'Antuono on the map. This was a very exciting opportunity for two young culinary students to be able to anchor the kitchen of a family Trattoria. Frank and Jean made sure the operation was a family haven for years and we are still family until this day.

Little did I know that when I met Mark in 1983, he would become one of the most influential friends, Chefs, and mentors of my life. In fact, he is also the Godfather of both of my daughters.

After graduating from Johnson & Wales University with an Associate's degree in Culinary Arts and a Bachelor's degree in Food Service Management, I met up with Chef Mark again in Boston. I was working at The Top of the Hub and he was working at the Sheraton. The most remarkable time of my journey in Boston was living with the Sapienza family. Mark's dad, Tony, taught me even more commitment to family traditions and celebrations. Mr. Sapienza would be cooking throughout the week and then sharing Sicilian specialties with his family and myself. Sicilian food from the heart.

After a few years, I moved from Boston to Chicago with Stouffer's Restaurant to become an Executive Chef. I knew Chicago was a great food city, a great sports city, and a great restaurant city. But I had no clue I was about to meet the woman of my dreams.

I opened my own restaurant in the Old Town district of Chicago named Fedora's. The restaurant garnered 3 stars from the *Chicago Tribune* and *Chicago Sun Times*. It was also named one of the "Top 10" restaurants opened in 1988 by the *Chicago Sun Times*. It was during this time that I really developed and perfected my French-American Cuisine.

Around town, there was talk of a new bartender that worked across the street who had just moved here from Hawaii. Her name was Jacque and I courted her with my food. I would have a bus boy walk across the street to give her plates of food every day. After a while, she had accumulated almost 50 of my fine China plates and needed to return them. Six months later, we were married.

I had never been to Hawaii before our wedding, but I knew it was paradise. I knew I was going to learn a lot about the culture and food, but I never expected to learn about the true meaning of "Ohana". Ohana means family in Hawaiian, and family has always been at the forefront of mine and Jacque's relationship. Over the years, we have been able to create our own "Ohana" traditions and celebrations.

I love sharing Ohana whether it may be in the form of food, music, or culture. Ohana is a very special chapter of this book, and my life.

In 1994, after the birth of our first daughter, I moved my career and family to Lake Geneva, Wisconsin and established roots at The French Country Inn. It was at this time, I was really able to identify my cuisine as French American with Hawaiian Island influences. It was during this time, I created and featured dishes named after my wife, and daughters, Briana Kaiulani and Mackenna Anuhea, along with many others you will find in this book. The French Country Inn became a huge success with fine dining inside and a four-level dining patio on Lake Como to view the spectacular sunsets.

During these years, I was heavily involved with the American Culinary Federation-Geneva Lakes Chapter (ACF-GLC). In 1998, I furthered my culinary education and became a Certified Executive Chef, CEC.

In 2008, I opened the Lake Geneva School of Cooking and was committed to sharing 120 percent with my guests. We feature year round cooking classes inspired by seasonal ingredients. We love to support farmers markets and local farmers that are growing food for us to share. This book showcases these farm to table relationships I have cultivated while being a chef in the Geneva Lakes area for over 27 years.

At the Lake Geneva School of Cooking, I created Chef John's Signature Seasoning. Every food product should be seasoned and this seasoning will highlight all the beautiful flavors of seasonal food. Chef John's Signature Seasoning takes "good food to great food."

Lake Geneva School of Cooking offers me the opportunity to mentor the local Badger High School Prostart Culinary Program students sanctioned by the National Restaurant Association. We work with many of these young high school students and host an annual event, The Geneva Lakes Burger Throwdown. This tradition in Lake Geneva raises money for this terrific program. As I look back on my journey in culinary arts, starting at age 12, I hope that through mentoring, I can inspire other young adults to feel the same passion for food as I do.

As you read through *Recipes From the Seasons of My Life*, I hope you will recreate these dishes from my family traditions and celebrations while establishing your very own.

Right on, Right on! 120%! Bon Appetit!

Blue Cheese Beignets, Smoked Gouda Gougeres, and Cinnamon Beignets

Signature Popovers

When we opened the Lake Geneva School of Cooking in 2008, we wanted a signature dish. We wanted something people could enjoy with a glass of champagne or sparkling wine. We wanted to set ourselves up for the rest of the meal. When we first started, we served one large popover out of a traditional popover pan. Then we decided upon the smaller muffin pans—the mini popovers started. The smaller popovers were popping over the rim and became an instant hit.

Parmigiano Popover   18

Blue Cheese Beignet   20

Queso Popover   20

Smoked Gouda Gougeres   20

Oktoberfest Popover   20

Cinnamon Beignet   20

PARMIGIANO POPOVERS

In the beginning years of the Lake Geneva School of Cooking, this was the first popover we mastered. Our Parmigiano Popovers are a classic first course upon arriving to the school. Within weeks of opening, we began serving two to an order because one was not enough as everyone loved them. Now, we serve everyone two popovers to begin class.

SERVES 12

INGREDIENTS:

1½ cups milk

4 large eggs

1½ cups all-purpose flour

1 tsp salt

Nonstick spray

4 oz Parmigiano cheese, grated

PREPARATION:

1. Preheat oven to 400°F.
2. Place a popover or mini muffin pan with 24 cups in the oven.
3. In a small saucepan, heat the milk until just simmering.
4. In a large bowl, whisk the eggs until frothy. Slowly whisk in the hot milk so as not to cook the eggs. Gradually whisk the dry ingredients into the egg mixture, stirring until almost smooth.
5. Remove the popover pan from the oven and spray it with nonstick spray. While the batter is still slightly warm, fill each cup level to the top.
6. Use half of the Parmigiano to top each popover; set aside the rest. Bake for 15 minutes.
7. Rotate the pan 180° so that the popovers will rise evenly.
8. Turn oven to 350°F. Bake for 20 more minutes, or until golden brown. Top with remaining Parmigiano.

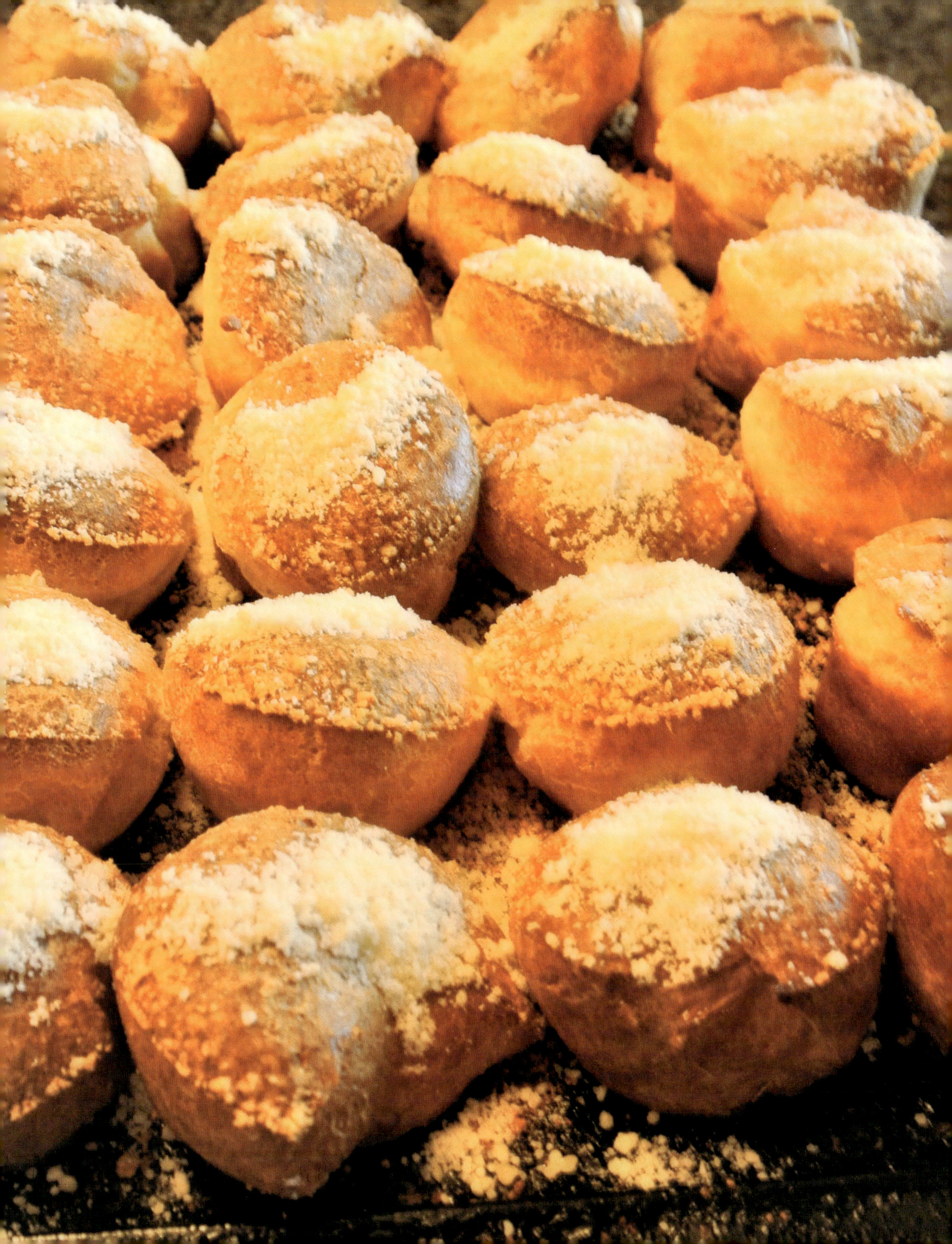

Popover Influenced Variations

As our school grew and we started hosting more classes and more holiday parties, we needed some variations to the Parmigiano Popover. We started to incorporate seasonal ingredients. For Mardi Gras, we would highlight New Orleans, creating the Blue Cheese Beignet. For Cinco de Mayo, we had Queso Popovers with Pepper Jack cheese. When we had a French theme, we prepared Smoked Gouda Gougeres. Entering the Fall season, we had the Oktoberfest Popover, which adds caraway seed and pretzel salt. With morning classes, we introduced the Cinnamon Beignet topped with powdered sugar. With these variations we now offer both sweet and savory popovers.

START WITH THE PARMIGIANO POPOVER RECIPE TO CREATE THESE VARIATIONS:

BLUE CHEESE BEIGNET:
1. Combine 2 oz crumbled Blue Cheese and 2 oz grated Parmigiano cheese.
2. Add 2 oz of mixed Blue Cheese and Parmigiano on top of the beignets before baking.
3. When golden brown, remove from oven, and top with remaining 2 oz mixed crumbled Blue Cheese and grated Parmigiano.

QUESO POPOVER:
1. Combine 2 oz of grated Pepper Jack cheese and 2 oz grated Parmigiano cheese.
2. Add 2 oz of mixed Pepper Jack and Parmigiano on top of the popovers before baking.
3. When golden brown, remove from oven, and top with remaining 2 oz of Pepper Jack and Parmigiano.

SMOKED GOUDA GOUGERES:
1. Combine 2 oz of grated Smoked Gouda and 2 oz of grated Parmigiano cheese.
2. Add 2 oz of Smoked Gouda and Parmigiano mixture together on top of the gougeres before going into the oven.
3. When golden brown, remove from oven, and top with remaining 2 oz of Smoked Gouda and Parmigiano.

OKTOBERFEST POPOVER:
1. Add 1 tsp of caraway seeds and 1 tsp of kosher salt to the milk and heat until just simmering.
2. Add 2 oz of grated Parmigiano cheese, 1 tsp of caraway seeds, and 1 tsp flaky sea salt on top of popover for Step 6 in Parmigiano Popover recipe.
3. When golden brown, remove from oven, and top with 2 oz of Parmigiano.

CINNAMON BEIGNETS:

This beignet is fashioned after a New Orleans-style beignet.
1. After you slowly whisk hot milk into egg mixture, add 3 Tbsp of sugar and 1 tsp of cinnamon. Then add flour and ¼ tsp of kosher salt.
2. Before going into oven, top with baked good crumbs such as, muffin, pound cake, or brownie.
3. When golden brown, remove from oven, and dust with 2 Tbsp of powdered sugar.

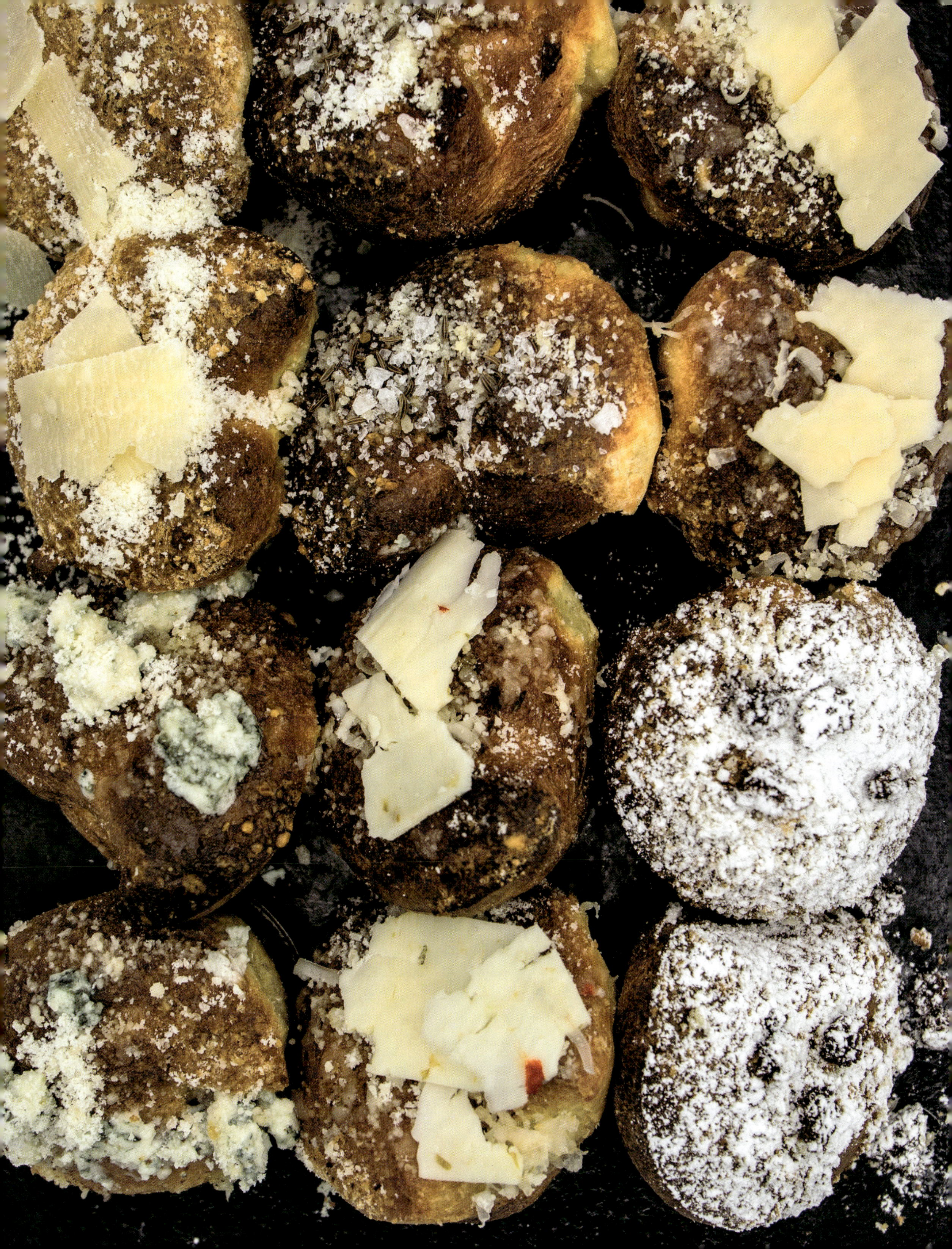

Rhubarb Strawberry Cobbler

Spring

Spring is a very exciting time of year for chefs as the farmers markets open up and we start harvesting local vegetables like asparagus and rhubarb. The days start to get longer and Spring provides some lighter cooking options coming off of the winter season. One of my favorite dishes in this chapter is the Pan Fried Calamari. This recipe was created in 1983 with my best friend, Chef Mark Sapienza. This chapter is filled with many dishes that are great to prepare and share with your family.

Grilled Asparagus with Mediterranean Chopped Egg   24

Grilled Asparagus with Prosciutto   26

Sweet Crab Cakes   28

Pan Fried Calamari   30

Colossal Shrimp Scampi   32

Homemade Potato Gnocchi   34

Spinach and Four Cheese Ravioli   36

Blackened Beef Tenderloin Crostini   40

Filet Medallion with Red Wine Sauce   42

Rhubarb Strawberry Cobbler   44

Vanilla Bean Crème Brûlée   46

Flourless Chocolate Pâté   48

GRILLED ASPARAGUS WITH MEDITERRANEAN CHOPPED EGG

As I grew up on the Bogan Ranch, one the first signs of Spring was asparagus sprouting out of our garden. I remember our family garden always grew the thickest asparagus. We would peel the asparagus to make it tender on the stalk end. We would also have eggs from our very own Rhode Island Red Hens. I always prefer to use local eggs, such as Yuppie Hill Farms, in our kitchen. We toss the asparagus and eggs with capers and Kalamata olives—this dish boasts beautiful color. This is a great dish that says "Spring" to start off this chapter.

SERVES 8

INGREDIENTS:

24 fresh asparagus spears

3 Tbsp extra virgin olive oil

Chef John's Signature Seasoning, to taste

½ Tbsp fresh lemon juice

4 hard-boiled large eggs (see note), shelled and coarsely chopped

16 Kalamata olives, quartered lengthwise

½ Tbsp drained capers

2 Tbsp Panko bread crumbs

1 Tbsp fresh parsley, chopped

8 leaves of romaine, medium size

4 cups romaine, chiffonade

2 tsp Aged Balsamic

PREPARATION:

1. Rinse asparagus. Cut tough stem off. Peel ends 3- to 3½-inches up stalk (see page 192).
2. Mix asparagus with 1 Tbsp EVOO, fresh lemon juice, and Chef John's Signature Seasoning. Grill asparagus 2–3 minutes only.
3. Meanwhile, in a bowl, mix 1 Tbsp EVOO with chopped eggs, olives, capers, bread crumbs, and parsley. Mix gently to avoid mashing yolks. Season to taste with Chef John's Signature Seasoning.
4. Mound romaine chiffonade on romaine leaf. Drizzle lettuce with 1 Tbsp EVOO, Aged Balsamic, and Chef John's Signature Seasoning.
5. Arrange asparagus on greens and spoon egg salad over asparagus.

Note: Hard-boiled Egg Preparation

1. Place eggs in a 3- to 4-quart pan and cover with cold water.
2. Bring to a boil over high heat, reduce heat, and boil gently, uncovered, for about 15 minutes.
3. With a slotted spoon, lift eggs from water and immerse in cold water until cool.

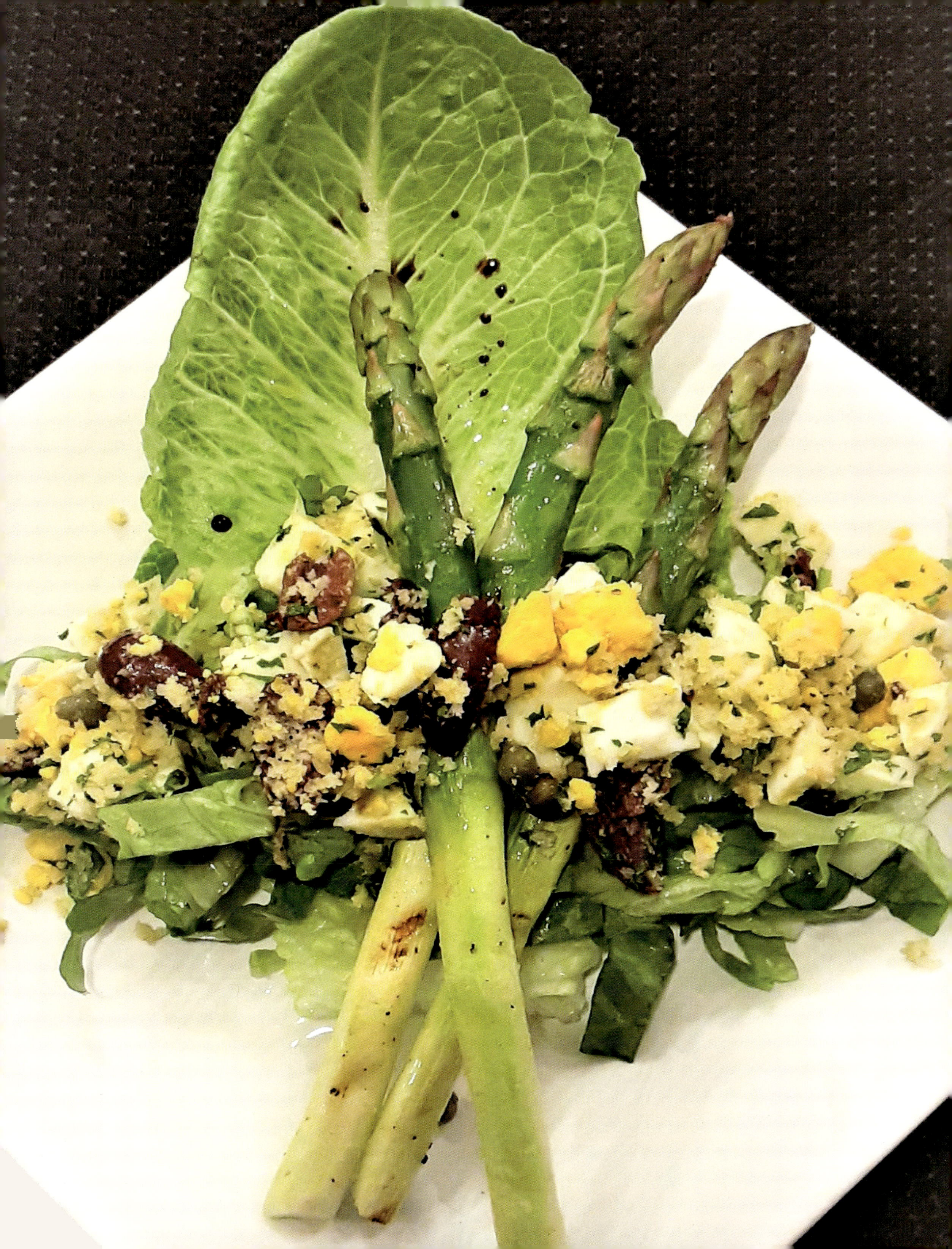

GRILLED ASPARAGUS WITH PROSCIUTTO

This is a great way to wrap asparagus with a pork product, Prosciutto. Instead of using bacon with the asparagus, we prefer Prosciutto because it does not flare up on the grill. The wrapped asparagus only takes three minutes to grill. You can toss in some beautiful Italian ingredients that complement the Prosciutto; we traditionally use Gorgonzola cheese, Aged Balsamic, a little garlic, and some mini croutons for some crunch.

SERVES 8

INGREDIENTS:

24 fresh asparagus spears

12 slices of Prosciutto, 8-inch slices

2 cloves garlic, finely minced

2 Tbsp extra virgin olive oil

Black pepper, freshly ground

1 Tbsp of extra virgin olive oil

1 tsp of fresh herbs, chopped (parsley, thyme, and oregano)

½ loaf baguette bread

8 hearts of romaine leaves

4 cups romaine, chiffonade

Chef John's Signature Seasoning, to taste

½ cup Gorgonzola cheese, crumbled

3 Tbsp of extra virgin olive oil

1 Tbsp of Aged Balsamic

PREPARATION:

1. Preheat oven to 350°F.
2. Cut tough stem off. Peel ends 3- to 3½ inches up stalk (see page 192).
3. Cut Prosciutto slices in half or 4-inch pieces. Wrap one 4-inch piece of Prosciutto around each asparagus spear.
4. Add minced garlic with 1 Tbsp of EVOO and brush each spear with EVOO mixture, making sure to coat tips well. Season with black pepper.
5. Preheat grill to medium-high heat. Place asparagus onto grill and cook for 2-3 minutes, turning occasionally. Remove from heat.
6. Cut or tear bread into small cubes. Toss with 1 Tbsp EVOO, Chef John's Signature Seasoning, and 1 tsp assorted fresh herbs. Toast in oven for 12 minutes or until golden brown.
7. Season romaine lettuce hearts and romaine chiffonade with 3 Tbsp EVOO, 1 Tbsp Aged Balsamic, and Chef John's Signature Seasoning.
8. Place romaine on plate and top with grilled asparagus, crumbled Gorgonzola, and croutons.

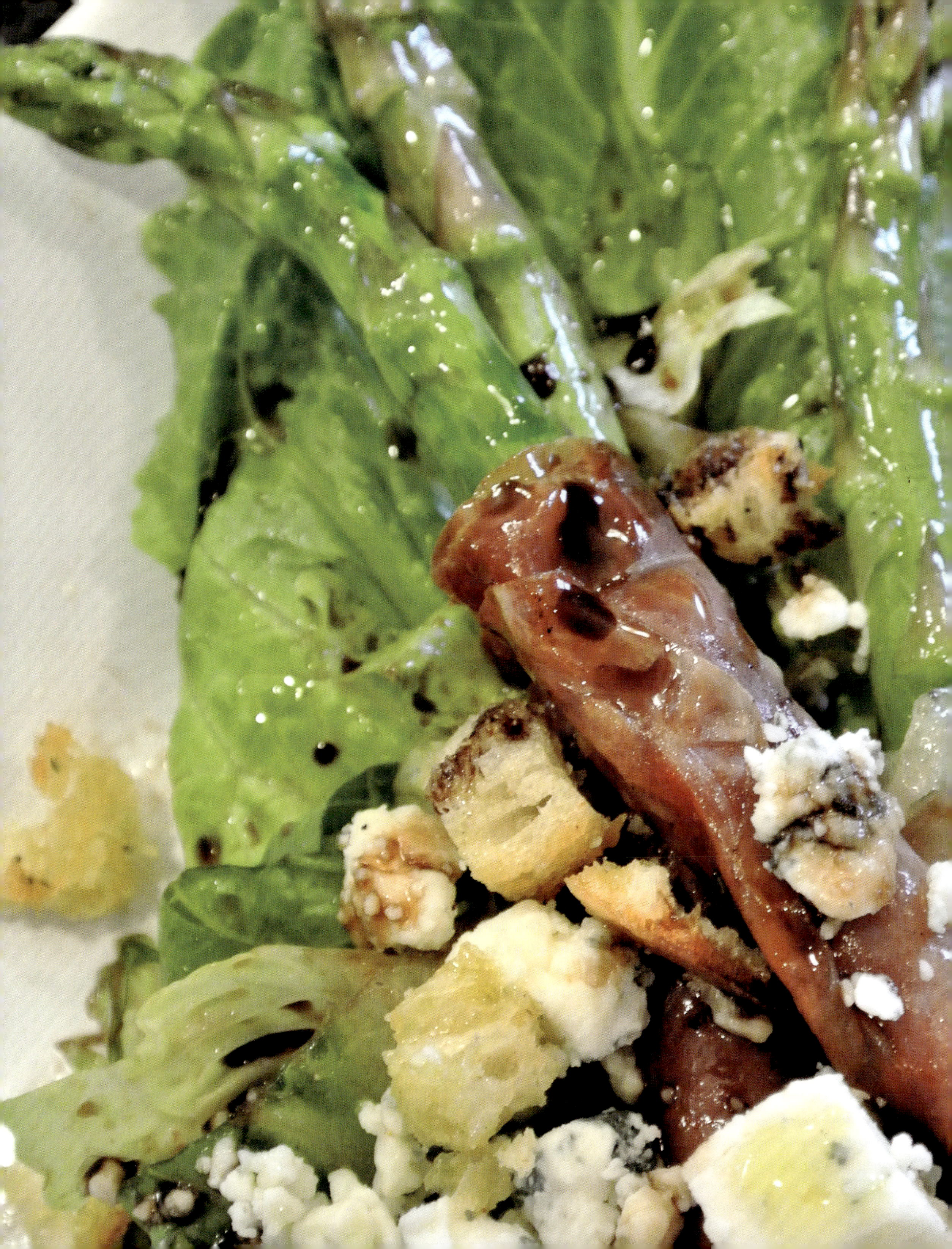

Sweet Crab Cakes
With Three Mustard Sauce

Our crab cakes are inspired by my mother, Teresa. The day after Thanksgiving, she would take all the left-over mashed potatoes and form little cakes, dredging them in flour and frying in butter. They were served crisp on the outside, and soft and tender on the inside. When we make our crab cakes, we do not use bread crumbs. We use the potato as a binder, mashed or riced, and sauté them until the cakes "poof" up and are light and fluffy. To ensure the perfect crab cake, we use sweet jumbo lump crab meat. When you start with quality ingredients, it just makes everything easier.

SERVES 8

INGREDIENTS:

16 oz jumbo lump crab meat

2 large egg yolks

2 Tbsp mayonnaise

1 Tbsp Dijon mustard

½ tsp Tabasco

1 tsp Worcestershire sauce

½ tsp cumin

⅓ tsp chili pepper flakes

Chef John's Signature Seasoning, to taste

1 cup riced potato

1 cup flour

¼ cup butter

¼ cup olive oil

PREPARATION:

1. Mix egg yolk, mayonnaise, mustard, Tabasco, Worcestershire, cumin, chili pepper flakes, Chef John's Signature Seasoning and potato.
2. Add jumbo lump crab meat and fold together. IMPORTANT: Be careful to not break up your crab lumps.
3. Portion 1½ oz scoops onto flour then dust tops of scoops with additional flour forming into cakes.
4. Sauté in fortified butter (butter and olive oil) for about 2-3 minutes on each side or until golden brown.

Serving Suggestion: *use Three Mustard Sauce (see recipe on page 194) as a base sauce and your favorite chili pepper puree*

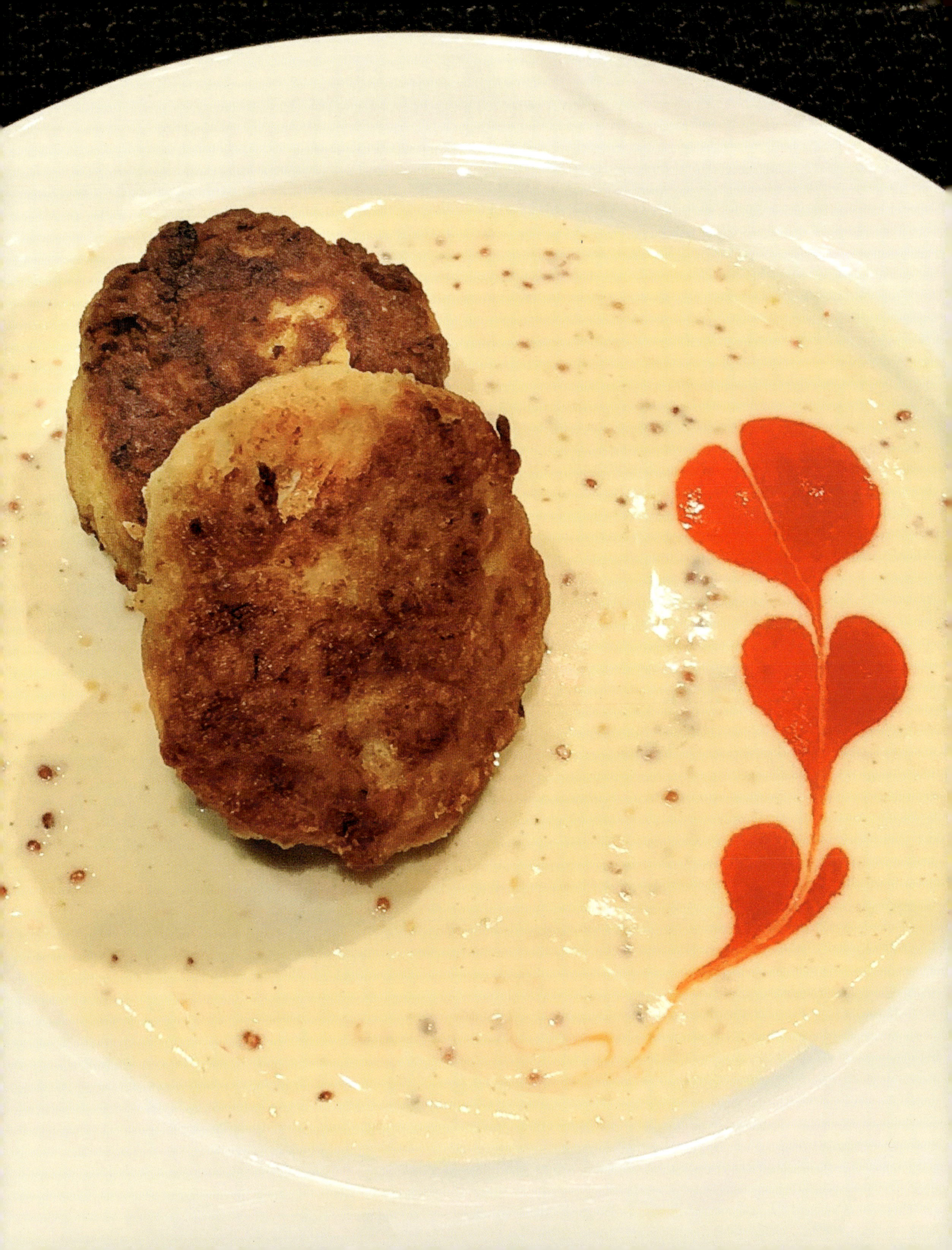

Pan Fried Calamari

This dish is a nod to my best friend, Chef Mark Sapienza from Boston. We created this dish in 1983 at the Trattoria D'Antuono in Providence, Rhode Island. It is a terrific dish and has been on every restaurant menu that I have created throughout the years. It is a favorite of my father, Larry, and I make this every time I see him. We have had great success with this dish over the years, and it still works. The Pepperoncini peppers give the calamari just enough kick, and the capers with the lemon give it just the right amount of seasoning. We do not serve our calamari with marinara or cocktail sauce. I hope you enjoy it as much as Chef Mark and I have.

SERVES 8

INGREDIENTS:

2½ lb calamari (tubes and tentacles)

2 cups flour

3 cups olive oil blend
(1 cup extra virgin olive oil and 2 cups 100% olive oil)

3 Tbsp extra virgin olive oil

3 Tbsp garlic, chopped

2 fresh lemons, halved

¼ cup Pepperoncini pepper rings

3 Tbsp capers

3 Tbsp fresh parsley, chopped

Chef John's Signature Seasoning, to taste

PREPARATION:

1. Clean calamari tentacles and tubes, slice tubes into ¾-inch rings.
2. Prep (chop/slice) all garnishes (garlic, lemons, Pepperoncini peppers, capers, and parsley).
3. In a large, deep sauté pan, heat olive oil blend to 335°F.
4. Lightly dredge calamari with flour seasoned with Chef John's Signature Seasoning in small batches. Do not dredge too many at once.
5. Fry rings and tentacles in small batches in olive oil blend at 335°F until golden brown (about 20-30 seconds), making sure your oil doesn't get too cold or hot. (Do not crowd pan, they will not become crispy). Remove crispy calamari from oil and lightly season with Chef John's Signature Seasoning.
6. Discard hot oil carefully.
7. In same pan, heat 3 Tbsp EVOO; add garlic and crispy calamari, sauté for 2 minutes.
8. Toss in Pepperoncini rings, capers, lemon juice, chopped parsley, and Chef John's Signature Seasoning.

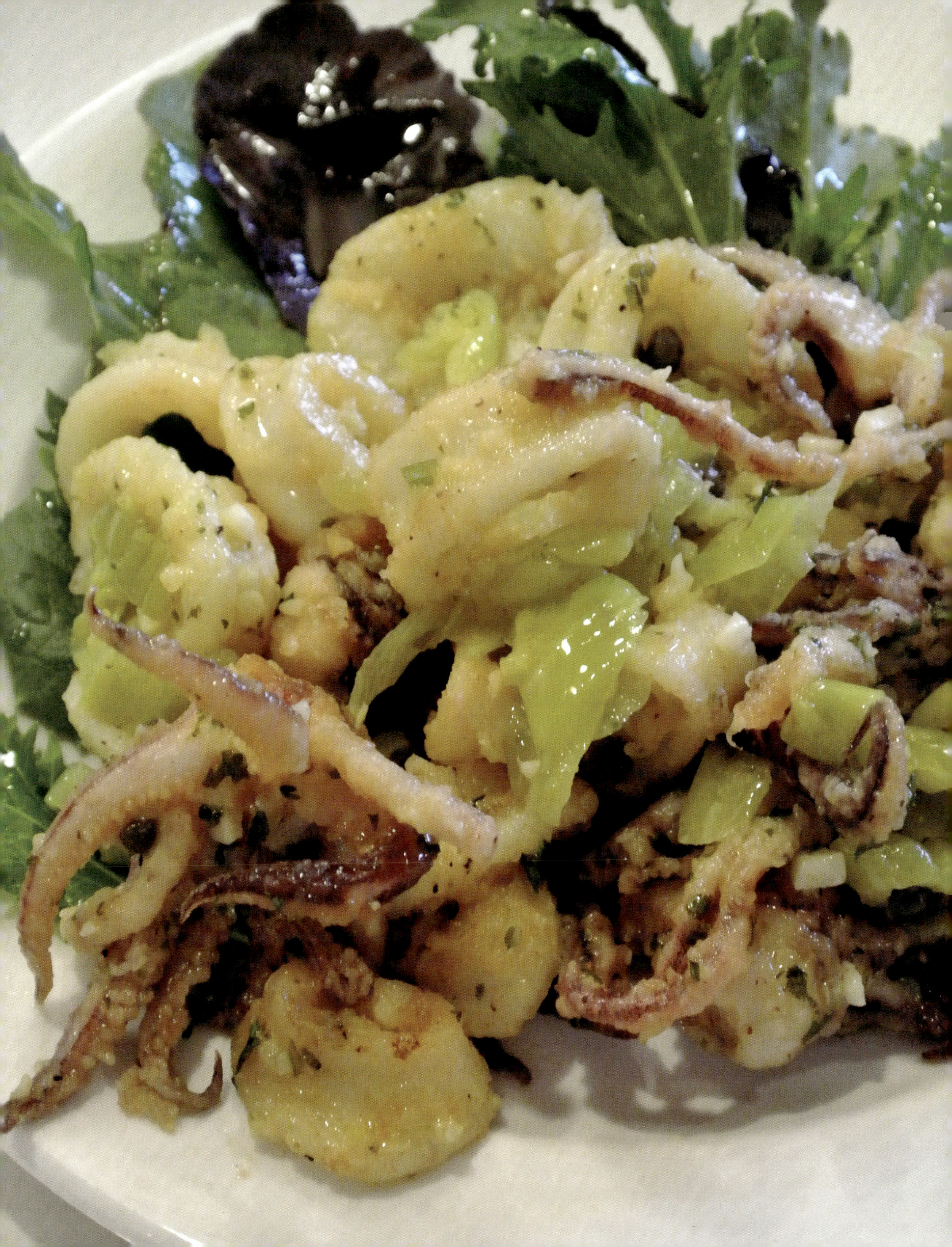

Colossal Shrimp Scampi

The key to this dish is the Colossal Shrimp. We use U-10 count shrimp, which means under 10 shrimp per pound (approximately 2 oz each). They are easier to peel, they are gorgeous, and they are colossal. Also, the size allows the edges of the shrimp to crisp up while they are sautéing. We sprinkle a pinch of chili pepper flake in our Shrimp Scampi lemon white wine sauce—just enough to add a little character and heat. It is a nice finish to this dish.

SERVES 8

INGREDIENTS:

16 shrimp (U-10 ct) peeled and deveined

2 Tbsp butter

2 Tbsp extra virgin olive oil

1 medium shallot, finely diced

2 cloves garlic, sliced

Pinch chili pepper flakes

2 Tbsp white wine

½ lemon, juiced

2 Tbsp butter

2 Tbsp fresh parsley, chopped

1 lb angel hair pasta

2 Tbsp kosher salt

Chef John's Signature Seasoning, to taste

SHRIMP PREPARATION:

1. In a large sauté pan, melt 2 Tbsp butter with 2 Tbsp EVOO over medium-high heat.
2. Season the shrimp with Chef John's Signature Seasoning and cook until they have caramelized on the edges, about 2-3 minutes. Turn over and repeat while adding the shallots, garlic, and chili pepper flakes. Sauté for about 1-2 minutes more.
3. Remove shrimp from pan; let rest on a side plate.
4. Add wine and lemon juice to the pan, bring to a simmer. Let reduce to half. Add 3 Tbsp of butter and swirl the pan until melted.
5. When the butter has melted, return the shrimp to the pan, along with the parsley, stir well and season with Chef John's Signature Seasoning. Let rest.

PASTA PREPARATION:

1. Bring a large pot of water to boil. Add 2 Tbsp kosher salt and the angel hair pasta.
2. Stir the pasta, making sure the pasta does not stick together, cover. When the water returns to a boil, cook for 3-4 minutes, until pasta is al dente. Reserve 1 cup pasta water. Drain.
3. Toss pasta with EVOO, reserve pasta water, and Chef John's Signature Seasoning. Spool pasta onto plate and top with shrimp and pan drippings.

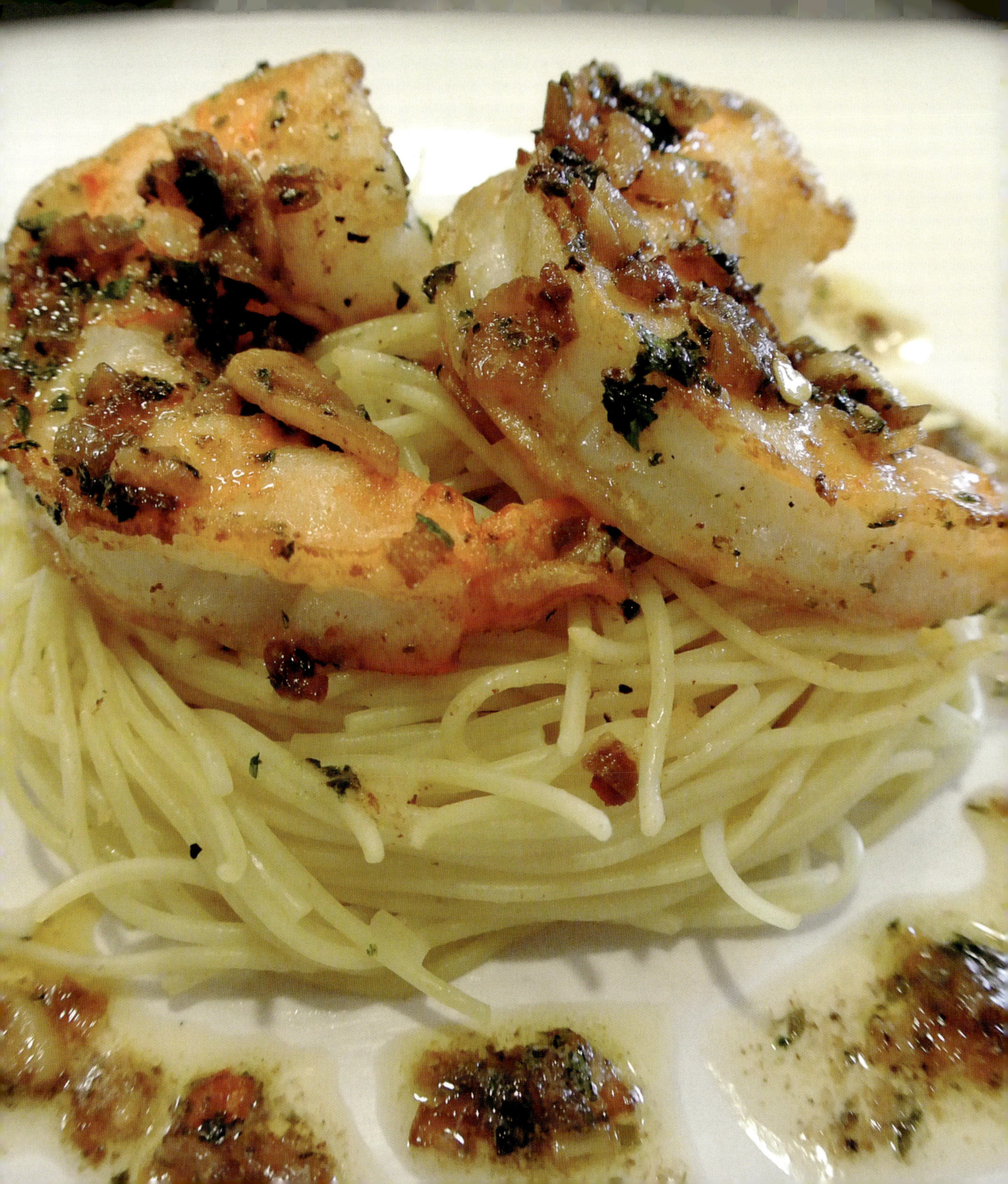

Homemade Potato Gnocchi

Homemade Gnocchi is a great dish to prepare in the Spring while there isn't an abundance of fresh vegetables available at the farmers market. I love making this dish using roasted russet potatoes and kosher salt. Homemade Gnocchi is so light, and totally different from a purchased Gnocchi. These are like fluffy potato pillows. They can be served with many different toppings and sauces. We prefer them with a little Truffle Oil and a sprinkling of Parmigiano-Reggiano cheese.

SERVES 8

INGREDIENTS:

½ cup kosher salt

4 baking potatoes, medium to large

2 cups plus 3 Tbsp flour

2 Tbsp extra virgin olive oil

1 large egg

½ tsp nutmeg

¼ cup corn meal

Chef John's Signature Seasoning, to taste

2 Tbsp butter

2 Tbsp extra virgin olive oil

2 cloves garlic, chopped

1 tsp assorted fresh herbs, chopped (parsley, thyme, and oregano)

1 Tbsp Black Truffle Oil

3 Tbsp Parmigiano-Reggiano cheese

PREPARATION:

1. Preheat oven to 375°F.
2. Sprinkle salt on baking sheet, fork/pierce each potato, and place on the baking sheet. Again, sprinkle salt over each potato and bake until a knife easily pierces to the center of each potato, approximately 1 hour. When cool enough to handle, scoop out the potatoes and pass them through a potato ricer. You should have approximately 4 cups of riced potato.
3. Add 1 cup of flour, 2 Tbsp EVOO, egg, nutmeg, and Chef John's Signature Seasoning. Mix well while continuing to add an additional cup of flour.
4. Dust the kitchen counter with flour. Turn out the dough on the kitchen counter and knead mixture until smooth. If the dough is too sticky, add another Tbsp of flour.
5. Dust a baking sheet with corn meal. Divide the dough into 6 pieces. On a lightly floured surface, roll each piece into a ½-inch thick rope. Cut each rope into 1-inch pieces. Roll each 1-inch piece with fork tines or a Gnocchi paddle. Place on baking sheet with corn meal. Bring a large pot of salted water to a boil. Add the Gnocchi and cook 2 minutes or until they float to the surface. Remove the Gnocchi with a slotted spoon, draining them well.
6. Melt butter with 2 Tbsp EVOO. Add garlic and sauté gently.
7. Add cooked Gnocchi, fresh herbs, Black Truffle Oil, Parmigiano-Reggiano, and Chef John's Signature Seasoning. Toss together.

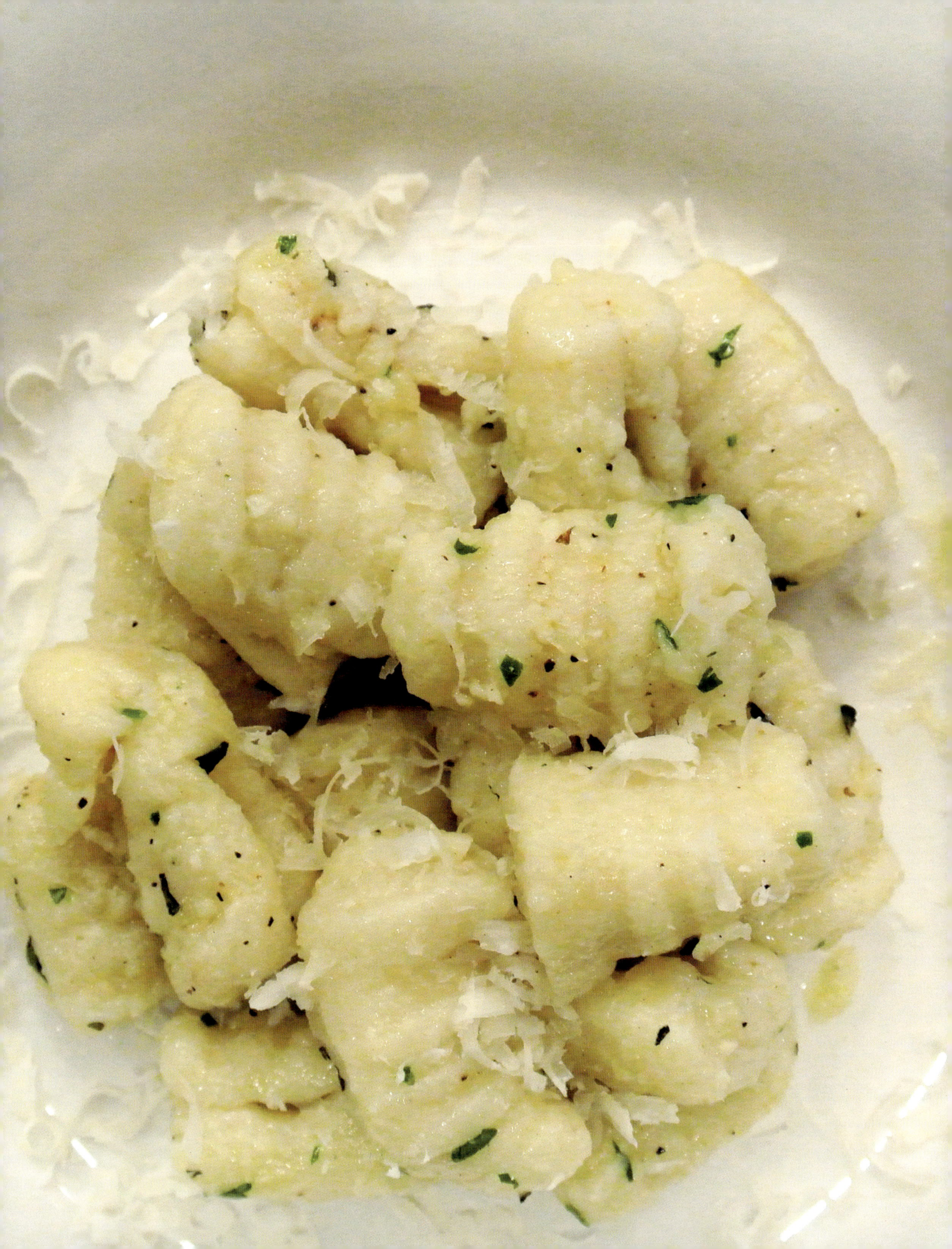

Spinach and Four Cheese Ravioli
With Tomato Basil Reduction

When making the pasta dough for our ravioli, I like to make sure to roll it out thin. Because of this, the filling ingredients inside the ravioli are more visible after we plate it. In this dish, you can see the green spinach, cheese, and herbs. We have plated this dish with fresh spinach on a bed of Tomato Basil Reduction.

SERVES 8

INGREDIENTS:

1 container (15 oz) Ricotta cheese

8 oz Fontinella cheese, shredded

8 oz Asiago cheese, shredded

½ cup Parmesan cheese, grated

2 cups fresh spinach, finely chopped

2 Tbsp parsley, chopped

2 Tbsp fresh Italian herbs, chopped (parsley, basil, thyme, and oregano)

1 whole egg

1 egg yolk (reserve egg white)

1 Tbsp water

Chef John's Signature Seasoning, to taste

Pasta Dough (see recipe on page 201)

PREPARATION:

1. To make filling, combine all cheeses, fresh spinach, parsley, herbs, Chef John's Signature Seasoning, and 1 egg plus 1 egg yolk in a bowl and stir until smooth. (Reserve egg white).
2. To fill ravioli, spoon a heaping Tbsp of filling in center of each pasta sheet. Lightly beat egg white with 1 Tbsp water. Using a small pastry brush, moisten edges of ravioli with beaten egg wash.
3. Top each ravioli with another pasta sheet and seal edges together; press out any air bubbles.
4. Bring a large pot of water to a boil and drop in filled raviolis. Cook 2-3 minutes or until tender.

Serving Suggestion: Tomato Basil Reduction as a base sauce

Tomato Basil Reduction

INGREDIENTS:

¼ cup extra virgin olive oil

1 clove garlic

4 ripe tomatoes, chopped and seeded

8 fresh basil leaves, chopped

½ cup white wine

½ cup heavy cream

¼ cup Parmesan cheese, grated

Chef John's Signature Seasoning, to taste

PREPARATION:

1. In a sauce pan, heat EVOO over medium heat. Sauté garlic about 2 minutes, or just until it begins to color a bit.
2. Add tomatoes and basil, deglaze pan with white wine.
3. Bring to a simmer and let sauce reduce about 2 minutes. Using an immersion blender, puree ingredients together.
4. Add heavy cream and stir in Parmesan until it melts and season with Chef John's Signature Seasoning.

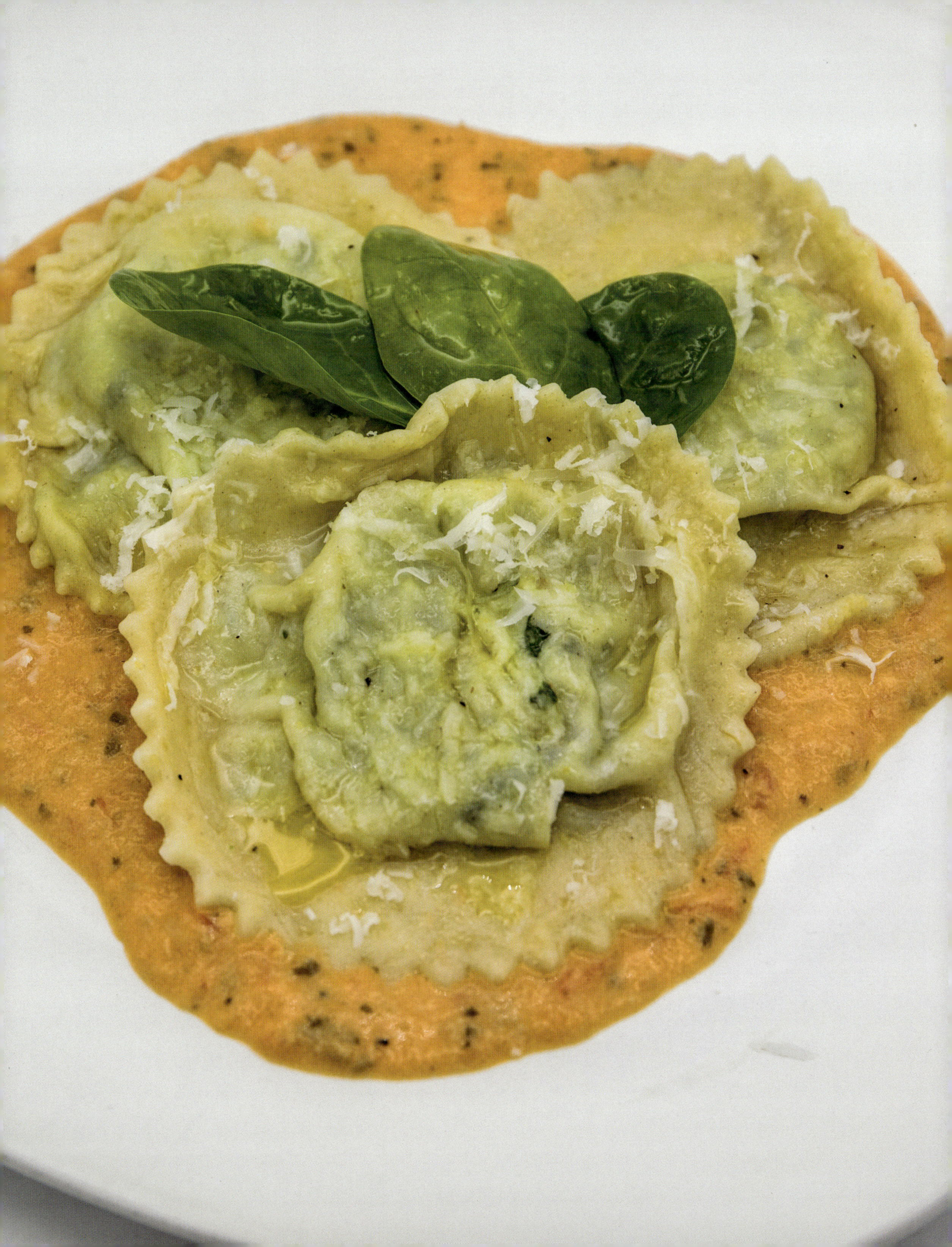

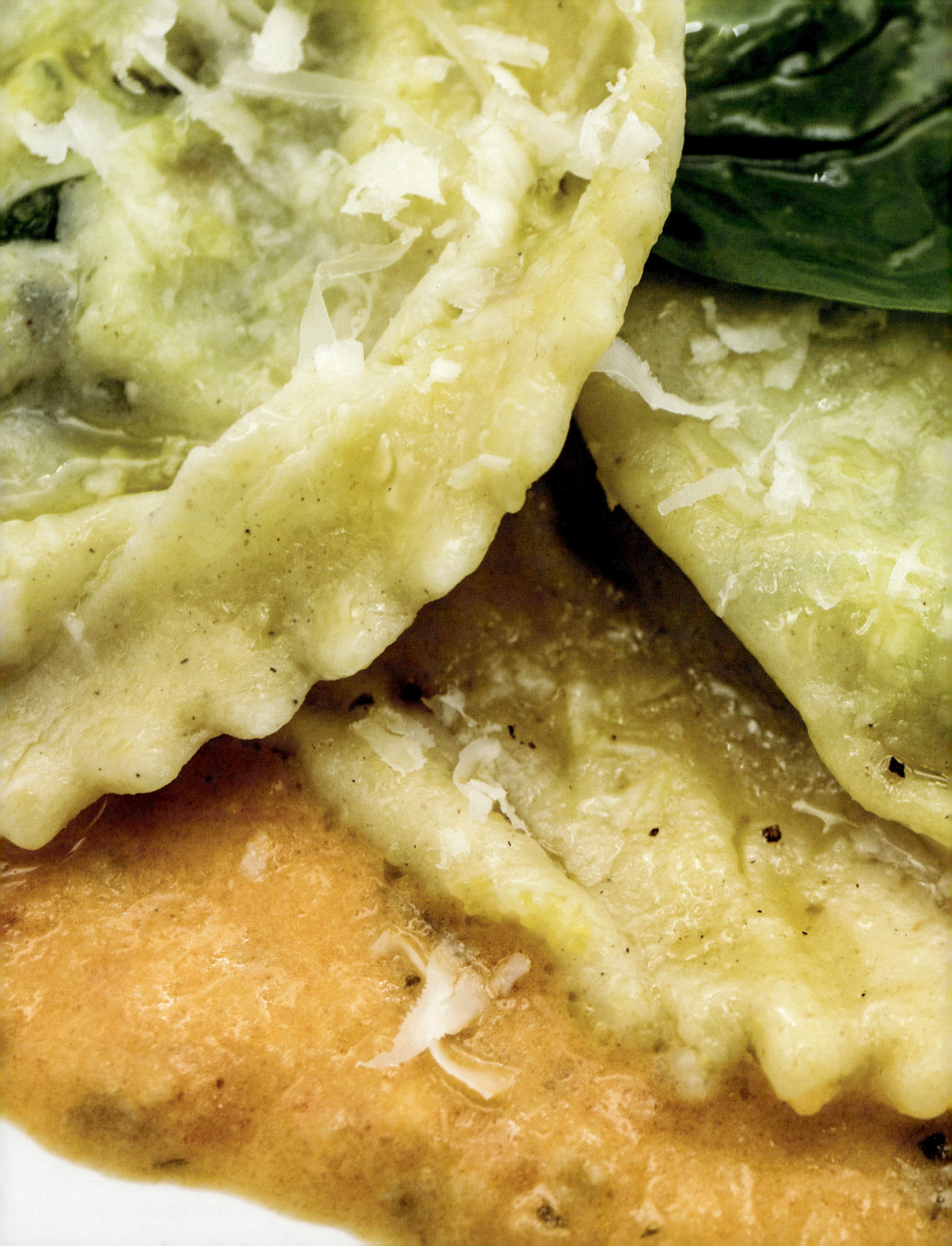

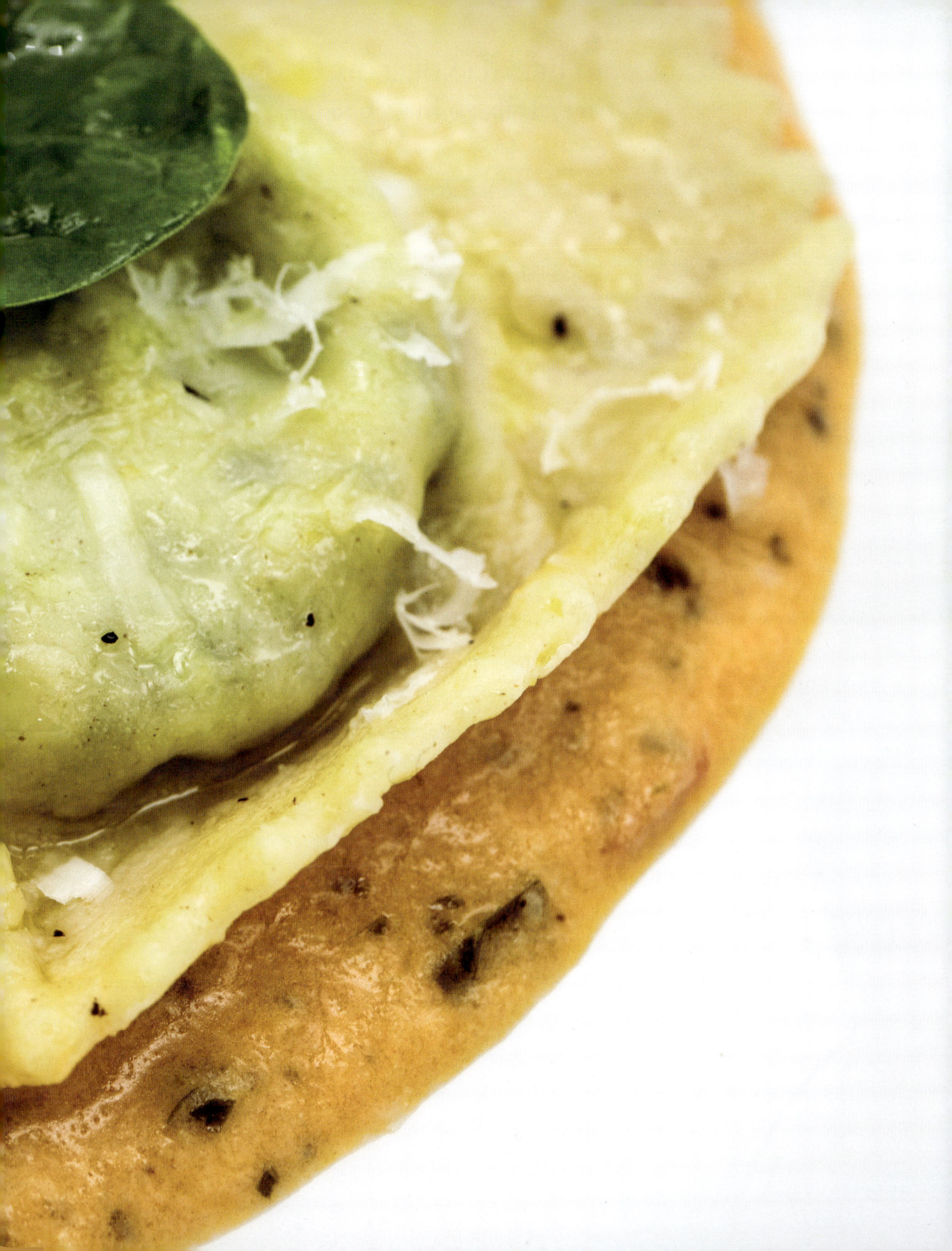

BLACKENED BEEF TENDERLOIN CROSTINI
WITH CRUMBLED BLUE CHEESE

In this dish we utilize the heads and tails of the whole tenderloin of beef. We roll them in a Cajun spice blend and blacken them in a pan to get a beautiful exterior crust on it. The tenderloin is served rare to medium rare. We then slice the beef and settle it on a crostini with white bean puree. Our preparation tops the beef with roasted peppers and crumbled Blue Cheese. The addition of the crumbled Blue Cheese helps cut the heat of the blackened Cajun spice.

SERVES 12

INGREDIENTS:

- 2 lbs beef tenderloin
- 3 Tbsp extra virgin olive oil
- 1 Tbsp Cajun spice
- 2 cloves garlic
- 24 slices of French bread, on the bias
- 1 cup bean puree
- ½ cup roasted peppers, sliced
- Chef John's Signature Seasoning, to taste
- ¼ cup crumbled Blue Cheese

PREPARATION:

1. Preheat oven to 375°F.
2. Coat beef tenderloin with 2 Tbsp EVOO, Cajun spice, and Chef John's Signature Seasoning. Sear tenderloin for 2-3 minutes on each side; 4 sides total, 8-12 minutes total.
3. Let rest until room temperature and slice into 1 oz slices on the bias.
4. Toast French bread slices, 8-10 minutes. Rub with garlic and brush with 1 Tbsp EVOO.
5. Place bean puree on French bread and top with a slice of beef, roasted pepper slices, and finish with crumbled Blue Cheese.

WHITE BEAN PUREE

INGREDIENTS:

- 1 can (15 oz) cannellini beans, drained
- 2 cloves garlic, minced
- 2 Tbsp chopped fresh herbs (parsley, thyme, and oregano)
- 2 Tbsp fresh lemon juice
- ⅓ cup extra virgin olive oil
- Chef John's Signature Seasoning, to taste

PREPARATION:

1. Placed cannellini beans, garlic, fresh herbs, and lemon juice in a food processor and pulse until well combined and smooth.
2. Slowly add in EVOO until thickened. If mixture is too thick, add additional lemon juice.
3. Add Chef John's Signature Seasoning. Refrigerate until served.

ROASTED RED PEPPER

INGREDIENTS:

- 1 red, orange, or yellow pepper

PREPARATION:

1. Roast pepper for 10 minutes on open flame, turning over occasionally until skin is charred.
2. Remove from flame and cover with plastic wrap until the pepper is cool enough to handle.
3. Remove the skin, stem, and seeds under water. Slice pepper into ¼-inch-thick slices and set aside until served.

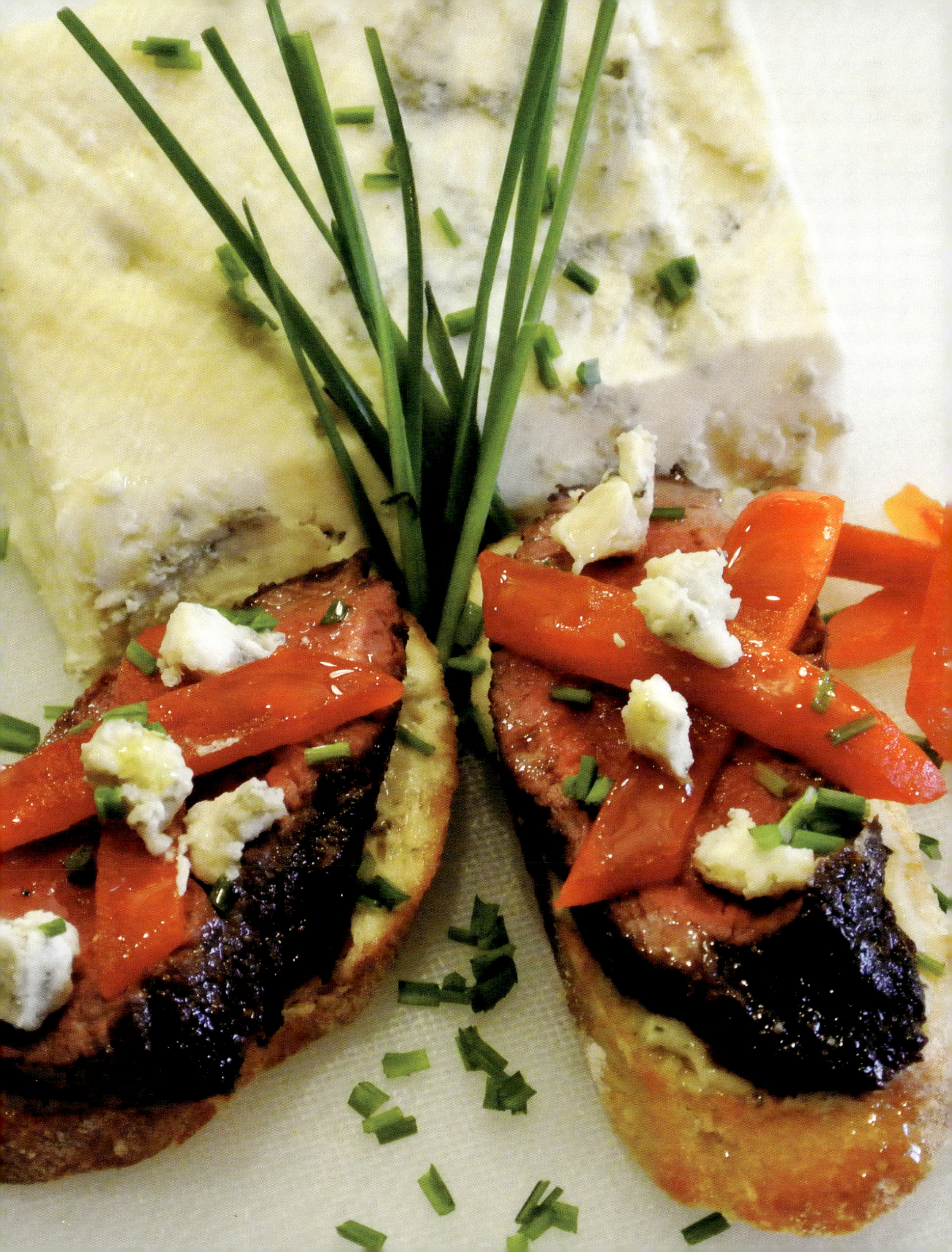

FILET MEDALLION WITH RED WINE SAUCE

I love to visit New Orleans and enjoy the Cajun/Creole Cuisine. It's such a great food town. Not everything has to be spicy in the Big Easy as this dish was fashioned after a Merchand de Vin sauce, which translates into "Wine Merchant Sauce," made popular by the French wine merchants years ago. The key to this dish is preparing a caramel roux as you begin the recipe; this adds so much depth and color while utilizing the famous Dark Roux of N'Awlins cooking.

SERVES 8
INGREDIENTS:

- 8 Filet Mignon, 5 oz each
- 2 Tbsp olive oil
- ½ cup butter
- ¼ cup flour
- ½ cup onion, finely chopped
- 2 celery stalks, finely chopped
- 1 clove garlic, minced
- 1 cup mushrooms, finely chopped
- 1 tomato, seeded and chopped
- 2 Tbsp fresh parsley, chopped
- 1 tsp fresh thyme, chopped
- 1 cup red wine
- 2 cups beef stock reduction
- Chef John's Signature Seasoning, to taste

PREPARATION:

1. Season the Filet Mignon liberally with Chef John's Signature Seasoning. Set aside at room temperature.
2. In a saucepan over medium heat, melt the butter, then add flour and gently stir continuously to make a roux. Let cook for 15-20 minutes.
3. When the roux is about the color of caramel, add the onion and celery, cook for 2-3 minutes. Then add the mushrooms and garlic, continue cooking for 2-3 more minutes.
4. Add the remaining ingredients and simmer on low heat for 45 minutes. Season with Chef John's Signature Seasoning.
5. Heat the olive oil in a large sauté pan over medium-high heat. Sear the filets until lightly browned, 3-4 minutes while turning only once; continue cooking for another 2-3 minutes.
6. Place on sheet pan and let rest.
7. Just before plating, finish in 335°F oven for 7-10 minutes.
8. Serve warm with red wine sauce.

Serving Suggestion: Dijon Whipped Potatoes (see recipe on page 200) and Sautéed Squash (see recipe on page 198)

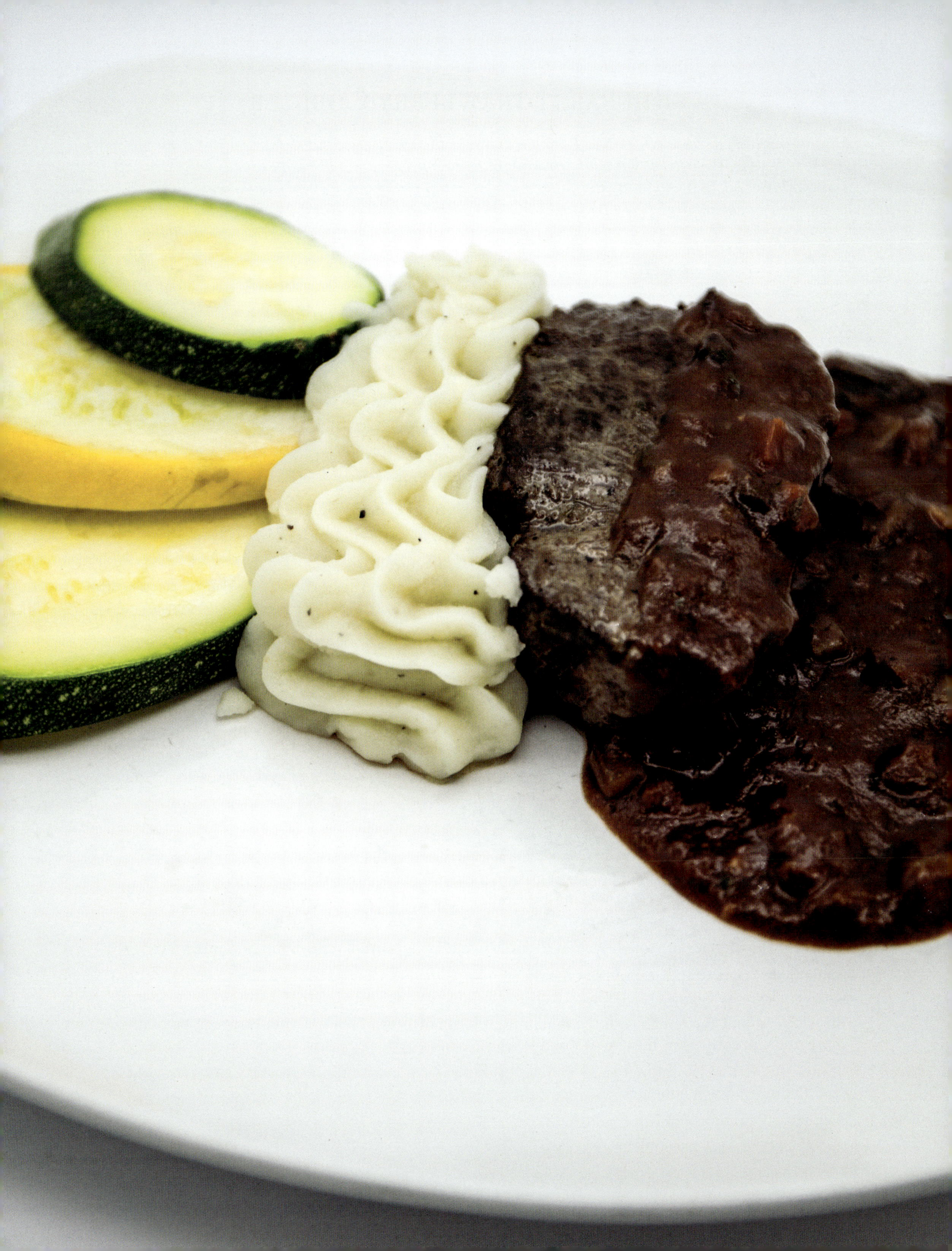

Rhubarb Strawberry Cobbler

Another ingredient from the Bogan Ranch was our rhubarb. Larry used to harvest this from our garden every year. We used to eat rhubarb straight from our garden. This would really pucker us up. My grandmother, Tid, would make rhubarb sauces and pies. The strawberry nod comes from my mother as she would take us strawberry picking. I was terrible at it, but my sister, Cindy, would help pick all the berries. I would cook with my grandmother and mother, and we put these two together to make a Rhubarb Strawberry Cobbler. It is a great combination. We create this dish with spring rhubarb from the Lake Geneva Farmers Market (shout out to Farmer Darlene).

SERVES 8-10

INGREDIENTS:

FILLING

4 cups rhubarb, 1-inch slices

½ cup granulated sugar

2 cups strawberries, sliced in half

3 Tbsp cornstarch

1 tsp pure vanilla

1 orange, zested

DOUGH

1⅔ cups all-purpose flour

3½ Tbsp sugar

½ Tbsp baking powder

1 pinch salt

6 Tbsp cold, unsalted butter, cut into small dice

1 cup plus 1 Tbsp heavy cream

1 large egg yolk

Raw sugar, for garnish

PREPARATION:

FILLING

1. Preheat oven to 350°F.
2. Mix the rhubarb and granulated sugar in a large bowl. Let mixture set for 20 minutes. Drain the rhubarb and discard any liquid.
3. Toss the rhubarb with the cut strawberries, cornstarch, vanilla, and orange zest. Mix well. Divide the mixture into baking dishes such as ramekins

DOUGH

1. In a large mixer bowl or a food processor, combine the flour, sugar, baking powder, and salt. Add the butter and mix briefly, just until the mixture resembles coarse crumbs. Add 1 cup heavy cream and blend until just moistened.
2. Turn the dough out onto a lightly floured surface and knead with flour 5-6 times to mix thoroughly.
3. On a lightly floured surface, roll out the dough to a ⅓-inch thickness. Using a biscuit cutter, cut out 3-inch circles. Place the circles on top of the fruit-filled ramekins. Re-roll dough and cut out heart shapes.
4. Brush the top of the dough with the remaining 1 Tbsp of heavy cream. Brush heart cut out with egg yolk. Sprinkle with raw sugar. Bake for 15 minutes.
5. Lower the oven temperature to 325°F. Bake 12 minutes more or until the crust is lightly browned and the fruit juice is bubbling.
6. Let rest 20 minutes.
7. Serve warm with Vanilla Bean ice cream.

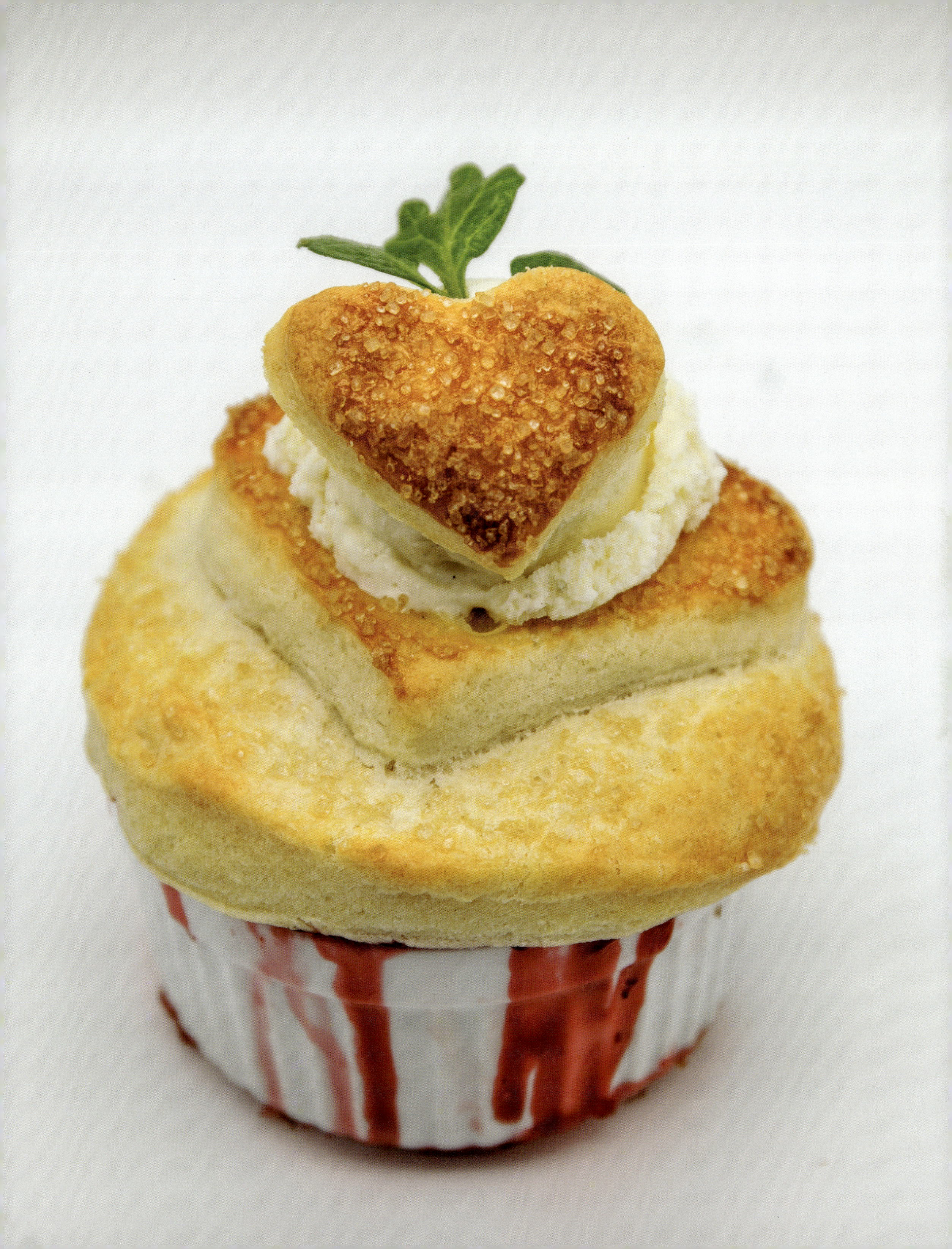

Vanilla Bean Crème Brûlée

Who doesn't love to use a blow torch? I love the aromatic of burnt marshmallow and toasted, caramelized sugar. In French, Crème Brûlée means burnt cream. Ideally, you sprinkle sugar onto the Crème Brûlée and use a blow torch to caramelize the sugar, creating a topping that would crack open like ice on a frozen pond. It should "shard up" with the first crack of the spoon. While I was growing up, I always enjoyed Crème Brûlée as the perfect finish at my favorite steak houses.

SERVES 8-10

INGREDIENTS:

4 cups heavy cream

10 large egg yolks

½ Vanilla Bean, split and scraped

1 cup granulated sugar

Raw sugar to caramelize top

PREPARATION:

1. Using a wire whisk, vigorously whisk egg yolks with granulated sugar in a large bowl until mixture becomes light in color and sugar has dissolved a bit; set aside.

2. In a medium size saucepan, combine heavy cream with Vanilla Bean, which has been carefully split down the center, its fragrant black seeds scraped from the pod, and combining both with the cream. Bring the mixture to a simmer.

3. Gradually pour the cream mixture into the egg/sugar mix, whisking gently by hand to combine. Strain custard through a fine mesh strainer.

4. Preheat oven to 350°F. Place individual ramekins in a baking pan, large enough to hold 8 to 10 six-ounce custard cups and deep enough to allow the water for the bain-marie to be added reaching at least halfway up the sides of the dishes.

5. Fill ramekins ¾ full with vanilla custard. Place pan in preheated oven and pour hot water into baking pan so water level reaches halfway up the sides of the ramekins. Cover pan with a sheet of heavy-duty aluminum foil, sealing edges to retain steam. Cook 35-40 minutes or until custard is set.

    To test for doneness, gently shake the individual ramekins; if center is still a bit liquid-like or wobbly, return custards to oven and continue to cook, checking every 3 to 4 minutes, until it has just set.

6. Remove ramekins from baking pan and chill custard in refrigerator 3-4 hours or until chilled through.

7. To serve, put a thin layer of raw sugar atop each custard. Using a blow torch, caramelize sugar working from the outside in towards the middle, keeping the torch in constant motion. Sugar should be golden brown and caramelized.

Serving Suggestion: Chantilly Cream (see recipe on page 195) and Berry Garnish

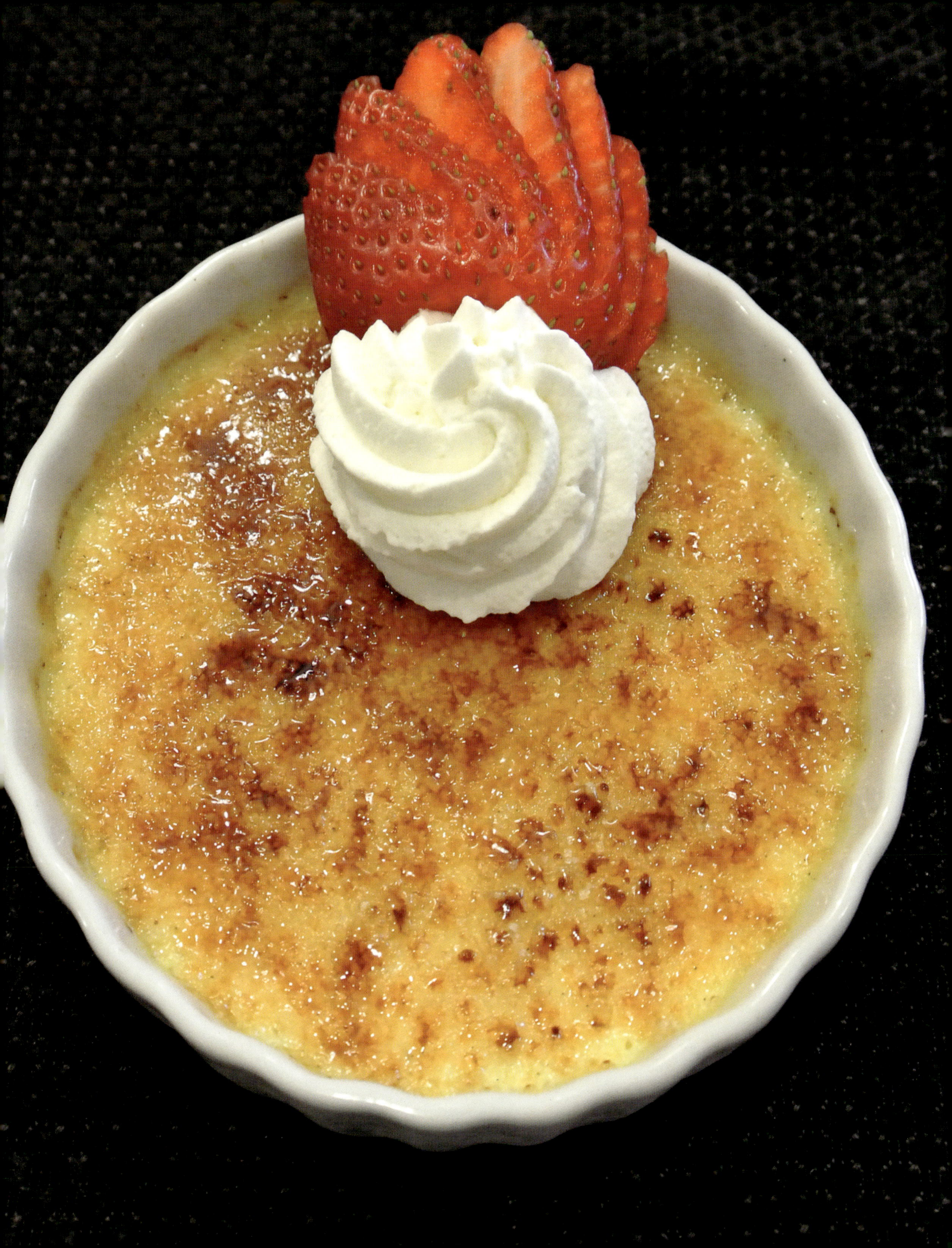

Flourless Chocolate Pâté

We created this recipe in 1988 at my restaurant Fedora's in Old Town, Chicago. This is a gluten-free dish, but back then we did not have to advertise it as such. It is a light dish, like a chocolate soufflé, where eggs are the leavening agent. You get the rich chocolate flavor with no flour and a great aromatic. I love when you take a spoonful, close your mouth and eyes, and breathe through your nose; you get a rich chocolate flavor.

SERVES 16-18

INGREDIENTS:

10 oz bittersweet chocolate

8 oz butter

1 cup coffee

1 cup sugar

½ tsp pure vanilla

1 tsp cinnamon

1 oz dark rum

5 large eggs

PREPARATION:

1. Preheat oven to 350°F.
2. Butter a 8x10 baking casserole dish.
3. Combine butter and chocolate in bowl and melt over a hot water bath.
4. In separate bowl, mix coffee, sugar, vanilla, cinnamon, and rum; add to melted chocolate. Let cool slightly.
5. Whisk eggs and add to chocolate and coffee mixture whisking constantly to thicken.
6. Bake in buttered casserole dish, covered in foil for 35 minutes or until the top just dries out.
7. Let cool for 20 minutes.
8. Scoop out portion onto plate and top with Chantilly Cream. Garnish with Berry Coulis.

***Serving Suggestion:** Crème Anglaise, Berry Coulis, Chantilly Cream, and Berry Garnish (for recipes see pages 195-197)*

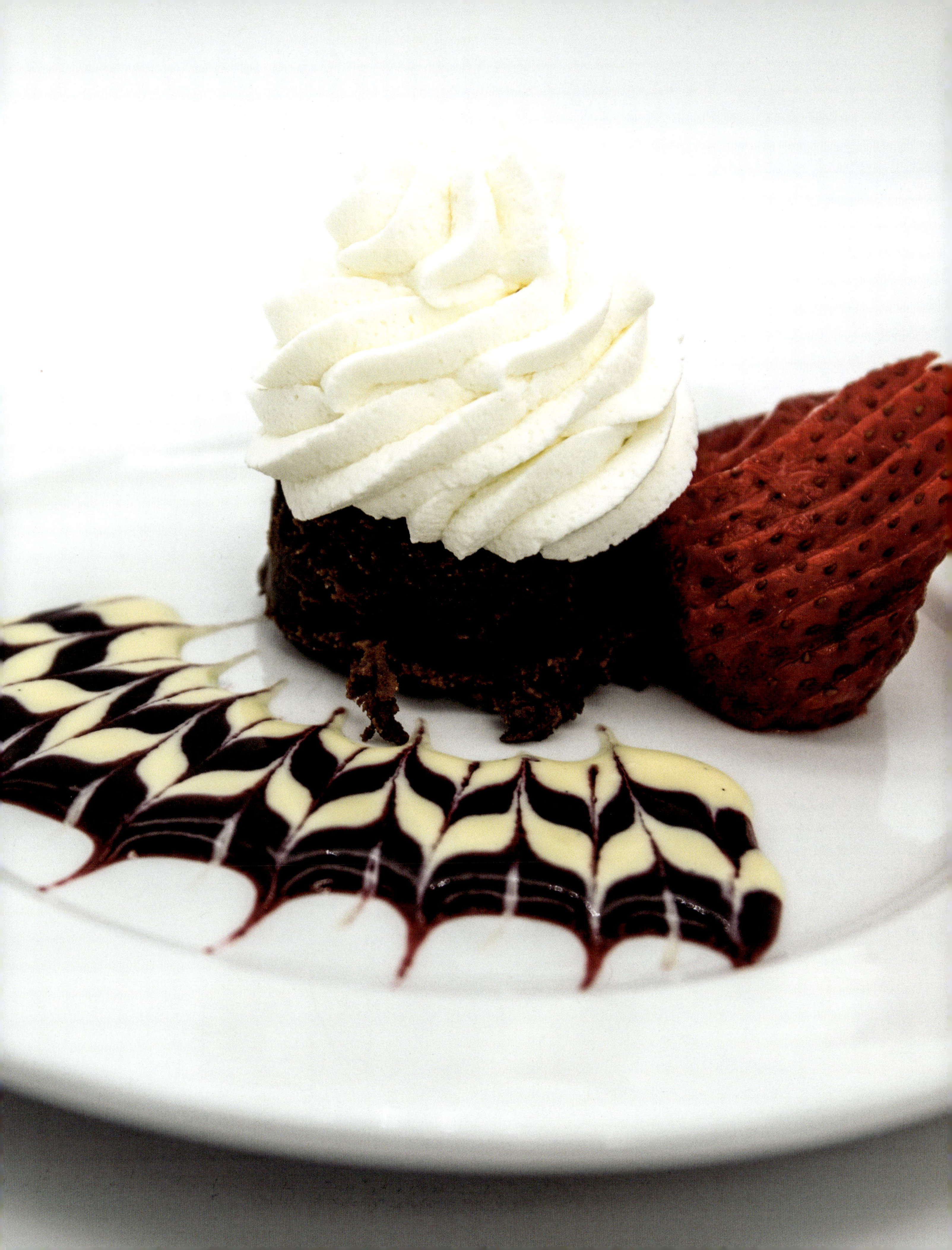

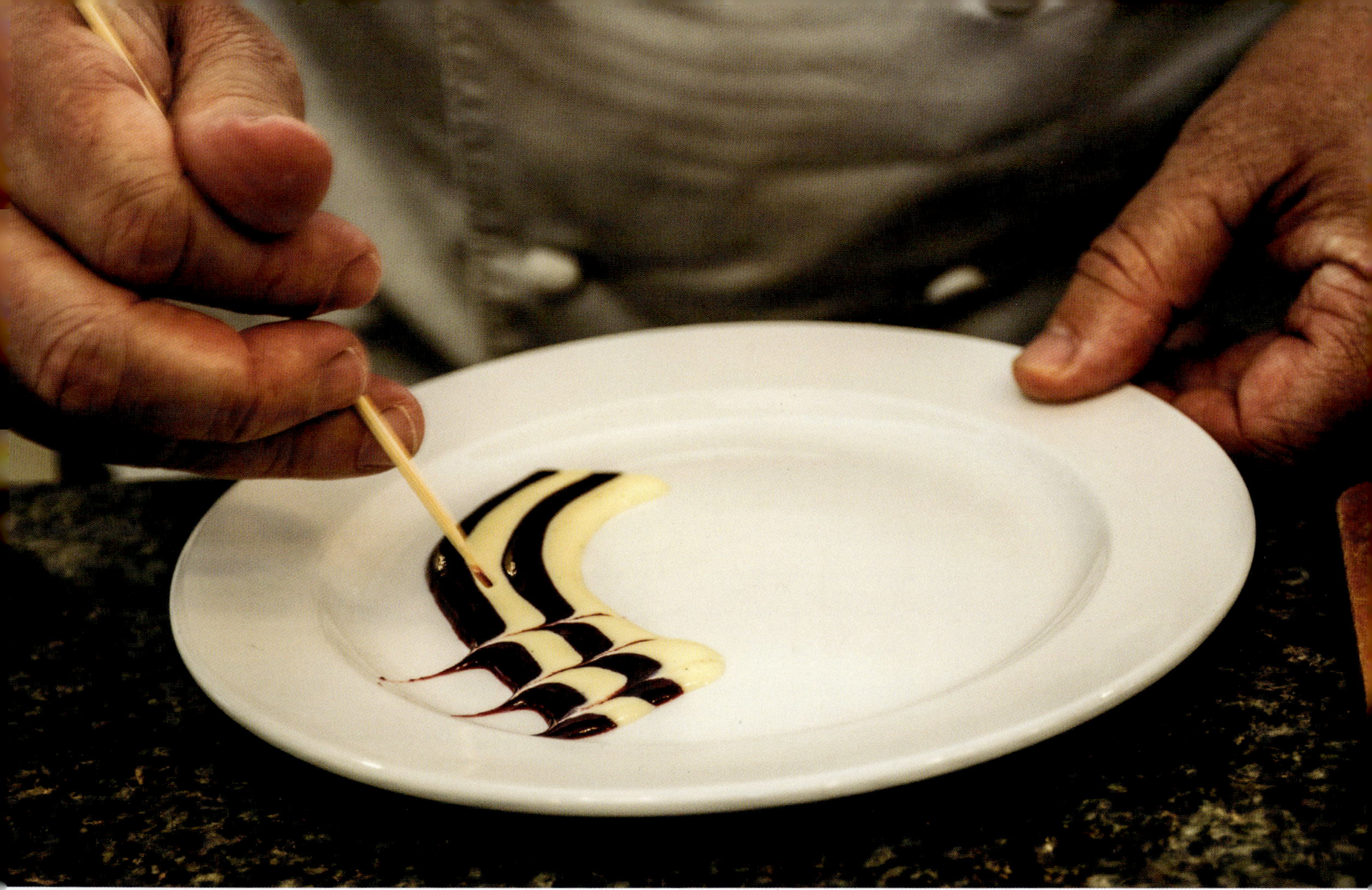
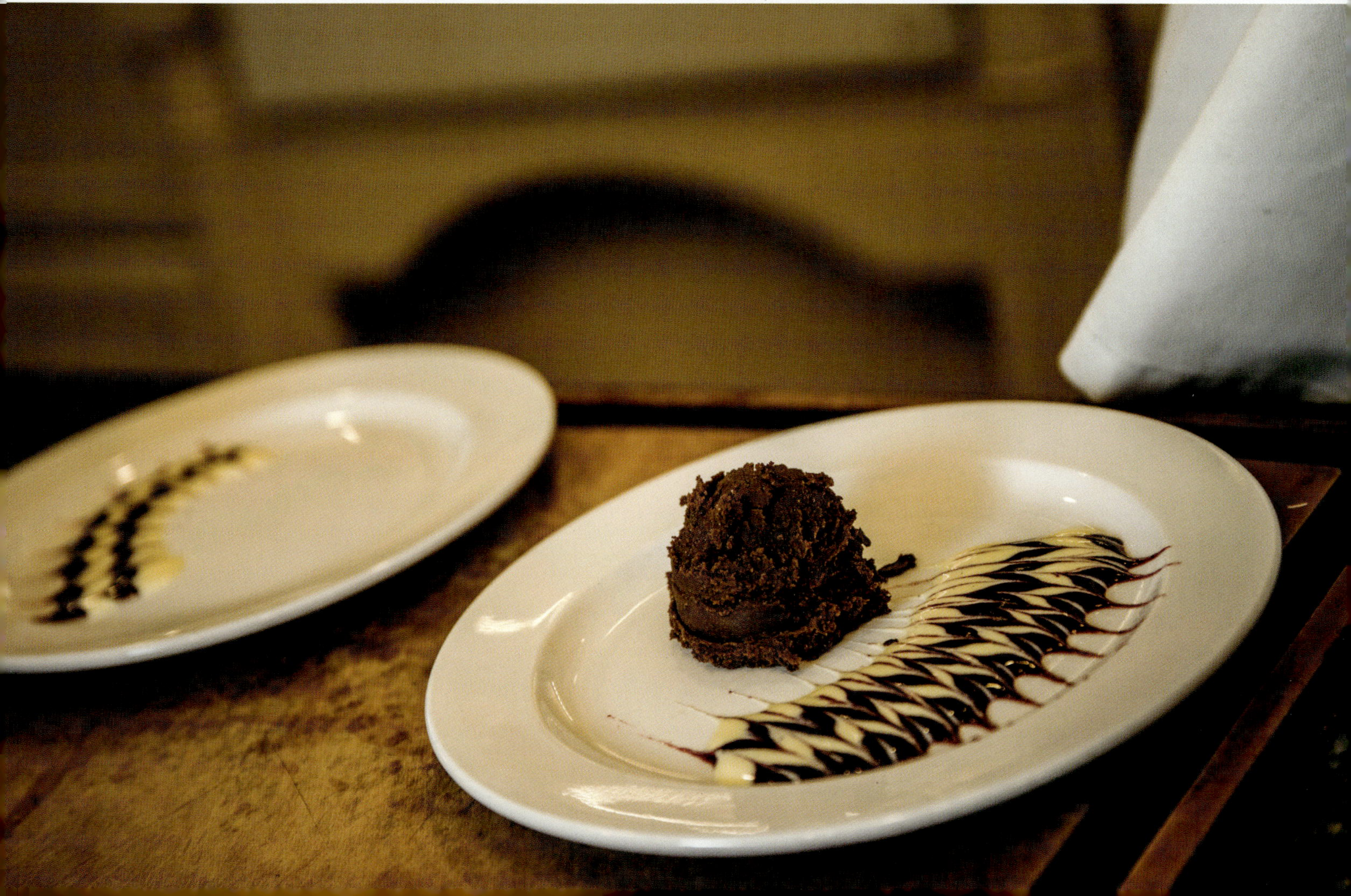

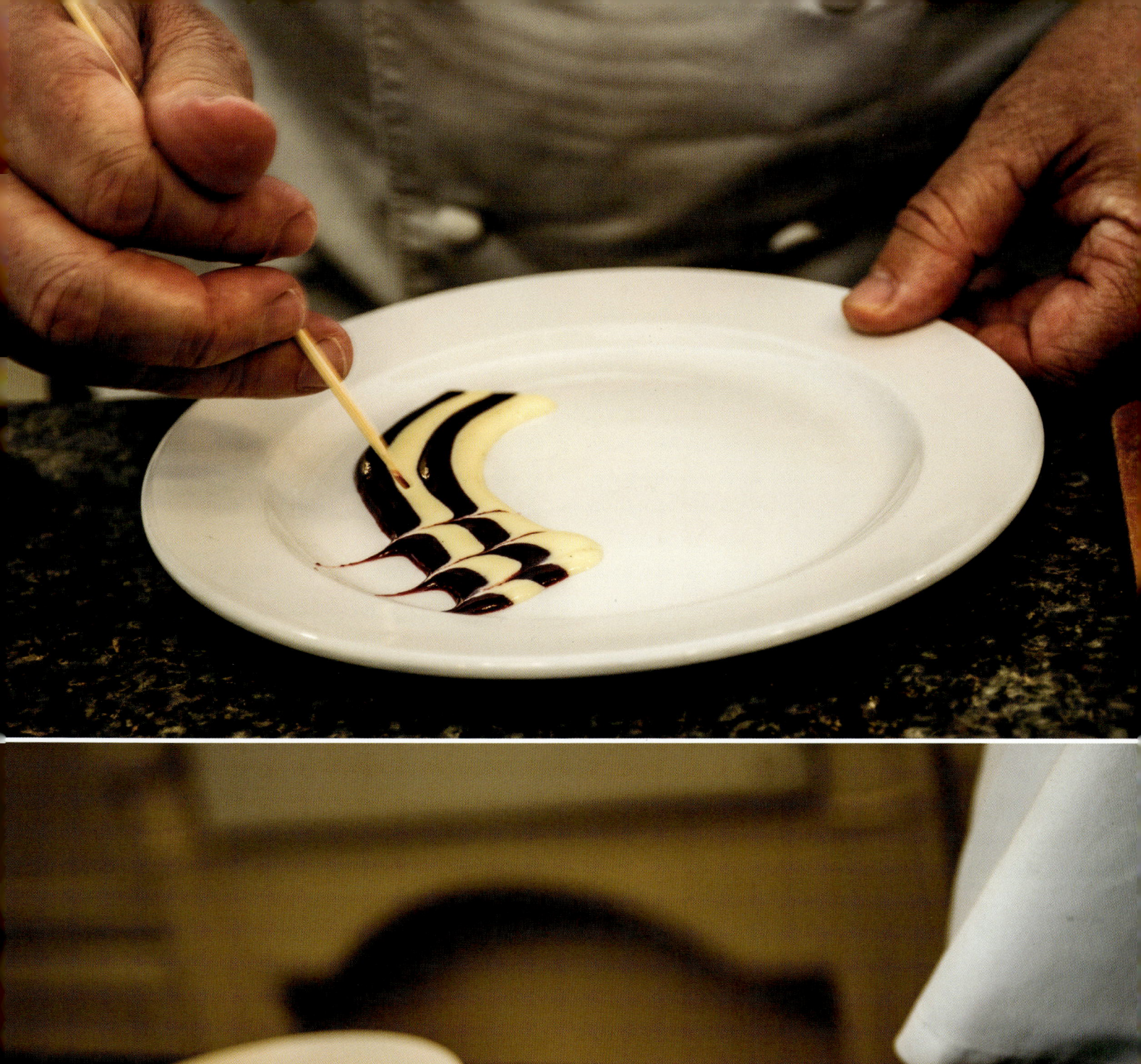

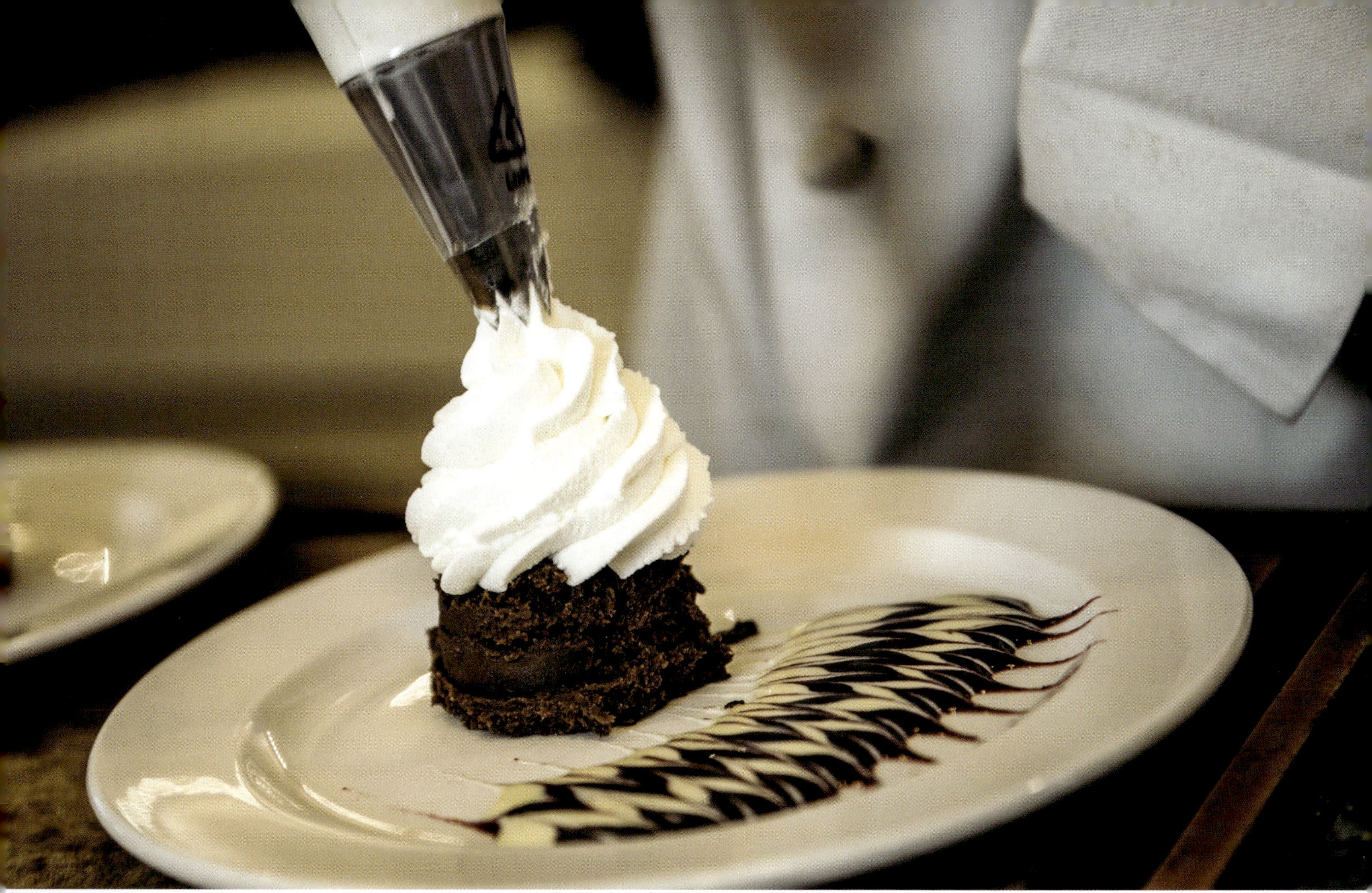

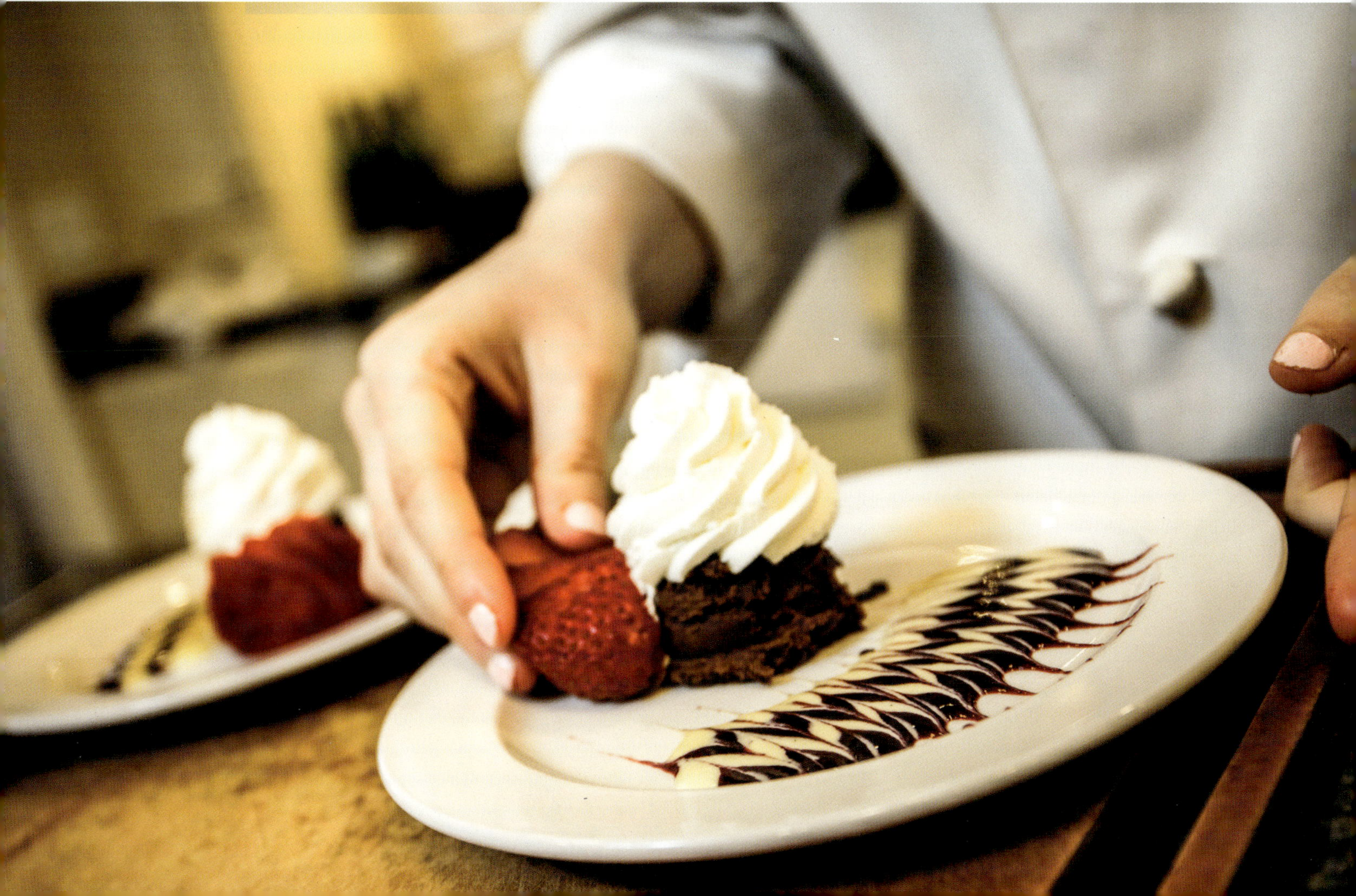

Preparing "Ahi" Tuna

Hawaiian Ohana

This is my most personal chapter of the book. In 1989, I met a beautiful young lady from Hawaii, my wife, Jacque. We got married in 1990, and over the years we have traveled to her home, the island of Oahu, and celebrated Ohana with my mother-in-law, Nancy. Ohana means "family" in Hawaiian and I love celebrating my family. I've also had the pleasure of bringing Ohana, chefs and musicians from Hawaii to Wisconsin to help share and celebrate the Hawaiian culture. Chef David Paul, from David Paul's Lahaina Grill in Maui, came to be a guest chef at the French Country Inn for our Hawaiian Ohana festival. The amazing band Maunalua have been here many times to share the culture and the love of Hawaiian music. Bobby Moderow, the lead singer of Maunalua, taught me "the Aloha of the Ohana and the Aina" which means, "the love of the family and the land," which is a Hawaiian spiritual motto that I still like to follow to this day. In this chapter we have dishes named after my wife, daughters, and grandson, along with dishes influenced by Nancy. I have great memories in this chapter and I hope you will share some of these recipes with your Ohana. Aloooooooooooha!

Tahitian Lanai Banana Muffins   56

Aina Haina Mango Avocado Salsa   58

Jacque's Kona Crusted Chateaubriand   60

Shrimp Briana Kaiulani with Macadamia Nut Pesto   62

Mackenna Anuhea "Ahi" Tuna Napoleon   64

Henry Kekoa's Harvest Risotto Cakes   68

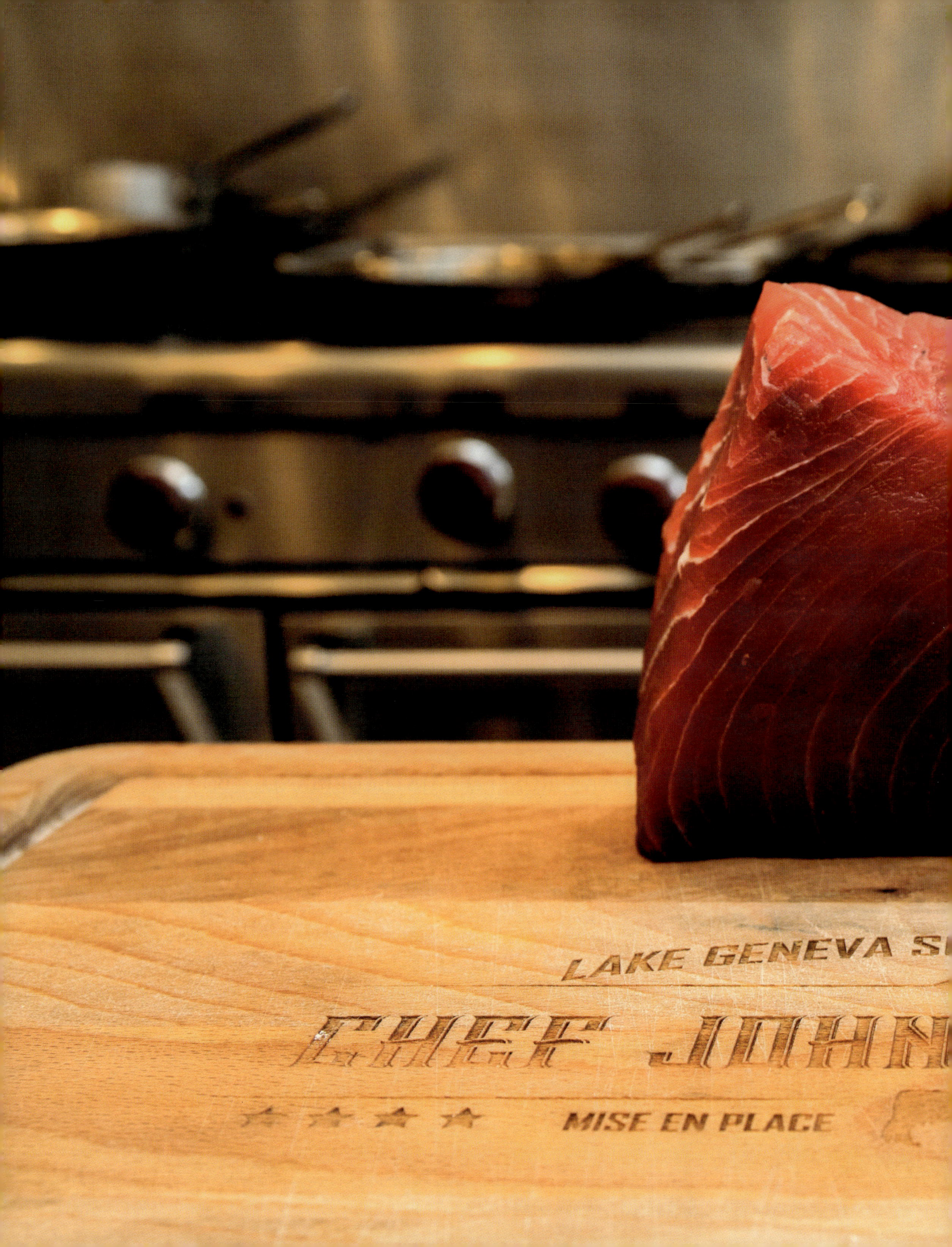
LAKE GENEVA
CHEF
MISE EN PLACE

"Ahi" Tuna Loin

Tahitian Lanai Banana Muffins

There was a great local restaurant in the Waikikian Hotel named Tahitian Lanai that featured Hawaiiana. The tables were situated around a beautiful pool and lagoon, and they were known for their Tahitian Lanai Banana Muffins. Every meal started with a basket of these highly sought after banana muffins. It was an amazing atmosphere of hospitality and Hawaiian culture. I hope you can close your eyes and feel the tropical breeze while enjoying these exceptional muffins.

SERVES 2 DOZEN

INGREDIENTS:

2 cups sugar

1½ cups butter, room temperature

2 cups mashed bananas

6 large eggs, beaten

½ tsp banana extract

½ tsp pure vanilla extract

4 cups cake flour

1 tsp baking soda

¼ tsp salt

Nonstick spray

PREPARATION:

1. Preheat oven to 350°F.
2. Cream sugar and butter together in large bowl with mixer on medium speed for 10 minutes.
3. Add mashed bananas, eggs, and banana and vanilla extracts; mix for 5 minutes.
4. Add cake flour, baking soda, and salt, mix for another 5 minutes.
5. Spray muffin pans with nonstick spray and fill with batter, about ⅞ full.
6. Bake for 20-25 minutes until golden brown. Serve warm.

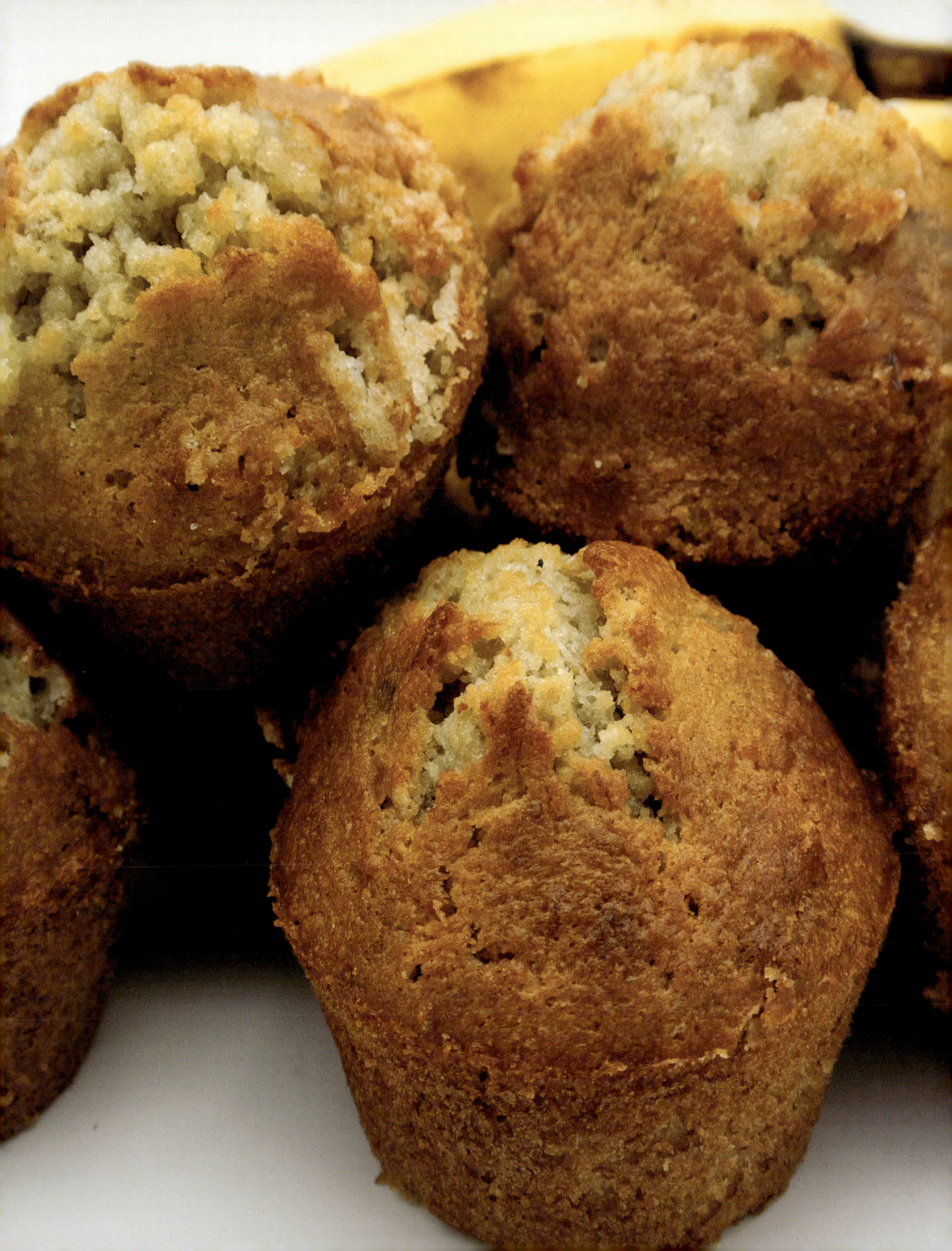

AINA HAINA MANGO AVOCADO SALSA

We used to pick mangos right off the tree in Nancy's backyard in Aina Haina. We always stayed at her house when we visited, and I would create new Hawaiian influenced dishes for us to share. We would have sit-down, 6-course meals with 8 people, but also pupu (appetizer) parties where Nancy would invite 80 people! Mango avocado salsa was created for these parties with mangos from Nancy's backyard and avocados from the neighbors. Ripe mangos can be very sweet, so the addition of some heat like chili pepper flakes, and Jalapeño and Poblano peppers, help balance the heat with the sweet.

SERVES 8

INGREDIENTS:

1 fresh Poblano pepper

1 medium red onion, medium dice

2 large red tomatoes, medium dice

¼ fresh Jalapeno, finely chopped

3 large ripe avocados

2 large mangos, medium dice

1 fresh lime, juiced

Chili pepper flakes, to taste

¼ cup fresh cilantro, chopped

Chef John's Signature Seasoning, to taste

PREPARATION:

1. Lay Poblano pepper on grill over medium heat. Turn every minute or so until charred, 7-10 minutes. Remove from flame, place in pan, and cover with plastic wrap until cool enough to handle. Remove the skin by peeling off the outer char. Remove the stem and seeds while rinsing off. Chop into small dice and place in large bowl.
2. Add red onions, tomatoes, and Jalapeno.
3. Split avocados in half, take out seed, and remove the flesh from the skin. Chop into a medium dice and add to bowl.
4. Add mango to bowl.
5. Squeeze fresh lime over salsa and season with chili pepper flakes, cilantro, and Chef John's Signature Seasoning.

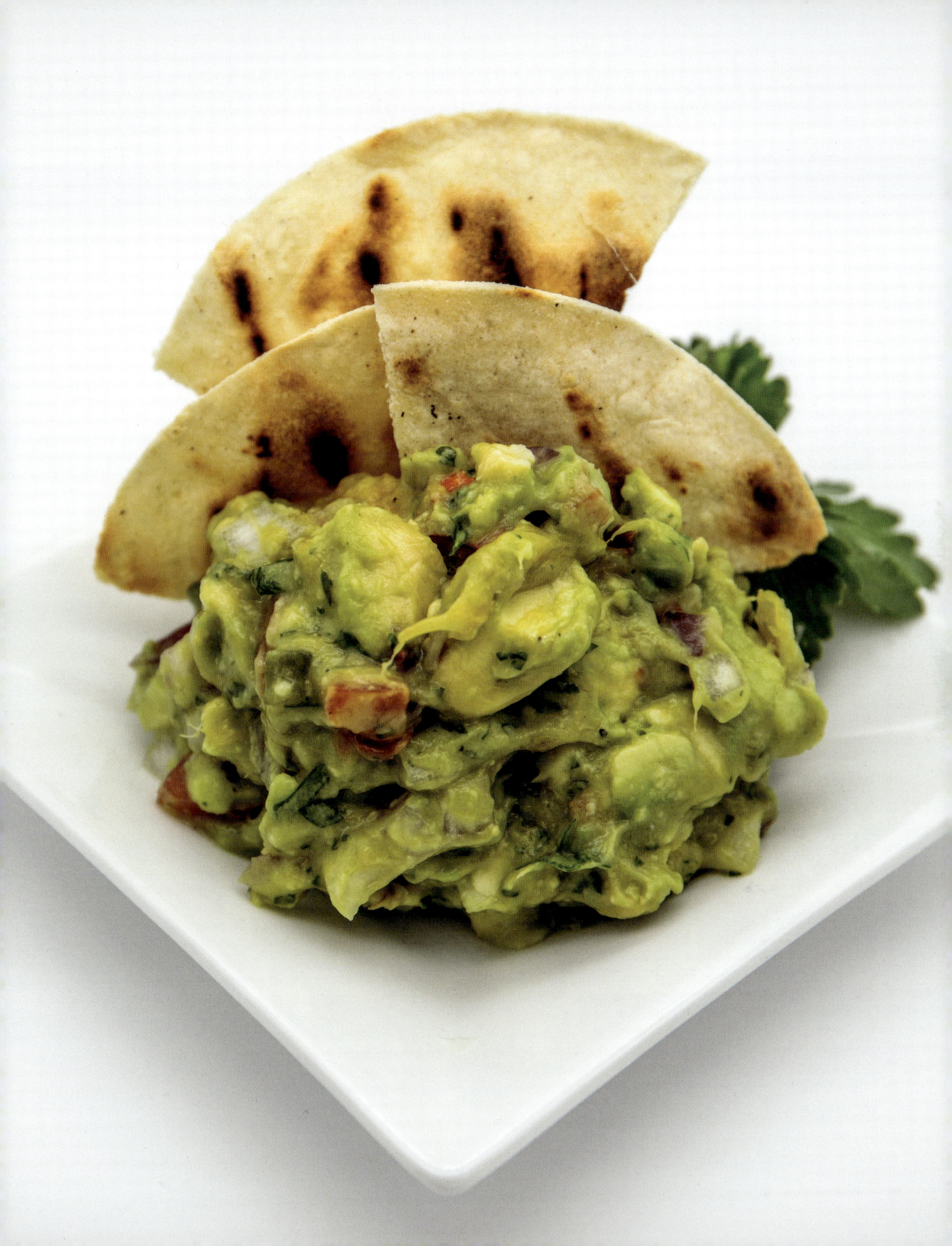

Jacque's Kona Crusted Chateaubriand
With Mushroom and Port Wine Reduction

In 1991, this was one of the first dishes I created while visiting Oahu. Nancy would invite 8 of her friends over and we would have a sit-down, 6 course meal where I would prepare my newly created recipes inspired by the islands. This Kona Crusted Chateaubriand was named after my wife, Jacque, during our first dinner party on the lanai. We take a whole beef tenderloin and roll it in Chef John's Signature Kona Coffee Rub. We then sear the beef creating a crust and the juices of the meat caramelize with the coffee. We continue to serve this dish today for many different occasions. It is ono-licious!

SERVES 8

INGREDIENTS:

1 Beef Tenderloin, 3-4 Lbs

¼ cup Chef John's Signature Kona Coffee Rub

2 oz olive oil

PREPARATION:

1. Preheat oven to 350°F.
2. Completely trim tenderloin of all silver skin.
3. Season with Chef John's Signature Kona Coffee Rub.
4. Heat olive oil in large roasting pan until hot (just before smoking point).
5. Carefully place tenderloin in pan, making sure not to splash oil.
6. Sear all sides, about 3-4 minutes per side. Finish in oven to desired doneness (10-15 minutes), or a thermometer registers 120°F (rare-medium rare).
7. Remove from oven; let set before slicing. Approximately 3 slices per person.

Mushroom and Port Wine Reduction

INGREDIENTS:

4 Tbsp butter

¼ cup shallots, chopped

1 clove garlic, chopped

3 cups mushrooms, sliced ¼ inch

1 cup Port wine

¼ tsp fresh thyme, chopped

¼ tsp fresh rosemary, chopped

2 cups beef stock reduction

Chef John's Signature Seasoning, to taste

PREPARATION:

1. Gently sauté shallots and garlic in butter for 3 minutes, add mushrooms and sauté until mushrooms are lightly browned, about 5 minutes.
2. Deglaze pan with Port wine. Reduce by half.
3. Add thyme, rosemary, and beef stock reduction; reduce and simmer 15-20 minutes or until desired consistency. Season with Chef John's Signature Seasoning.

PLATING:

1. Slice desired amount of meat from tenderloin.
2. Fan the tenderloin slices attractively on plate and spoon Mushroom and Port wine reduction over top.

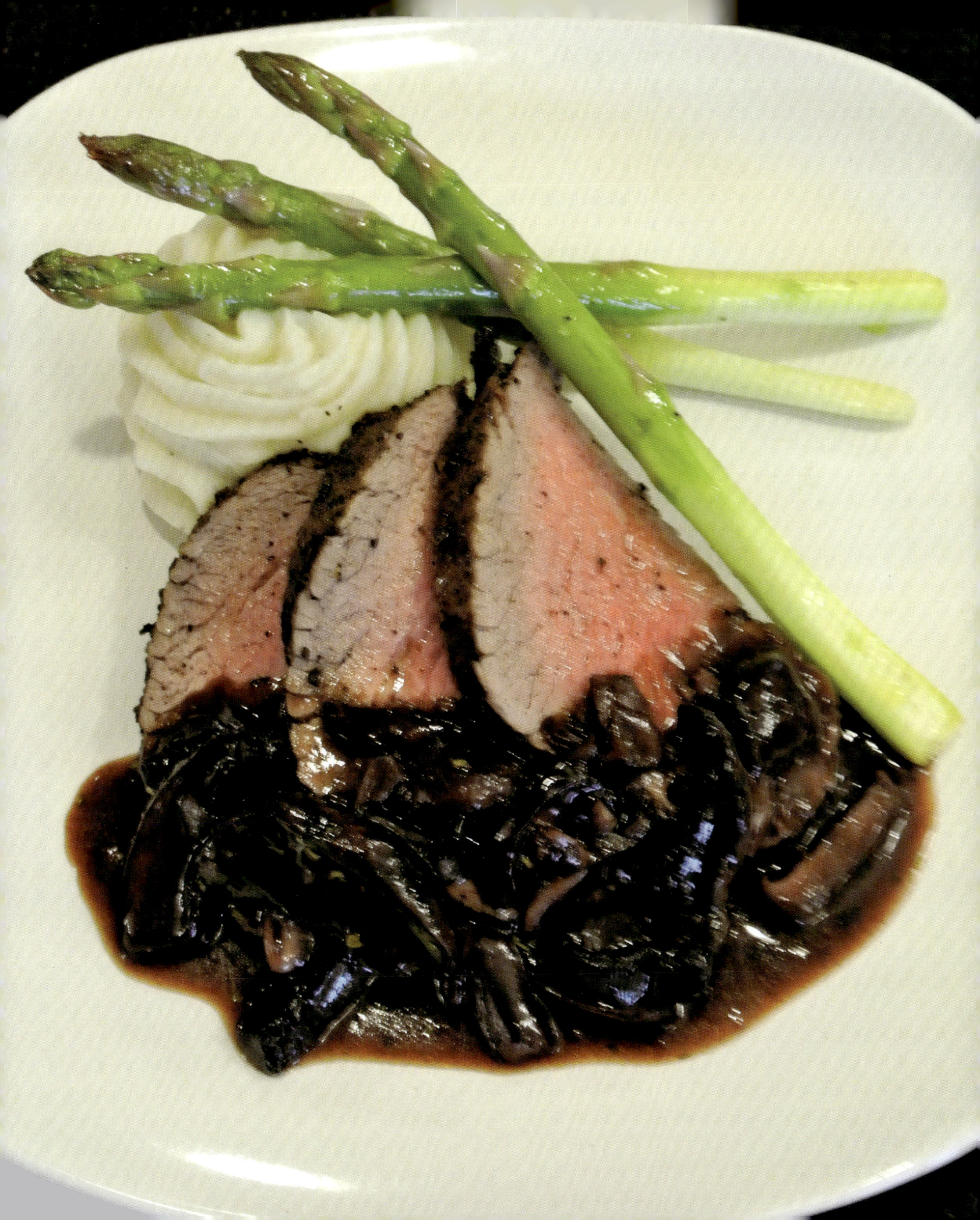

Shrimp Briana Kaiulani
With Macadamia Nut Pesto and Angel Hair Pasta

This dish was originated in 1993 for my first daughter, Briana Kaiulani Lee, who was named after Princess Kaiulani of Hawaii. We served this dish at the dinner and pupu parties at Nancy's house. Using Colossal Shrimp is ideal for this recipe. I love the aromatic of the fresh basil. It is a very traditional pesto, but instead of pine nuts, we make it with Macadamia Nuts for a Hawaiian flare. We coat the shrimp with the Macadamia Nut Pesto, and then we add white wine and lemon to the remaining pesto to make a sauce to drizzle over the pasta. We serve this with angel hair pasta, which is a nod to my first daughter who was, and still is, our angel.

SERVES 8

INGREDIENTS:

16 shrimp (U-10 ct.)
1 cup Macadamia Nut Pesto
½ fresh lemon, juiced
2 oz white wine

1 lb angel hair pasta, cooked al dente (3-4 minutes)
8 fresh basil leaves, chiffonade
¼ cup Parmigiano-Reggiano cheese, grated

PREPARATION:

1. Peel and devein shrimp (slice through shrimp to almost butterfly), wash thoroughly.
2. Coat shrimp with ¼ of pesto.
3. Place shrimp on hot grill; 2 minutes on front side and then turn shrimp over and grill 1 minute on other side.
4. Take shrimp off the grill and let rest 5 minutes to finish cooking.

PLATING:

1. Spool a mound of angel hair pasta in center of plate.
2. Place shrimp on side of angel hair, end to end to create a heart shape.
3. Warm remaining pesto with lemon and white wine, drizzle around shrimp and pasta.
4. Garnish with basil chiffonade, and grated Parmigiano-Reggiano.

Macadamia Nut Pesto

INGREDIENTS:

½ cup Macadamia Nuts, toasted
2 garlic gloves
2 cups basil leaves, chopped
¾ cup extra virgin olive oil

1 lemon, juiced
3 Tbsp Parmigiano-Reggiano cheese
Chef John's Signature Seasoning, to taste

PREPARATION:

1. Put Macadamia Nuts and garlic in food processor and pulse to a fine chop.
2. Add the basil leaves and work them to a coarse chop.
3. As the mixture becomes finely chopped and adheres to the blade, add EVOO, a little at a time, continuing to blend the mixture to a puree.
4. When the puree is smooth, add the lemon juice, Parmigiano-Reggiano, and Chef John's Signature Seasoning.

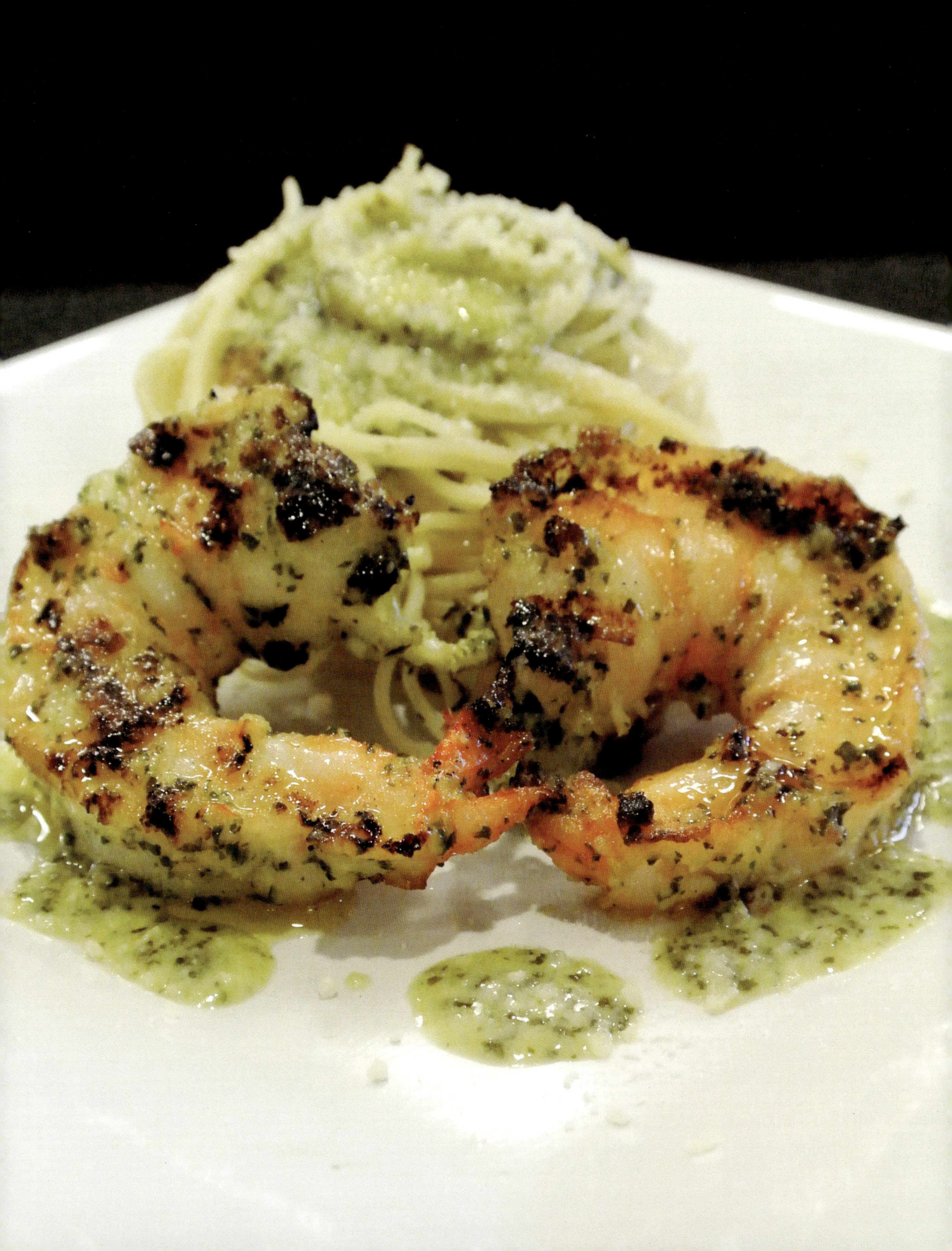

Mackenna Anuhea "Ahi" Tuna Napoleon

We created this dish in 1997, naming it after my second daughter, Mackenna Anuhea Teresa. Anuhea means "kissed by the morning dew" in Hawaiian. Inspired by the meaning of her middle name, we take the "Ahi" Tuna loin and lightly "kiss" it in the hot sesame oil. We serve this Napoleon style (layered) with sesame seared vegetables, crispy fried wontons, Deviled Soy Marinade, and Wasabi Shoyu Reduction. We joke that Mackenna has some "devil" soy marinade in her, while my first daughter, Briana, has more "angel" hair pasta in her.

SERVES 8

INGREDIENTS:

2 "Ahi" Tuna Loins, 10-12 oz each

¼ cup sesame seeds

¼ cup sesame oil

16 fried Wonton triangles

2 cups Crispy Rice Noodles

8 oz Deviled Soy Marinade

4 oz Wasabi Shoyu Reduction

12 oz Sesame Seared Vegetables

PREPARATION:

1. Prepare the Wonton Wraps and Crispy Rice Noodles.
2. Prepare Deviled Soy Marinade.
3. Prepare the Wasabi Shoyu Reduction.
4. Prepare Sesame Seared Vegetables.
5. Coat "Ahi" with sesame seeds.
6. Sear "Ahi" rare in hot sesame oil on all sides, 3-4 minutes total. The "Ahi" should still be rare-medium rare.
7. Slice each loin into 12 even slices (24 slices total).

PLATING:

1. Place 1 oz seared vegetables in center of plate. Place Wonton Wrap, top with 1 oz seared vegetables.
2. Place 2 slices of "Ahi" on top of seared vegetables. Splash "Ahi" with hot Deviled Soy Marinade. Repeat with Wonton, vegetables and 1 slice of "Ahi."
3. Drizzle Wasabi Shoyu Reduction on plate. Garnish with Crispy Rice Noodles.

Deviled Soy Marinade

INGREDIENTS:

5 oz soy sauce

6 oz pineapple juice

4 oz Cream Sherry

¼ Jalapeno pepper, finely chopped

¼ tsp white pepper

¼ tsp chili pepper flakes

½ Tbsp ginger, chopped

½ Tbsp garlic, chopped

¼ cup brown sugar

PREPARATION:

1. Combine ingredients, bring to a simmer for 10 minutes, remove from heat, let rest 1 hour.

Wonton Wraps and Crispy Rice Noodles

INGREDIENTS:

8 Wonton wraps (4-inch squares)

2 oz rice sticks, finished as 2 cups rice noodles

2 quarts Canola oil

PREPARATION:

1. Prepare Wontons by slicing a 4-inch square in ½ diagonally to form a triangle shape.
2. Preheat oil at 345°F.
3. Fry Wonton wraps in hot oil and drain.
4. Heat oil to 385°F.
5. Fry the rice noodles in hot oil and drain.

Wasabi Shoyu Reduction

INGREDIENTS:

¼ cup Wasabi powder

3 Tbsp water

3 Tbsp Shoyu (Japanese soy sauce)

PREPARATION:

1. Whisk ingredients together, and then place in sauce bottle.

Sesame Seared Vegetables

INGREDIENTS:

1 oz sesame oil

3 oz red cabbage, julienne

3 oz carrots julienne

3 oz pea pods, julienne

1 oz white wine

Chef John's Signature Seasoning, to taste

PREPARATION:

1. Heat sesame oil and sear cabbage for about 3 minutes. Add carrots and cook for 2 minutes, then add pea pods and cook for 1 more minute.
2. Deglaze with white wine.
3. Remove from heat immediately, season with Chef John's Signature Seasoning.
4. Serve al dente.

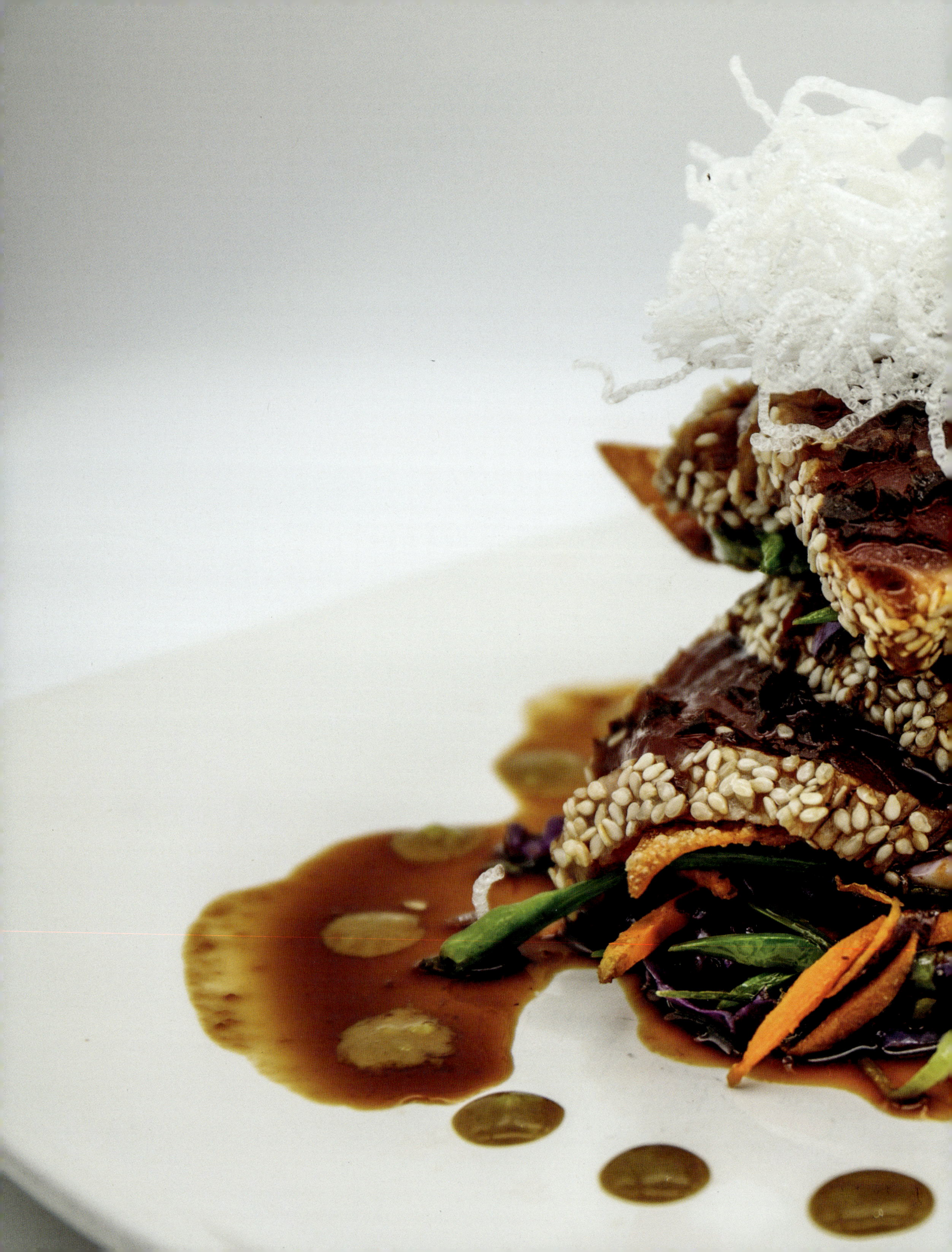

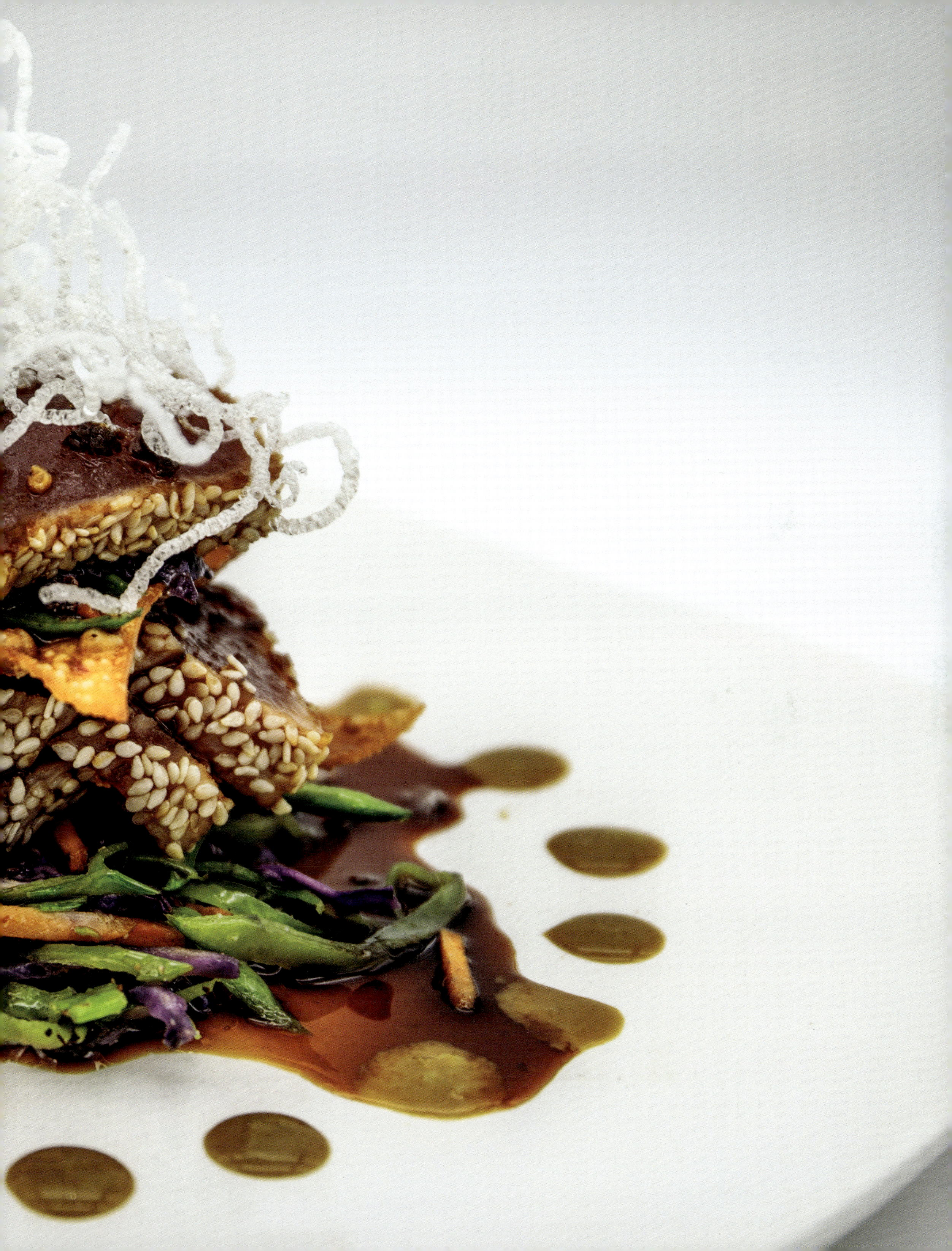

Henry Kekoa's Harvest Risotto Cakes

This dish was inspired by my grandson, Henry Kekoa Lee. In Hawaiian, Kekoa means strong. He was born in October, so a lot of harvest vegetables were available at the farmers market during this time. Wanting to incorporate these beautiful vegetables, we paired them with our classic Risotto. Being that he was younger, we wanted to make sure he enjoyed this meal, so we made little Risotto "cakes" and pan fried them until the edges were crispy. It was so tasty that we all could not get enough! We love to serve this with Aged Balsamic and Parmigiano-Reggiano shavings.

SERVES 10-12

INGREDIENTS:

¼ cup extra virgin olive oil

1 Tbsp garlic, chopped

1 cup onion, small dice

2 cups harvest vegetables (i.e. broccoli, brussel sprouts, cauliflower), small diced

2 cups mushrooms, small dice

2 cups Arborio rice

1 cup white wine

6 cups hot chicken stock

2 tsp assorted fresh herbs (parsley, thyme, oregano)

Chef John's Signature Seasoning, to taste

2 Tbsp butter

1 cup Parmigiano-Reggiano cheese, grated

1 cup heavy cream

1 Tbsp Black Truffle Oil

1 cup flour

¼ cup butter

¼ cup olive oil

1 Tbsp Aged Balsamic

¼ cup Parmigiano-Reggiano shavings

PREPARATION:

1. In a deep, wide Dutch oven, heat the EVOO over medium heat. Add the onion, garlic, and harvest vegetables.
2. Cook, stirring until the onions and vegetables are translucent, about 8 minutes. Add mushrooms and sauté another 6 minutes.
3. Stir in the rice until thoroughly mixed. Add the wine, stir and cook until most of the liquid evaporates.
4. Add about 2 cups of the stock and cook, stirring constantly, until most of the liquid has been absorbed. Add 3 more cups of stock, one cup at time, stirring well and allowing the liquid to be absorbed.
5. Taste a few grains of rice. They should be tender and creamy. If the rice is not done or is a little dry, add more stock and stir well. Season with fresh herbs and Chef John's Signature Seasoning.
6. Finish Risotto with ½ cup stock and stir in the butter, cheese, heavy cream, and Truffle Oil.
7. Let Risotto chill to room temperature.
8. Scoop out ¼ cup portions of Risotto.
9. Dredge each scoop in flour and form into round cakes.
10. Sauté in butter and olive oil for about 4 minutes or until golden brown on each side.
11. Serve 2 on a plate, drizzle with EVOO and Aged Balsamic.
12. Top with Parmigiano-Reggiano shavings.

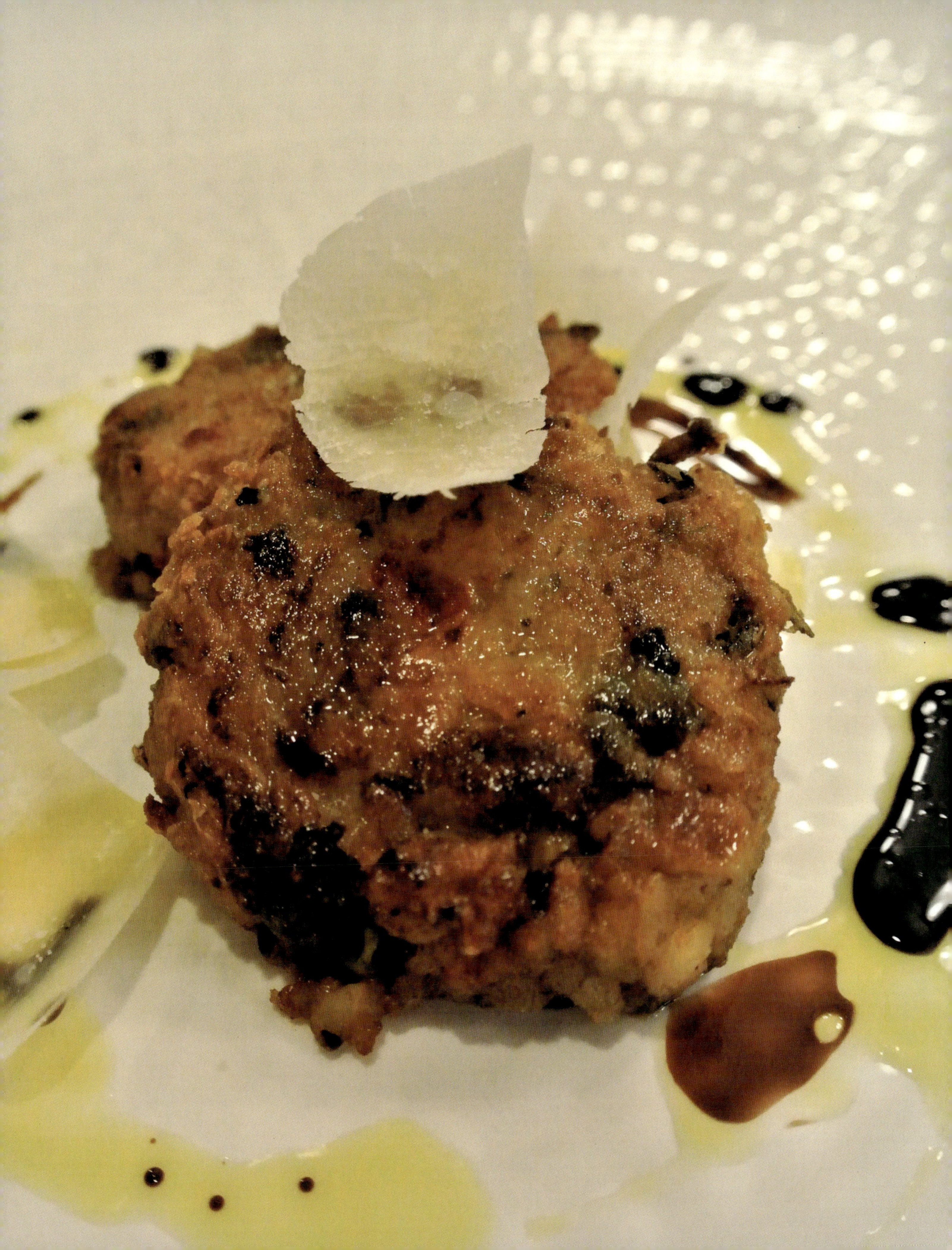

Hau'oli Lā Hānau

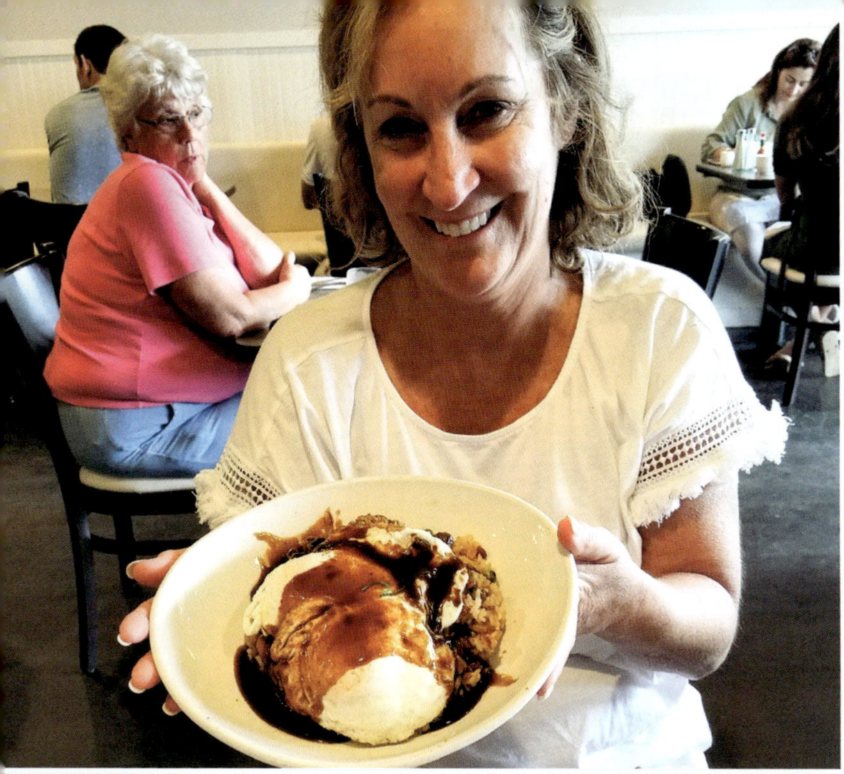

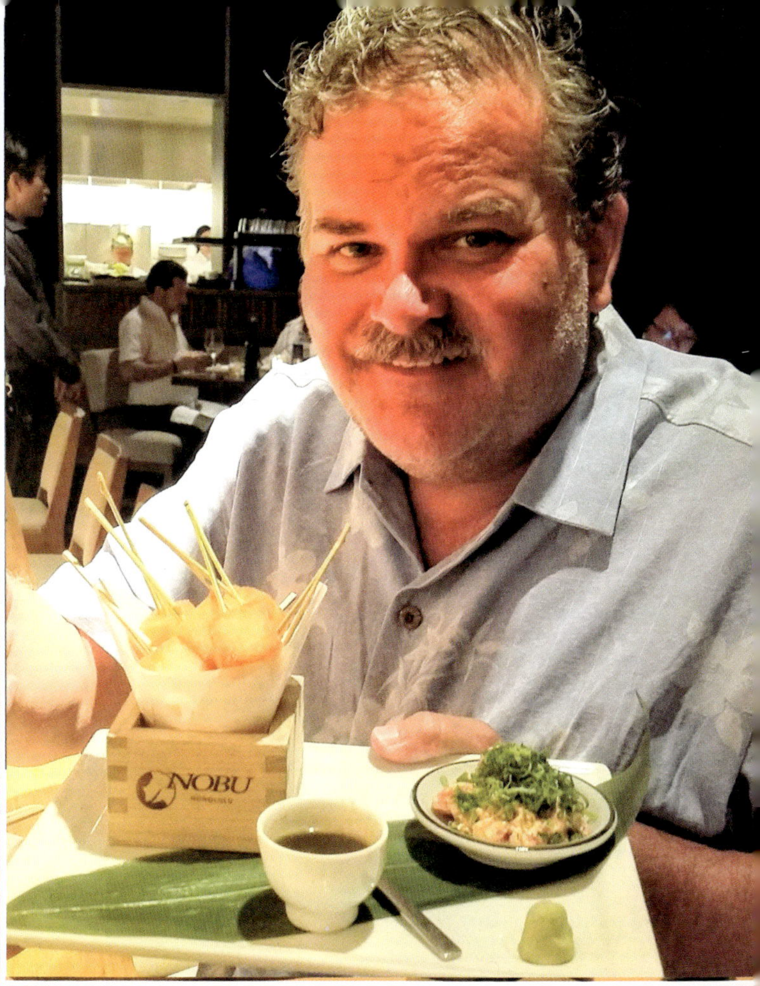
NOBU

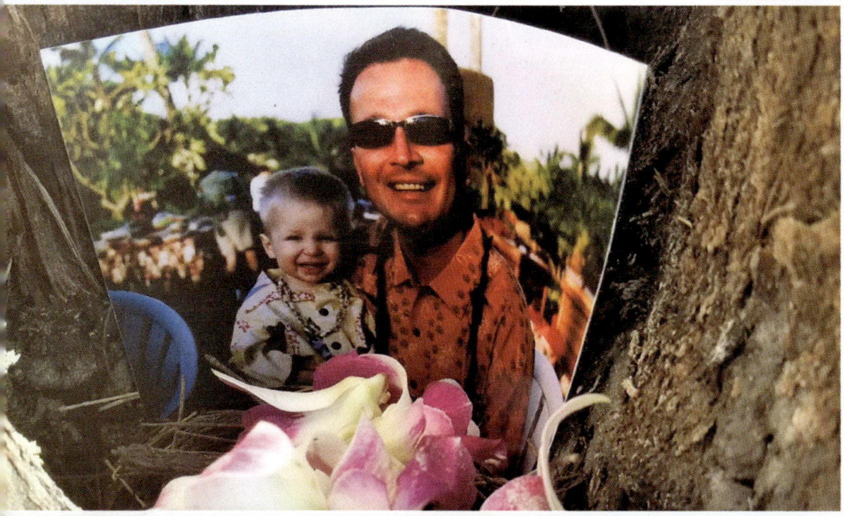

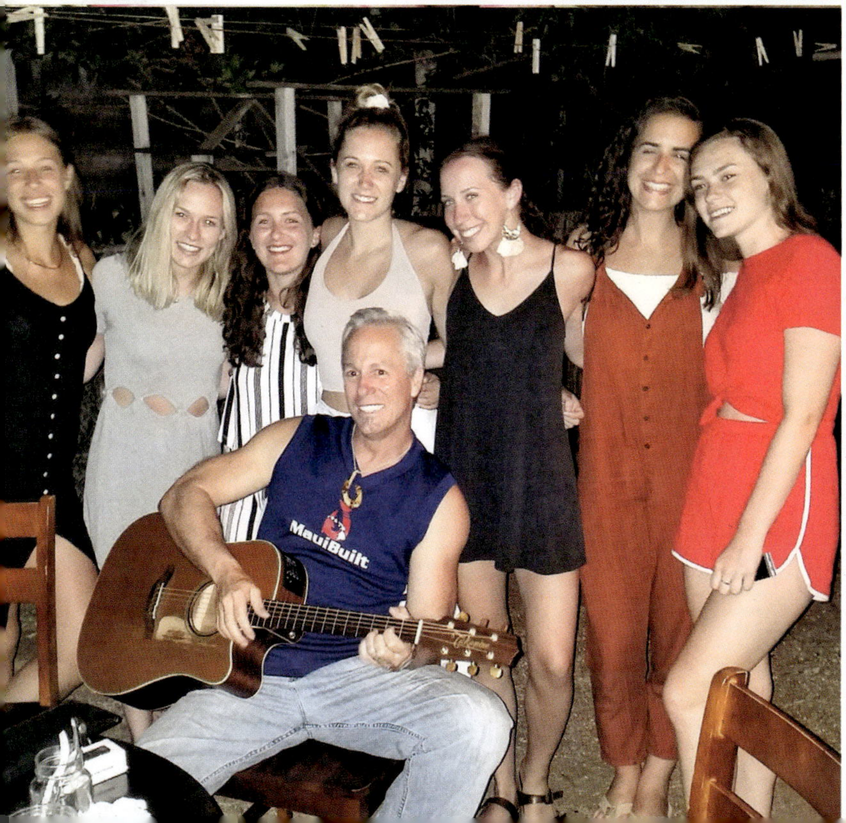
MauiBuilt

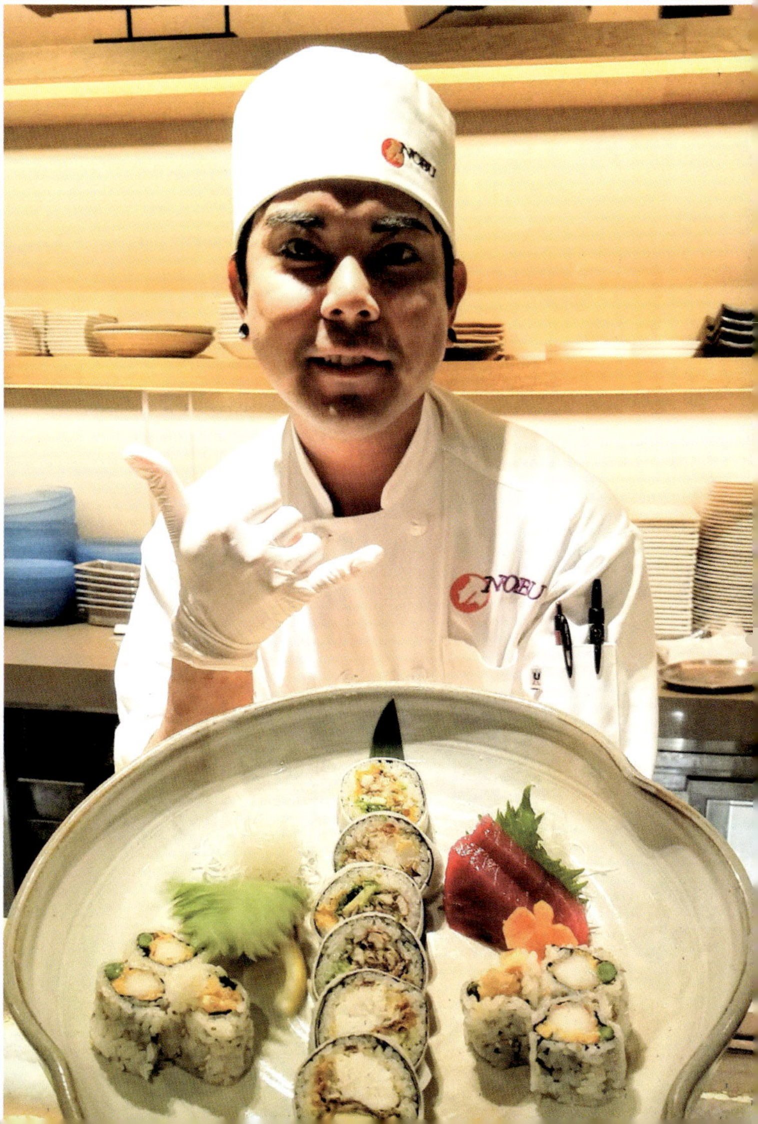
NOBU
NOBU

Chef John and the Lake
Geneva Cruise Line vessel,
Steam Yacht Louise.

Summer

Summer is by far the busiest time of the year in Lake Geneva. The town and lake are filled with locals and tourists alike. It is a beautiful sight. Over the years we have done many events on the lake, whether that be catering a Lakefront Croquet Party, July Shrimp Fest, or Expect a Miracle Extravaganzas. My favorite caterings involve the Lake Geneva Cruise Line aboard the Steam Yacht Louise. During the summer Lake Geneva has a wonderful farmers market and we love to incorporate local produce in our recipes. In addition, summertime is a great time to head out to the grill, and you will see an emphasis on grilling within this chapter.

Zucchini Fontinella   76

Panzanella   78

Ratatouille   80

Chicken Milanese   82

Grilled Chicken Au Poivre   84

Sautéed Shrimp and Zucchini   86

Braised Swordfish Steak Neapolitan   88

Grilled Stuffed Frenched Pork Rib Chop   90

Filet Mignon with Roasted Balsamic Onions   92

Balsamic Berries with White Chocolate Biscotti   94

Grilled Pound Cake with White Balsamic Peaches   96

Grand Marnier Dark Chocolate Mousse   98

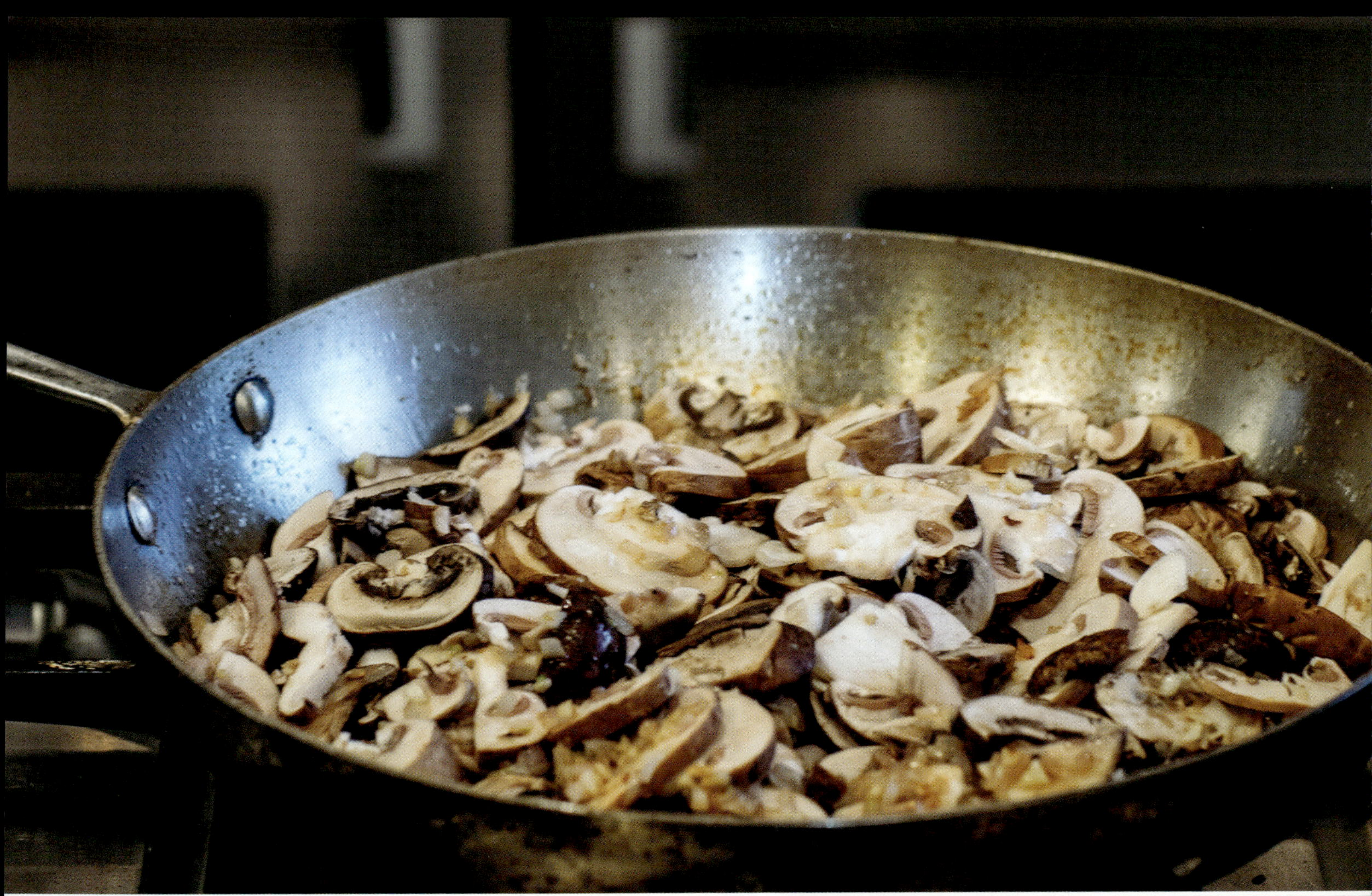
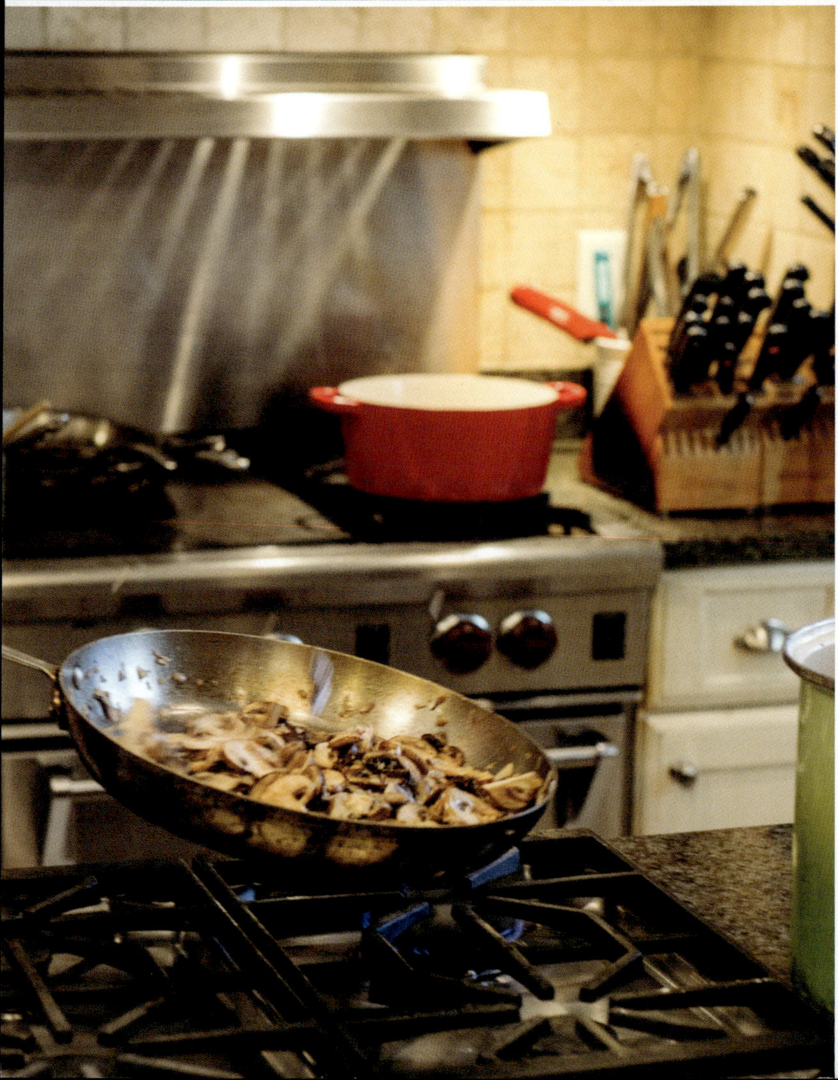
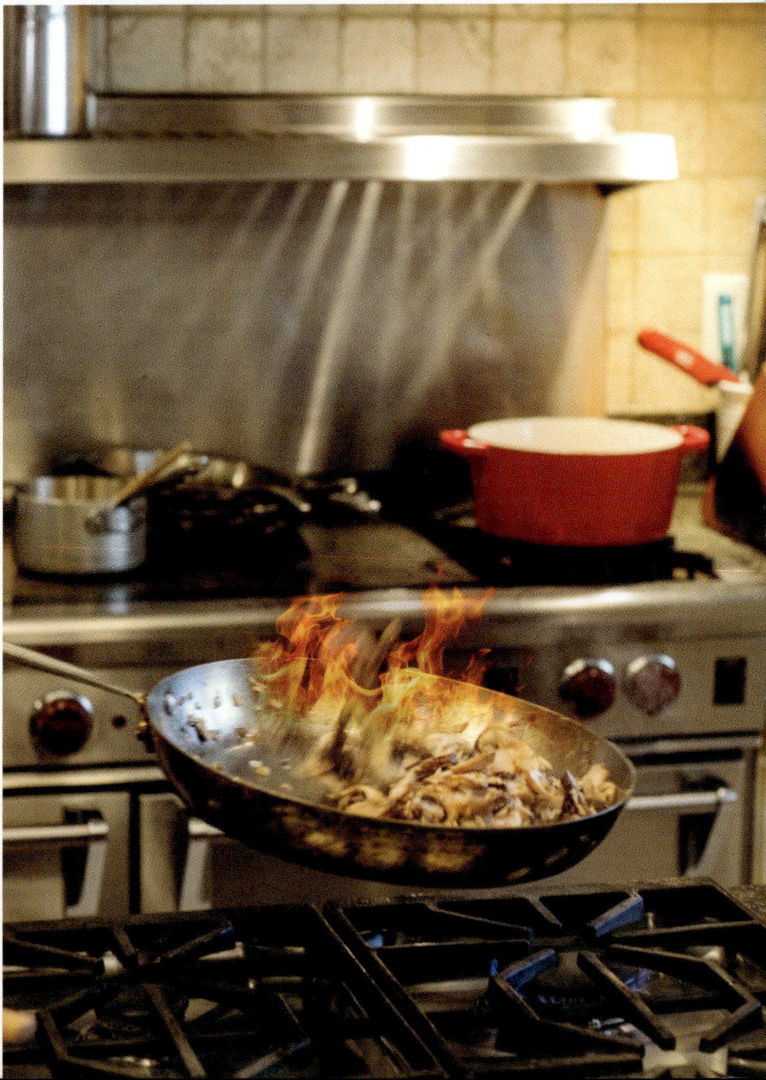

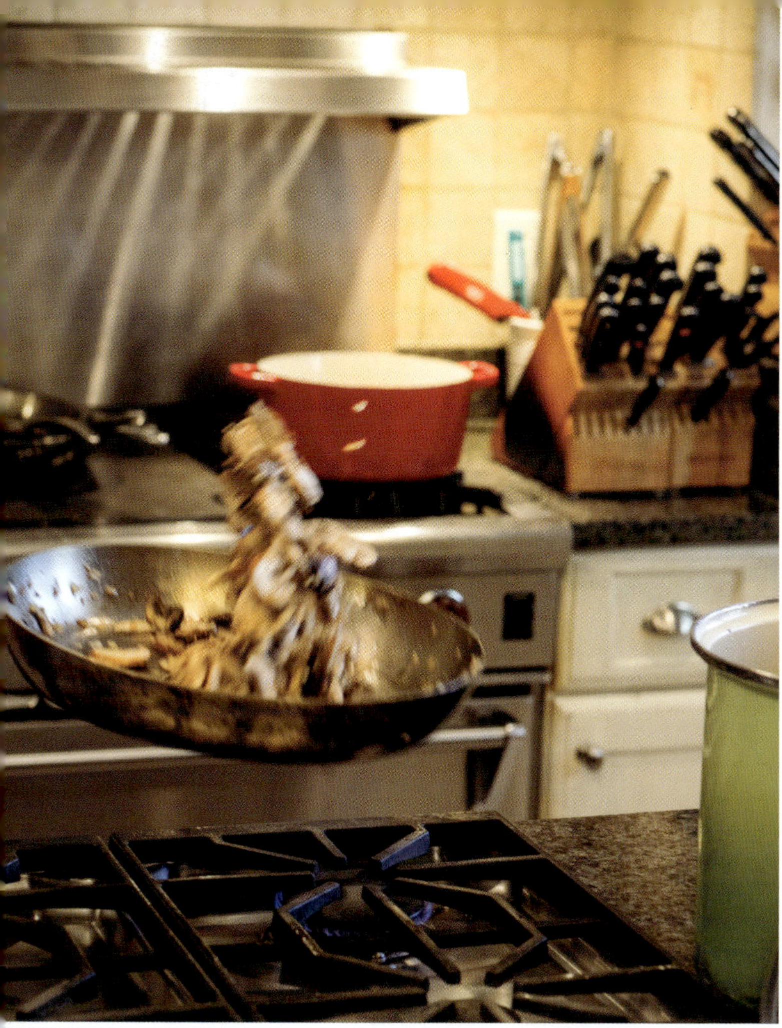
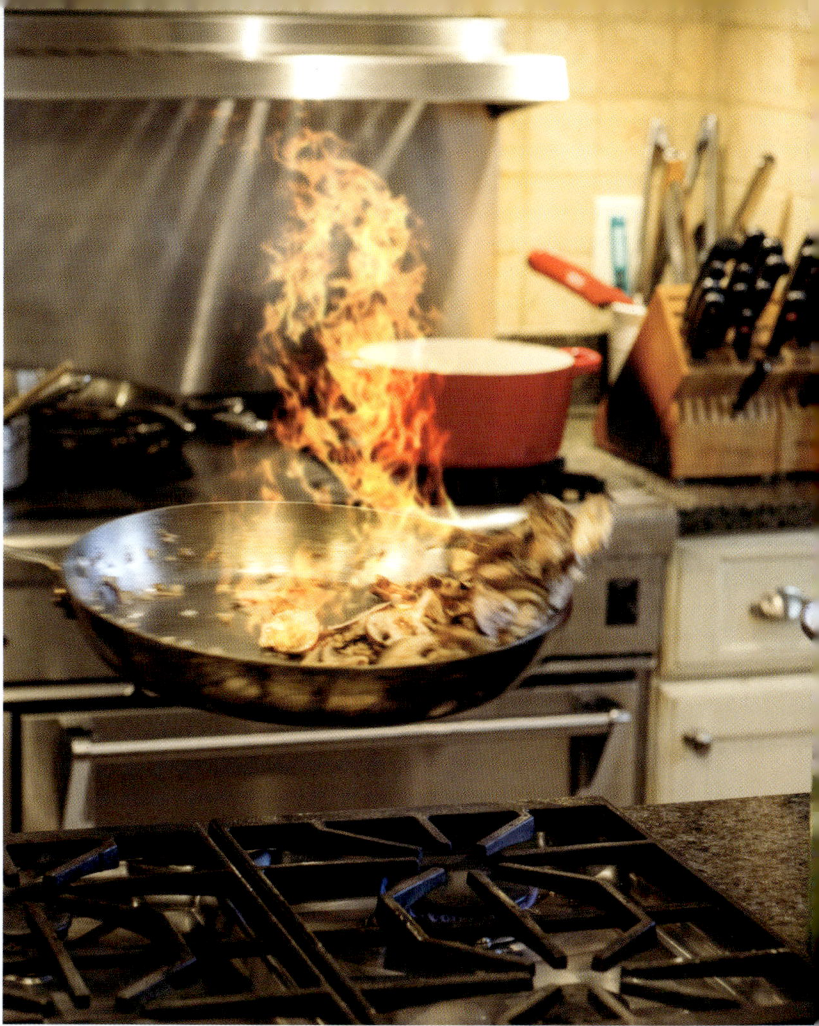
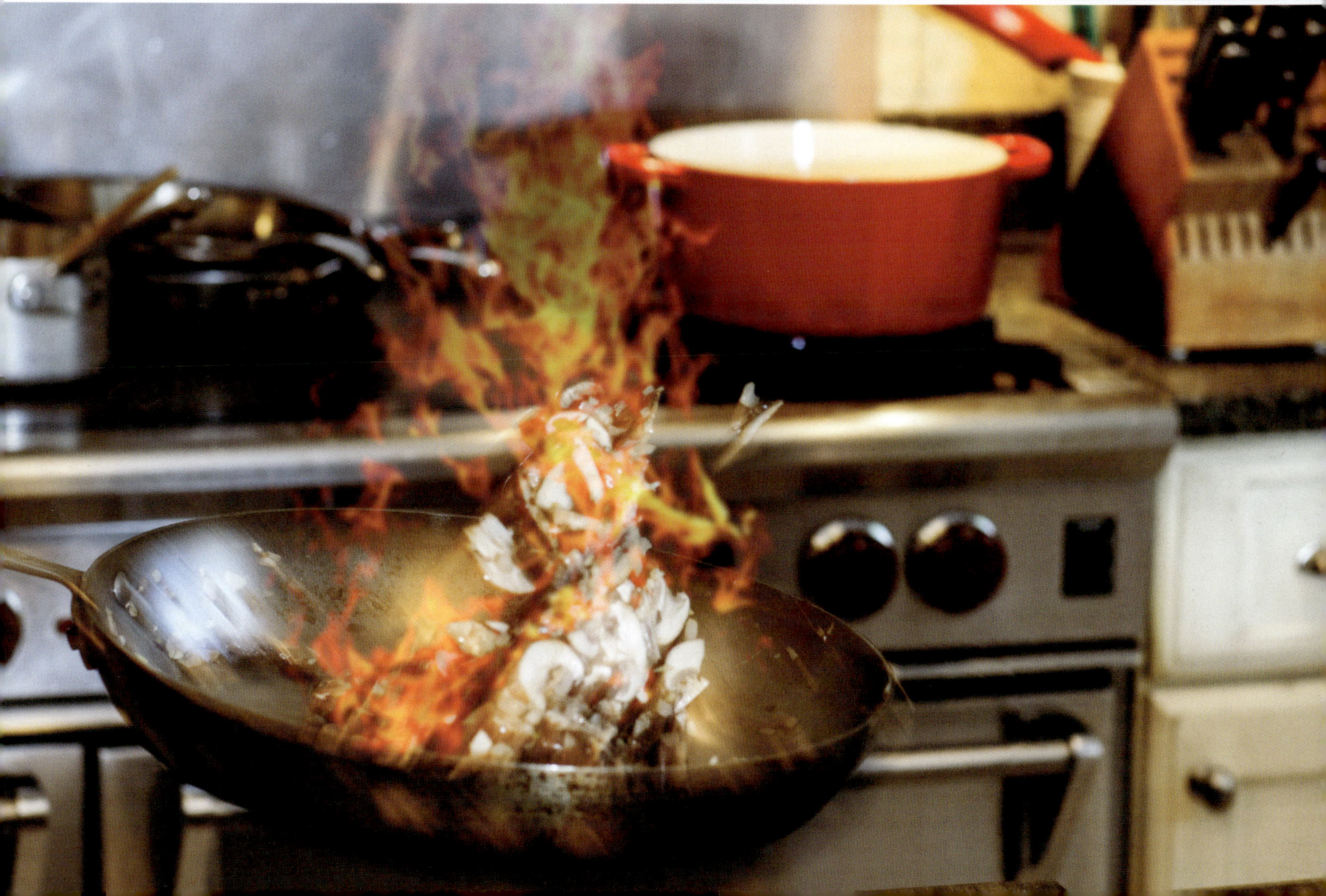

Zucchini Fontinella

Zucchini is a sure sign summer is arriving. I remember growing up, we would pick zucchini by the bushel in our garden. For this recipe, be sure to pick medium size zucchini before they get too large as they are ideal for this presentation. This is modeled as a zucchini grilled cheese where you have zucchini sandwiching Prosciutto and Fontinella cheese. This is a dish the whole family will enjoy. You can serve this creation with a salad or atop pasta for a light summer meal.

SERVES 8
INGREDIENTS:

- 4 medium zucchini
- 8 thin slices Prosciutto
- 16 leaves fresh sage
- 8 slices Fontinella cheese
- 3 large eggs, lightly beaten
- ½ cup all-purpose flour
- 2 Tbsp olive oil
- 2 Tbsp butter
- ½ Tbsp parsley, chopped
- 2 Tbsp Parmesan cheese, grated
- 1 lemon, cut into wedges
- Chef John's Signature Seasoning, to taste

PREPARATION:

1. With the zucchini lengthwise, cut a thin slice off each zucchini so they can lay flat and then be cut lengthwise into even ¼-inch-thick slices. You will need 16 slices total.
2. Arrange the Fontinella slices on the bottom half of 8 zucchini slices. Place sage leaf and Prosciutto on top of cheese. Finally, lay the remaining zucchini slices on top of each stack.
3. Pour the eggs into a deep plate. On another plate, season the flour with Chef John's Signature Seasoning.
4. Pick up each zucchini stack by both ends and hold it securely closed as you dip it first in the egg and then dredge in the flour until evenly coated.
5. In a large sauté pan, heat 2 Tbsp of butter and 2 Tbsp of olive oil over medium-high heat.
6. Cook the zucchini, turning once, until golden brown, about 2 minutes on each side.
7. Move zucchini to a plate and keep warm until all are cooked.
8. Slice zucchini cheese sandwiches in half "on the bias."
9. Serve with a sprinkling of parsley, Parmesan, and lemon wedges.

Serving Suggestion: Drizzle with extra virgin olive oil and Aged Balsamic

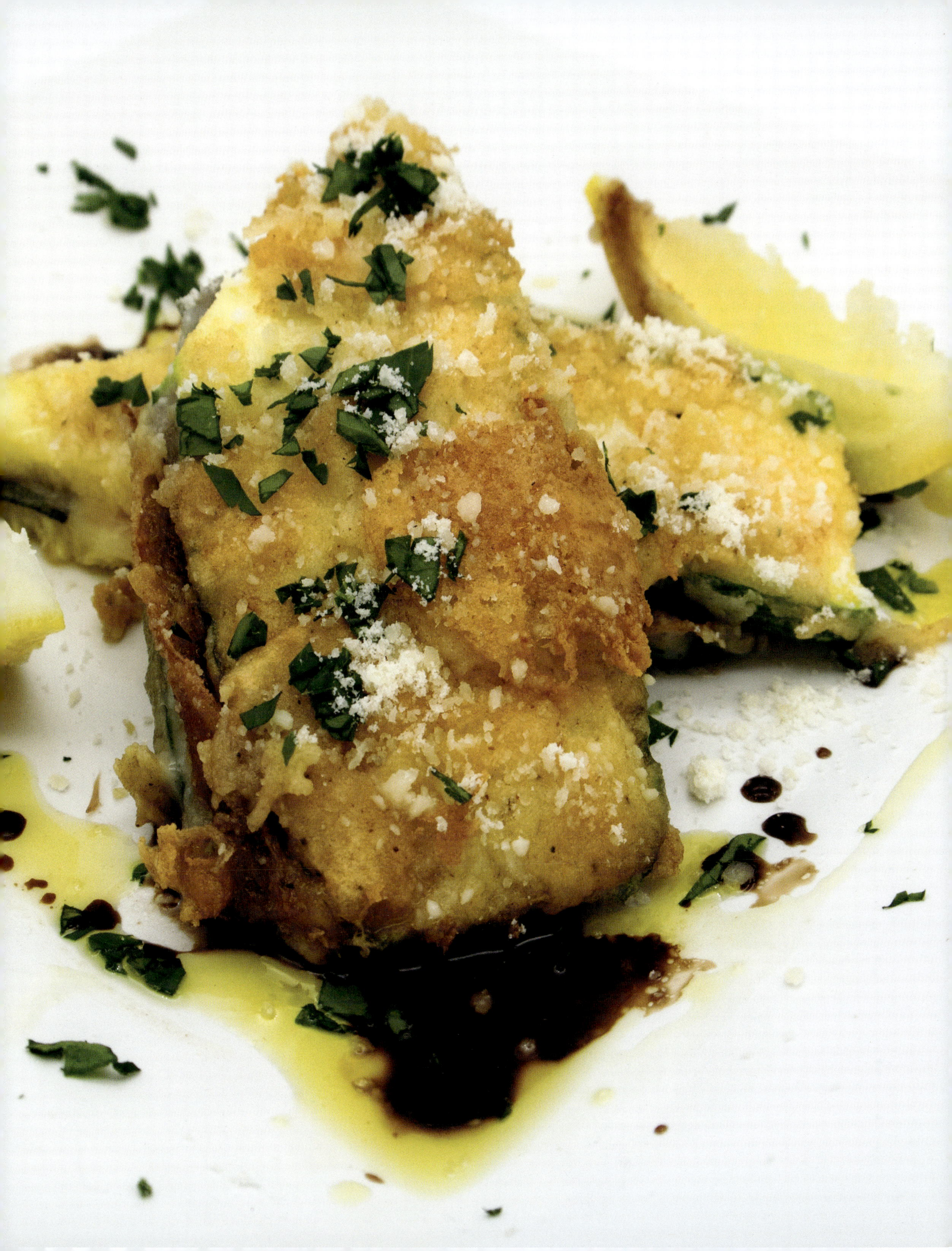

Panzanella

Through the years we have used many different types of tomatoes. Recently, there have been so many new heirloom cherry tomato varieties, like the yellow currants and Sungolds, and we like to highlight these different flavor profiles in this salad. We toss the tomatoes with croutons and a honey herb vinaigrette, and serve this on top of fresh baby greens. This is a great first course to kick off the summer tomato harvest.

SERVES 8

INGREDIENTS:

4 cups Italian bread (½ x ½ inch cubes)

2 Tbsp extra virgin olive oil

½ tsp Italian seasoning

4 cups cherry tomatoes, assorted shapes, colors, and sizes, halved

½ cup fresh basil, chiffonade

¼ cup Kalamata olives, quartered lengthwise

4 cups baby greens

¼ cup Parmigiano-Reggiano cheese shavings

DRESSING:

1 Tbsp lemon juice

¼ cup extra virgin olive oil

Chef John's Signature Seasoning, to taste

3 Tbsp honey

¼ tsp fresh thyme, chopped

½ tsp fresh oregano, chopped

PREPARATION:

1. Preheat oven to 375°F.
2. Toss bread cubes, EVOO, Italian seasoning, and Chef John's Signature Seasoning.
3. Spread out in an even layer on a baking sheet.
4. Bake 12-15 minutes until light golden brown.
5. Prep tomatoes by slicing in half depending on size.
6. Toss croutons with tomatoes, fresh basil, and Kalamata olives.
7. Whisk together dressing ingredients, pour over tomato/bread salad and fold in.
8. Allow the Panzanella to sit at room temperature for about a half hour before serving so that the flavors can meld.
9. Serve on top of seasoned baby greens with shaved Parmigiano-Reggiano.

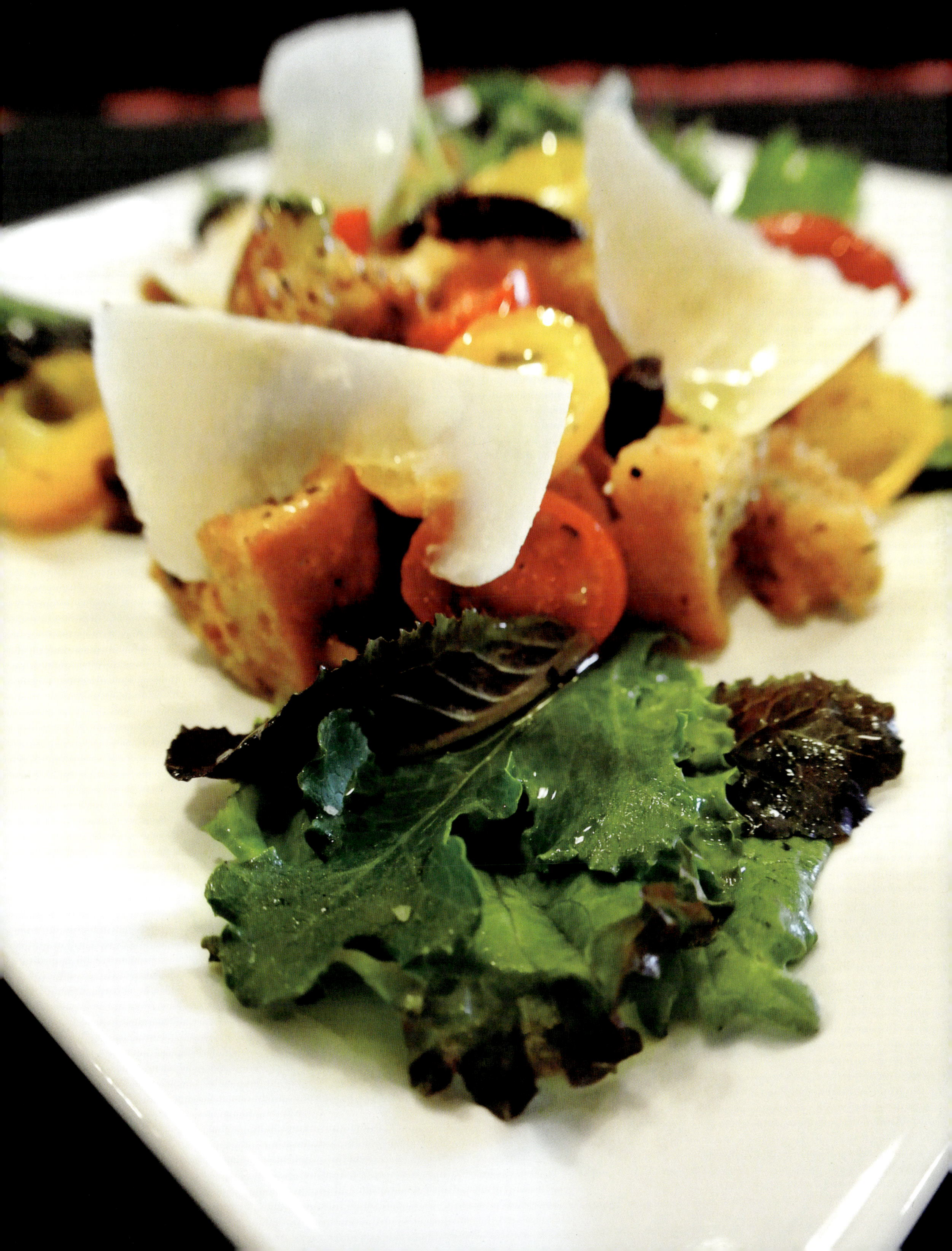

Ratatouille

I love the aromatic, taste, and colors of Ratatouille. To make a traditional Ratatouille, you will need Herbs de Provence, which has lavender that creates a great aromatic for the dish. I had the pleasure of traveling to the Provence region of France and viewing the gorgeous lavender fields. Traditionally, Ratatouille is topped with Gruyére cheese. We like to take it to the next level and top it with Gruyére cheese and Smoked Gouda. By putting this under the broiler it blends the two cheeses together and creates a gratinée. I like to serve this individually in a ramekin or cocotte.

SERVES 8

INGREDIENTS:

1 large eggplant

2 medium zucchini

2 Tbsp kosher salt

1 large onion

2 bell peppers

2 Tbsp extra virgin olive oil

2 cloves garlic, chopped

4 tomatoes, seeded and chopped

1 cup white wine

1 Tbsp Herbs de Provence

Chef John's Signature Seasoning, to taste

¼ cup olive oil

½ cup Gruyére cheese, grated

½ cup Smoked Gouda cheese, grated

PREPARATION:

1. Preheat oven to 375°F.
2. Peel and slice eggplant into ½-inch rounds; slice zucchini into ¼-inch-round slices.
3. Toss both with kosher salt and place in colander to drain for up to 15 minutes. Rinse salt off. Dry with paper towel or clean kitchen towel when ready.
4. While zucchini and eggplant are draining, slice onion and peppers. Heat EVOO in large sauté pan, sauté onion and peppers with Chef John's Signature Seasoning for about 8-10 minutes, until soft and golden.
5. Add garlic and tomatoes, sauté an additional 3 minutes.
6. Deglaze with wine and cook for another 5 minutes, add the Herbs de Provence. Let rest.
7. When eggplant and zucchini are drained and dried, in batches, sauté in olive oil until golden; transfer to sheet pan when done.
8. In a cocotte dish, arrange the sautéed zucchini and eggplant. Finish by topping with the pepper/tomato mixture and grated Gruyére and Smoked Gouda.
9. Bake for 10 minutes in the oven.
10. Then broil for 3-4 minutes, until golden brown.

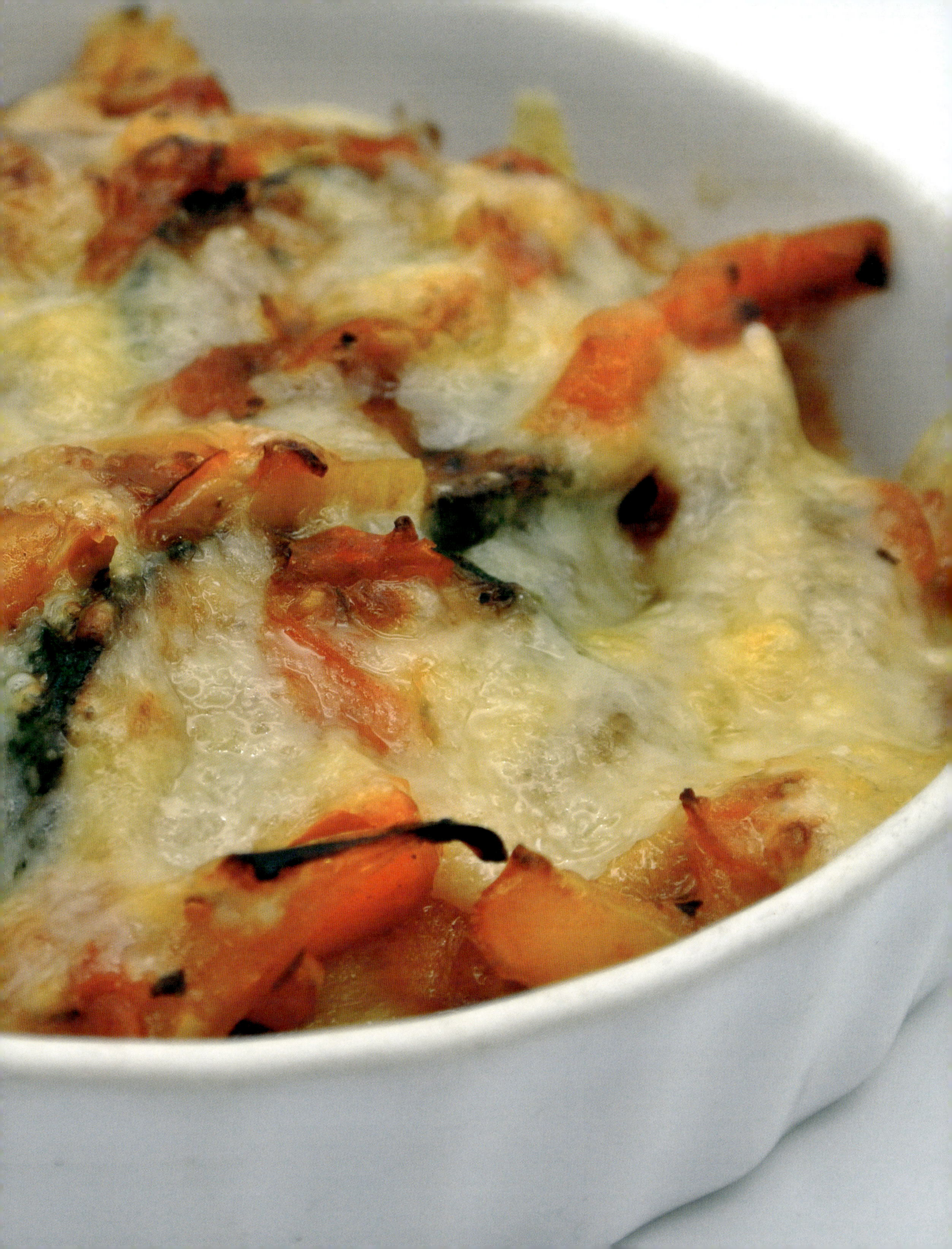

Chicken Milanese
With Cherry Tomatoes and Baby Greens

This dish is a simple preparation, ideal for summertime. We quickly sauté a pounded out chicken breast that has been lightly breaded to create a wonderful crust. Adding the fresh lemon at the end really brightens this dish. Roasting the cherry tomatoes will give the dish some extra sweetness and flavor. This is a great summer lunch on a warm afternoon.

SERVES 8

INGREDIENTS:

4 boneless skinless chicken breasts, sliced in half

1 cup flour

2 large eggs

2 Tbsp water

2 cups bread crumbs

¼ cup olive oil

¼ cup butter

Chef John's Signature Seasoning, to taste

PREPARATION:

1. Place the chicken breasts between two pieces of plastic wrap. Using a meat tenderizer, pound the chicken breast until they're about ¼-inch thick.
2. Set up a basic breading procedure with flour, egg wash (eggs and water whisked together), and bread crumbs, each in its own container; season each with a pinch of Chef John's Signature Seasoning.
3. Dip each piece of chicken into the flour, egg wash, and then dredge it in the bread crumbs, tapping off the excess.
4. Heat half of the olive oil and butter in a large sauté pan (big enough to hold 3-4 pieces of chicken in a single layer). Cook for about 4 minutes on the first side, or until evenly browned and crisp.
5. Flip and cook for an additional 2-3 minutes, or until evenly browned and the chicken is firm to the touch. Repeat with the remaining olive oil, butter, and chicken.

Cherry Tomatoes and Baby Greens

INGREDIENTS:

2 cups cherry tomatoes

4 Tbsp extra virgin olive oil

4 cups baby greens

1 Tbsp Aged Balsamic

Chef John's Signature Seasoning, to taste

PREPARATION:

1. Preheat oven to 400°F.
2. Place tomatoes in a small baking pan, drizzle with 2 Tbsp EVOO and a pinch of Chef John's Signature Seasoning. Roast for 15 minutes, stirring occasionally, until they're split, blistered, and super sweet.
3. Toss the greens with the remaining 2 Tbsp of EVOO, Aged Balsamic and Chef John's Signature Seasoning. Fold the tomatoes into the greens.

PLATING:

1. Place one piece of chicken on each plate and mound a handful of greens on each piece, making sure everyone gets plenty of tomatoes.

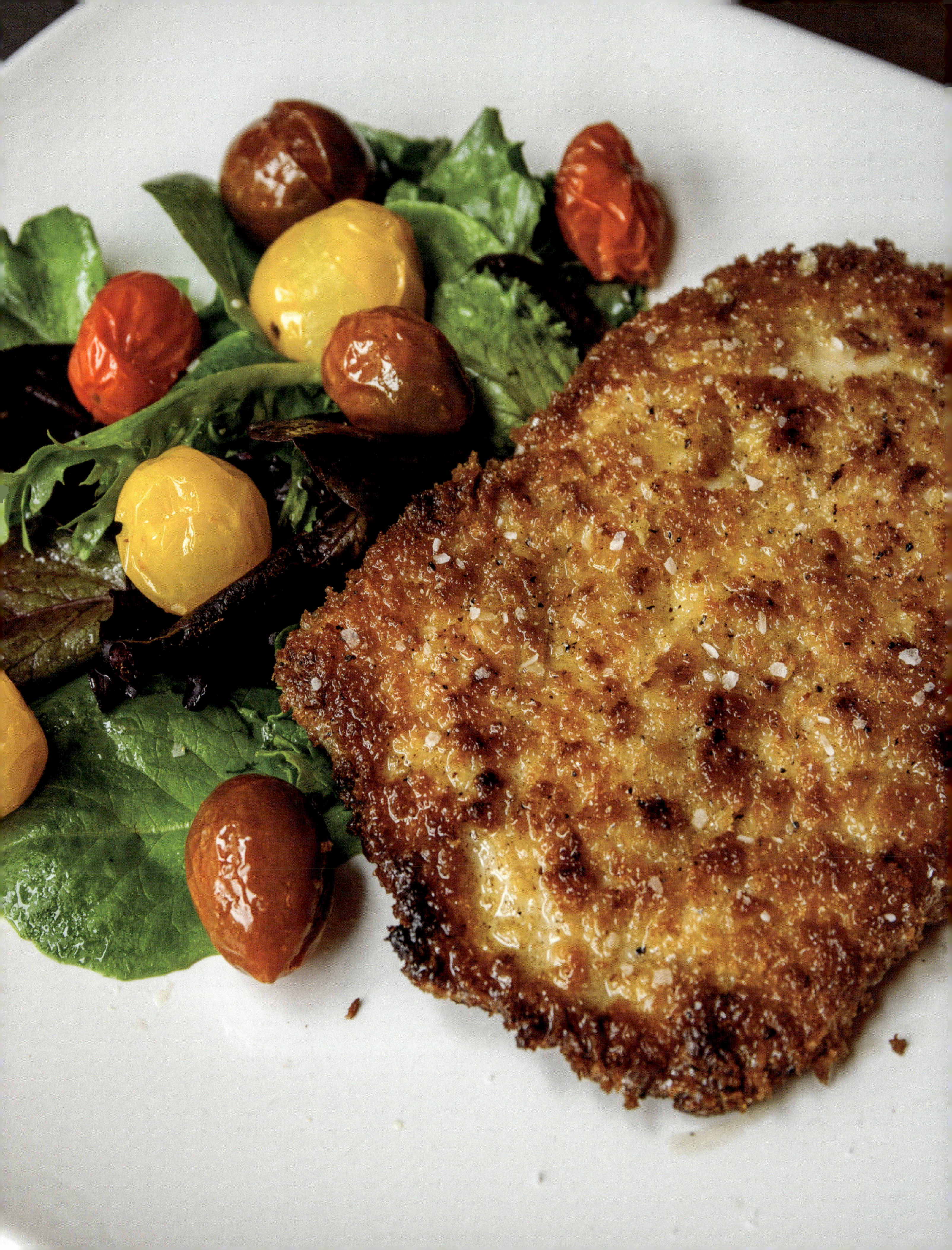

Grilled Chicken Au Poivre
With Cremini Mushroom Reduction

This is a wonderful entree to serve while entertaining dinner guests in the summertime. We start by coating the chicken breast in crushed green peppercorns and Chef John's Signature Seasoning. I love using green peppercorns in this dish because they are milder than a black peppercorn, ideally suited for chicken or pork. Enjoy a summer night outside while creating beautiful grill marks on the chicken breasts. The cremini mushroom reduction is naturally laid over the front edge of the chicken breast. Make sure to have an extra crispy baguette to soak up the reduction.

SERVES 8

INGREDIENTS:

8 chicken breasts, 5 oz each

1 Tbsp green peppercorns

3 Tbsp butter

¼ cup shallots, chopped

1 tsp garlic, minced

3 cups cremini mushrooms, sliced ¼ inch

2 Tbsp Dijon mustard

3 oz Cream Sherry

8 oz chicken stock

3 oz heavy cream

1 Tbsp fresh parsley, chopped

Chef John's Signature Seasoning, to taste

PREPARATION:

1. Crush green peppercorns (i.e., spice grinder or rolling pin).
2. Season chicken breasts with Chef John's Signature Seasoning and crushed peppercorns. Coat as much of the chicken with the peppercorns to your taste.
3. In a large 12-inch sauté pan, heat 3 Tbsp butter and sauté shallots and garlic for 2 minutes. Add cremini mushrooms, sauté an additional 4 minutes over medium heat.
4. Deglaze the pan with Cream Sherry. Let the flame catch the Sherry vapors and ignite. Swirl the pan slightly and let the flame burn out.
5. Add the Dijon mustard, chicken stock, and let reduce in half.
6. Add heavy cream, chopped parsley, and Chef John's Signature Seasoning. Reduce until desired thickness.
7. Set oven to 335°F.
8. Grill chicken over medium-high heat for 3 minutes; pick up and rotate, grill 3 minutes on the same side to create diamond char marks.
9. Turn over the chicken and grill 3 more minutes on back side.
10. Take the chicken off the grill and finish in oven for 8-10 minutes.
11. Serve with Cremini Mushroom Reduction.

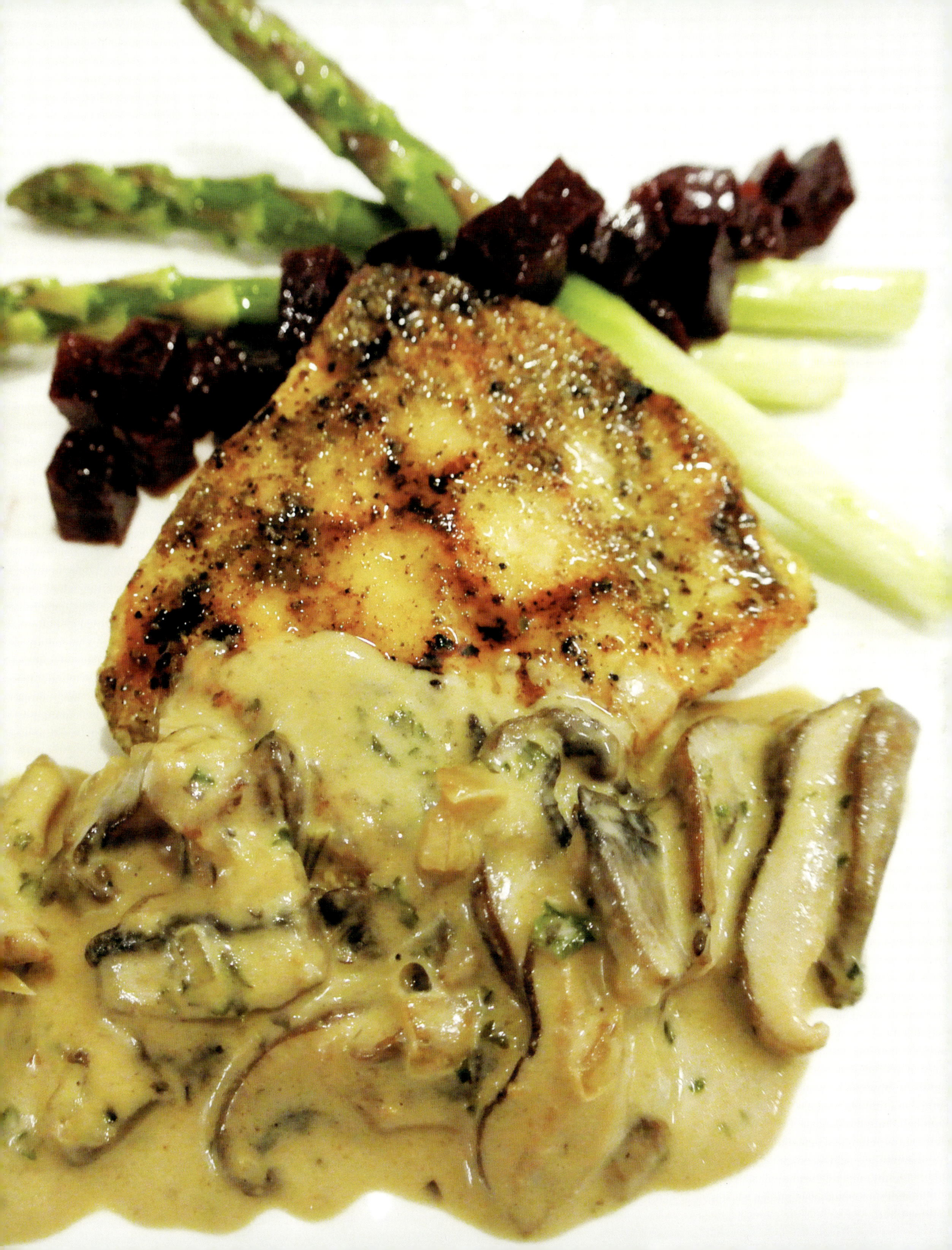

SAUTÉED SHRIMP AND ZUCCHINI

This is an ideal dish to serve in August when zucchini is in abundance. Sautéing the zucchini and deglazing with Vermouth and White Wine adds wonderful flavor. For an added crunch, the shrimp is dusted with bread crumbs and Parmesan cheese atop the zucchini compote.

SERVES 8

INGREDIENTS:

16 shrimp (U-10 ct.) peeled and deveined

½ cup all-purpose flour

Chef John's Signature Seasoning, to taste

½ tsp curry powder

⅛ tsp Cayenne pepper

4 Tbsp butter

1 cup onion, chopped

2 cloves garlic, chopped

4 zucchini, ½ inch dice

2 Tbsp Dry Vermouth

½ cup white wine

¼ cup bread crumbs

2 Tbsp butter, melted

½ cup Parmesan cheese, grated

1 Tbsp fresh lemon juice

PREPARATION:

1. Mix the flour, Chef John's Signature Seasoning, curry powder, and Cayenne pepper together in a pan.
2. Dredge the shrimp in the seasoned flour mixture.
3. Melt 4 Tbsp butter in a large sauté pan over medium-high heat. Add the shrimp and sauté them for about 2 minutes, turning once until they are golden brown, repeat on the other side. Transfer to a platter, squeeze fresh lemon over shrimp, and set aside.
4. Add the onions and garlic to the pan and sauté over medium-high heat for 2-3 minutes. Then add the zucchini and sauté an additional 3-4 minutes.
5. Deglaze the pan with Dry Vermouth. Let alcohol vapors burn out and add white wine and reduce by half. Season with Chef John's Signature Seasoning.
6. Divide the sautéed zucchini mixture and shrimp between 8 small ovenproof serving dishes.
7. Mix together the bread crumbs, 2 Tbsp melted butter, and Parmesan; divide and spoon the mixture evenly over each dish.
8. Place the dishes under the broiler until hot, bubbly, and browned on top.

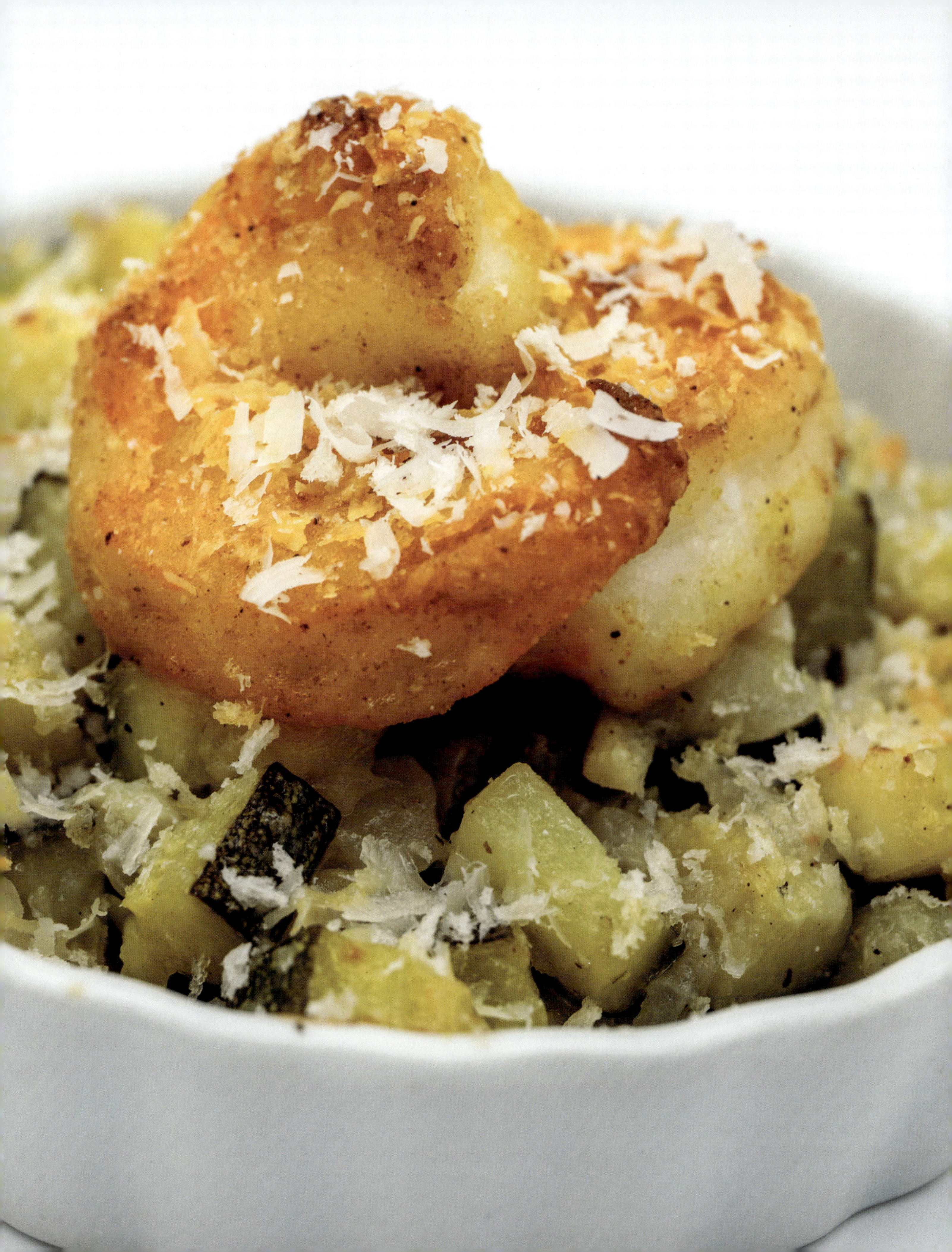

BRAISED SWORDFISH STEAK NEAPOLITAN

Early in my career, while I was working at the Top of the Hub in Boston, I prepared many swordfish dishes. I love swordfish for its meaty texture and the way it sears. I like to braise the fish, Neapolitan style, with capers, olives, and red and yellow peppers. I love the flavor profile of serving this over Saffron Basmati Rice. Swordfish is not often featured in the Midwest, yet I love to share this with my guests and open their eyes to this wonderful fish.

SERVES 8
INGREDIENTS:

8 swordfish steaks (4 oz, 1-inch thick)

½ cup flour

Chef John's Signature Seasoning, to taste

¼ cup olive oil

1 red pepper, medium slice

1 yellow pepper, medium slice

1 onion, medium slice

3 stalks celery, medium slice

1 cup white wine

4 tomatoes, seeded and chopped

½ cup Kalamata olives, quartered lengthwise

2 Tbsp drained capers

1 cup chicken stock

1 tsp sugar

½ tsp chili pepper flakes

PREPARATION:

1. Season the flour with Chef John's Signature Seasoning. Dredge the swordfish in flour, shaking off the excess.
2. In a large sauté pan, heat olive oil over medium-high heat. Lay swordfish in gently and sear until golden brown, about 2 minutes on each side. Remove from pan and let rest.
3. Turn down heat to medium. In the same pan, sauté the peppers, onion, celery, and garlic. Cover and cook until the vegetables are soft, about 5 minutes. Add the white wine and cook uncovered 5 minutes, scraping the flavor from the bottom of the pan.
4. Add the tomatoes, olives, capers, stock, sugar, and chili pepper flakes. Bring the sauce to a simmer and cook for 5 minutes.
5. Return the fish to the sauté pan. Baste the fish with the sauce so that the pieces are covered. Place in oven for 10 minutes on 335°F, or until the sauce is slightly thickened and the swordfish is very tender.

***Serving Suggestion:** Serve with Saffron Basmati Rice (see page 202 for recipe)*

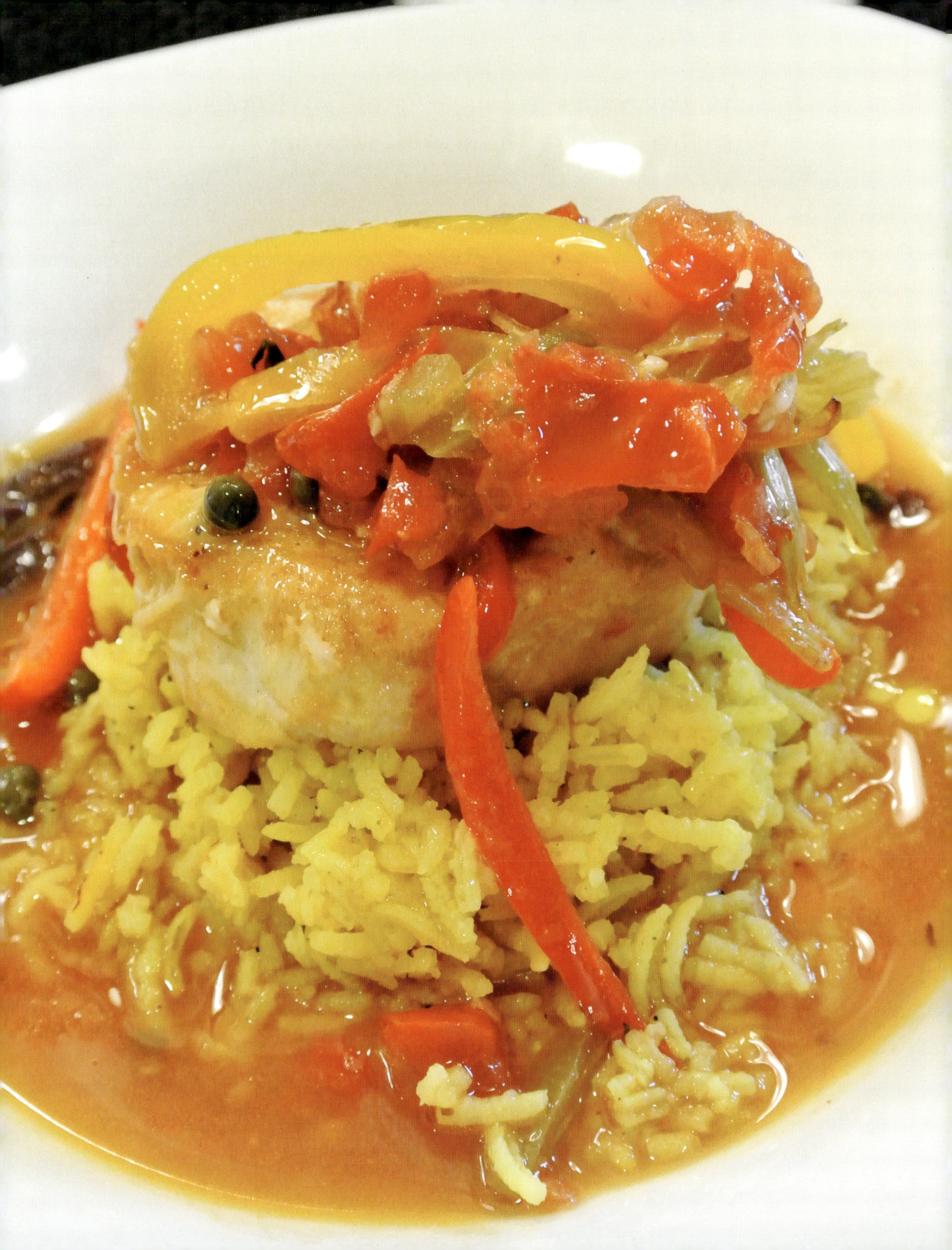

Grilled Stuffed Frenched Pork Rib Chop
With River Valley Mushrooms and Smoked Gouda

I love the presentation of this frenched pork rib chop. You start by purchasing the pork chop with a single bone (the rib bone) exposed and "Frenching" this exposed bone. Frenching means to trim all the meat off of the bone. You take away the grizzle and tendons so it makes a wonderful presentation, almost resembling a "lollipop." After this, the pork rib chops are stuffed with the mushrooms, Prosciutto, and Smoked Gouda, and grilled for "diamond" grill marks.

SERVES 8
INGREDIENTS:

8 frenched pork rib chops, 10-12 oz each

3 Tbsp butter

1 cup onion, small dice

2 cloves garlic, chopped

2 cups mushrooms, small dice

¼ lb Prosciutto, julienne

2 Tbsp fresh parsley, chopped

2 cups Smoked Gouda cheese, shredded

Chef John's Signature Seasoning, to taste

2 Tbsp extra virgin olive oil

PREPARATION:

1. In a medium sauté pan, melt 3 Tbsp of butter over medium-high heat. Add onions and garlic, sauté for 3 minutes.
2. Stir in mushrooms; sauté for an additional 5 minutes. Add Prosciutto, parsley, and Chef John's Signature Seasoning. Set stuffing mixture aside.
3. When the mixture has cooled slightly, add Smoked Gouda. Place half of the stuffing into pastry bag.
4. Cut a pocket in each pork rib chop, just large enough for pastry bag tip. Stuff about ¼ cup of the stuffing into each pork chop.
5. Season rib chops with EVOO and Chef John's Signature Seasoning, grill rib chops for 3 minutes, then rotate and grill an additional 3 minutes. Turn rib chops over and grill an additional 3 minutes on back side.
6. Pull off grill and let rib chops rest for 5-10 minutes.
7. Finish in 335°F oven for 8-10 minutes before serving.

Note: *"Frenching" is trimming the meat off the rib bones.*

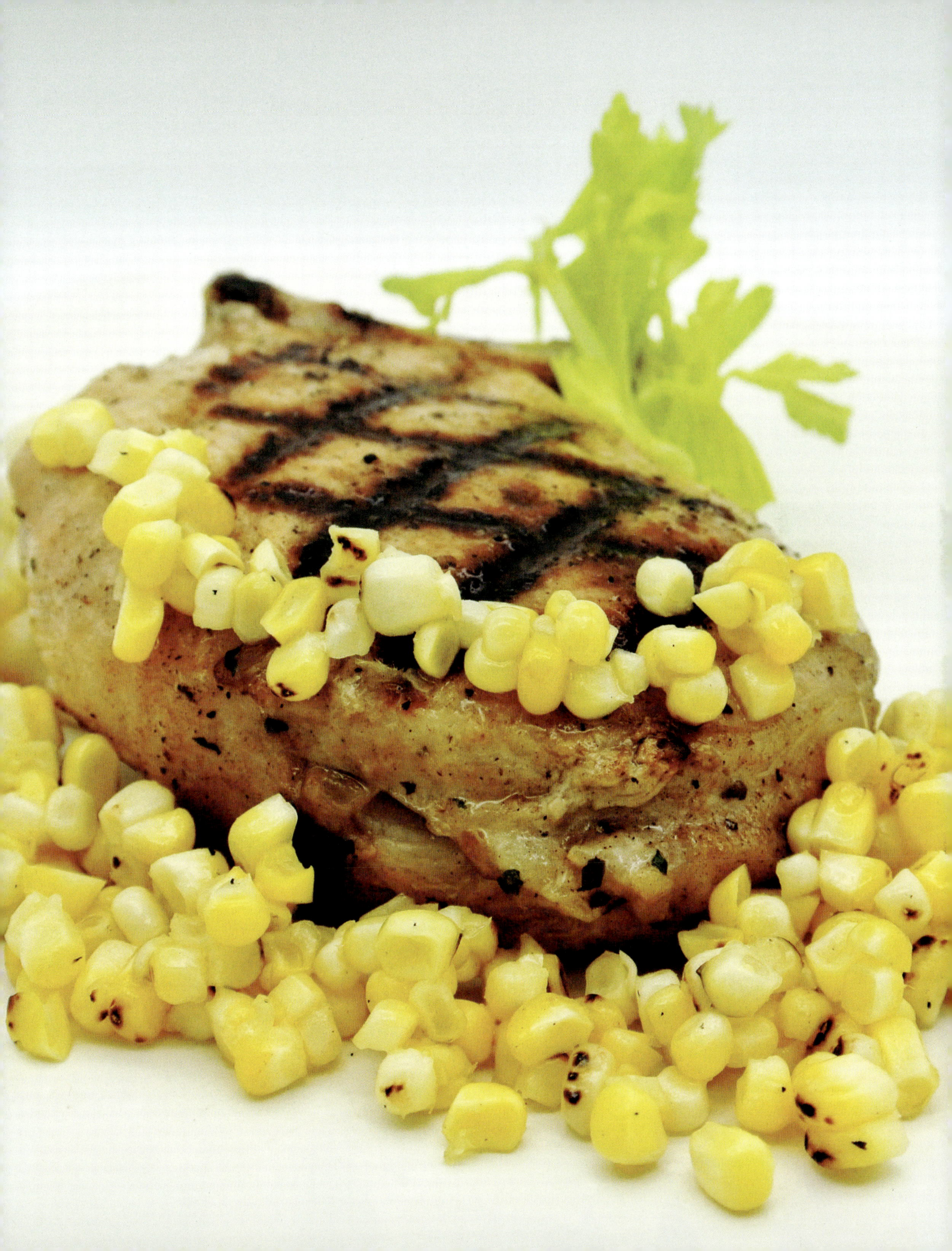

Filet Mignon with Roasted Balsamic Onions

I like referring to the balsamic onions in this dish as the Hawaiian "bird of paradise." Searing the red onions on each side pulls all the sugars out of the onion and caramelizes them. When you keep the core intact, the onion starts to uncurl and the "petals" of the onion start to open up. If you do this properly, it gets so sweet and gummy it almost tastes like a gummy bear. This is a masterful topping for grilled filet mignon.

SERVES 8

INGREDIENTS:

8 Filet Mignon, 6 oz each

2 sweet red onions

¼ cup plus 2 Tbsp extra virgin olive oil

Chef John's Signature Seasoning, to taste

2 Tbsp garlic, coarse chop

2 Tbsp fresh thyme, oregano, and rosemary, chopped

½ cup balsamic vinegar

1 Tbsp unsalted butter, cut into cubes

PREPARATION:

1. Preheat oven to 375°F.
2. Peel onions and cut into quarters or wedges leaving the onion root end intact. Peel exterior skin carefully.
3. Heat the ¼ cup EVOO in a large ovenproof sauté pan over medium-high heat.
4. Add the onions and cook until brown on both faces, about 7-9 minutes each side.
5. Season with Chef John's Signature Seasoning. Add the garlic and cook briefly until light brown. Add the herbs and ¼ cup balsamic vinegar, splashing over the onions, covering bottom of the pan.
6. Place the onions in the oven and roast until tender and browned (the wedges will tend to char along the edges), about 15 minutes.
7. Remove from oven. Deglaze with remaining balsamic vinegar and let rest.
8. Heat the grill over medium-high heat until hot.
9. Season filets with 2 Tbsp EVOO and Chef John's Signature Seasoning. Cook filets until charred, about 2 minutes, rotate filets and cook another 2 minutes on front side.
10. Turn over and grill 2 more minutes on the back side, let rest.
11. Place in 335°F oven to roast until desired temperature, about 7-8 minutes for medium rare.
12. Remove from oven and dot the top of the filets with butter, let melt.
13. Place filets on plate and finish with a roasted balsamic onion on each filet.

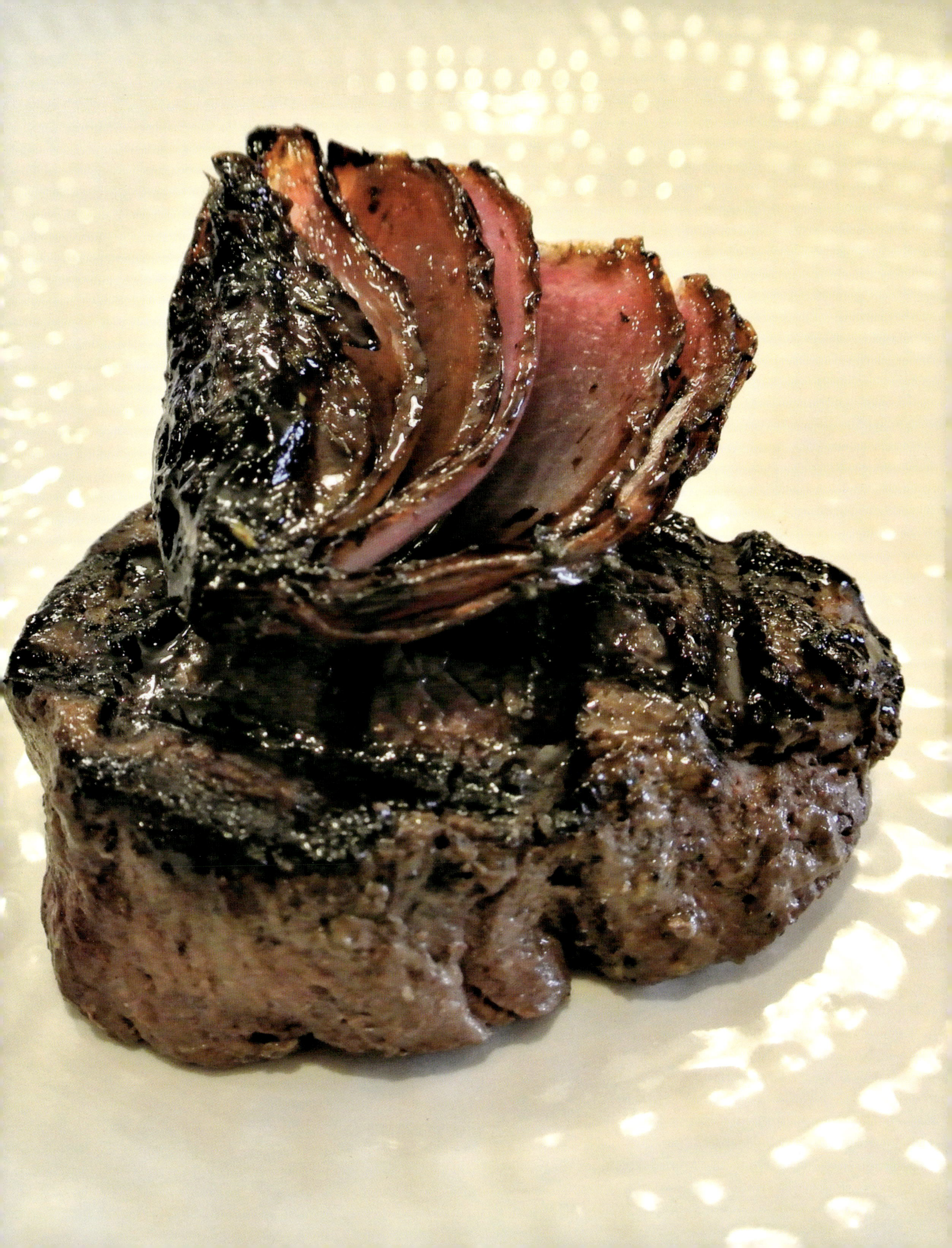

BALSAMIC BERRIES WITH WHITE CHOCOLATE BISCOTTI

Berries are a staple on a hot summer day. This dish is perfect for the Fourth of July. It can be easily taken to a picnic and shared with friends and family. Crumbling white chocolate biscotti and layering it with the balsamic berries adds some crunch, while the berries add a sweet tartness. After chilling the dessert for a few hours, this is an ideal summer treat.

SERVES 8

INGREDIENTS:

¼ cup superfine sugar

3 Tbsp Aged Balsamic

Sea salt, generous pinch

Black pepper, fresh ground, generous pinch

6 cups mixed berries

8 fanned strawberries

4 cups biscotti, gently crushed

1 cup Mascarpone cheese (flavored with 1 Tbsp maple syrup)

PREPARATION:

1. In a bowl, whisk together the sugar, Aged Balsamic, and a generous pinch of sea salt and fresh ground pepper.
2. Add the berries and toss gently until they are well coated. Let marinade for 10 minutes.
3. Gently place ⅓ cup of the berries into each serving glass and top with ¼ cup of biscotti, repeat the process again.
4. Top with dollop of Mascarpone and a fanned strawberry. Chill for minimum 2 hours then serve.

WHITE CHOCOLATE BISCOTTI

INGREDIENTS:

½ cup butter, softened

1 cup sugar

4 large eggs

1 tsp vanilla extract

3 cups all-purpose flour

1 Tbsp baking powder

¾ cup dried cranberries

¾ cup white chocolate chips

PREPARATION:

1. Preheat oven to 350°F.
2. In a mixing bowl, cream together the butter and sugar. Add eggs one at a time, beating well. Beat in vanilla.
3. Combine flour and baking powder; gradually add to creamed mixture. Stir in cranberries and white chocolate chips. Divide dough into three portions.
4. On ungreased baking sheets, shape each portion into a 10 x 3 x 2 inch rectangle.
5. Bake for 20 to 25 minutes, or until lightly browned. Cool for 5 minutes.
6. Transfer to a cutting board and cut diagonally with a serrated knife into ½-inch slices.
7. Place cut side down on ungreased baking sheet. Bake for 15-20 minutes, or until golden brown.
8. Remove from oven and place on wire racks to cool.

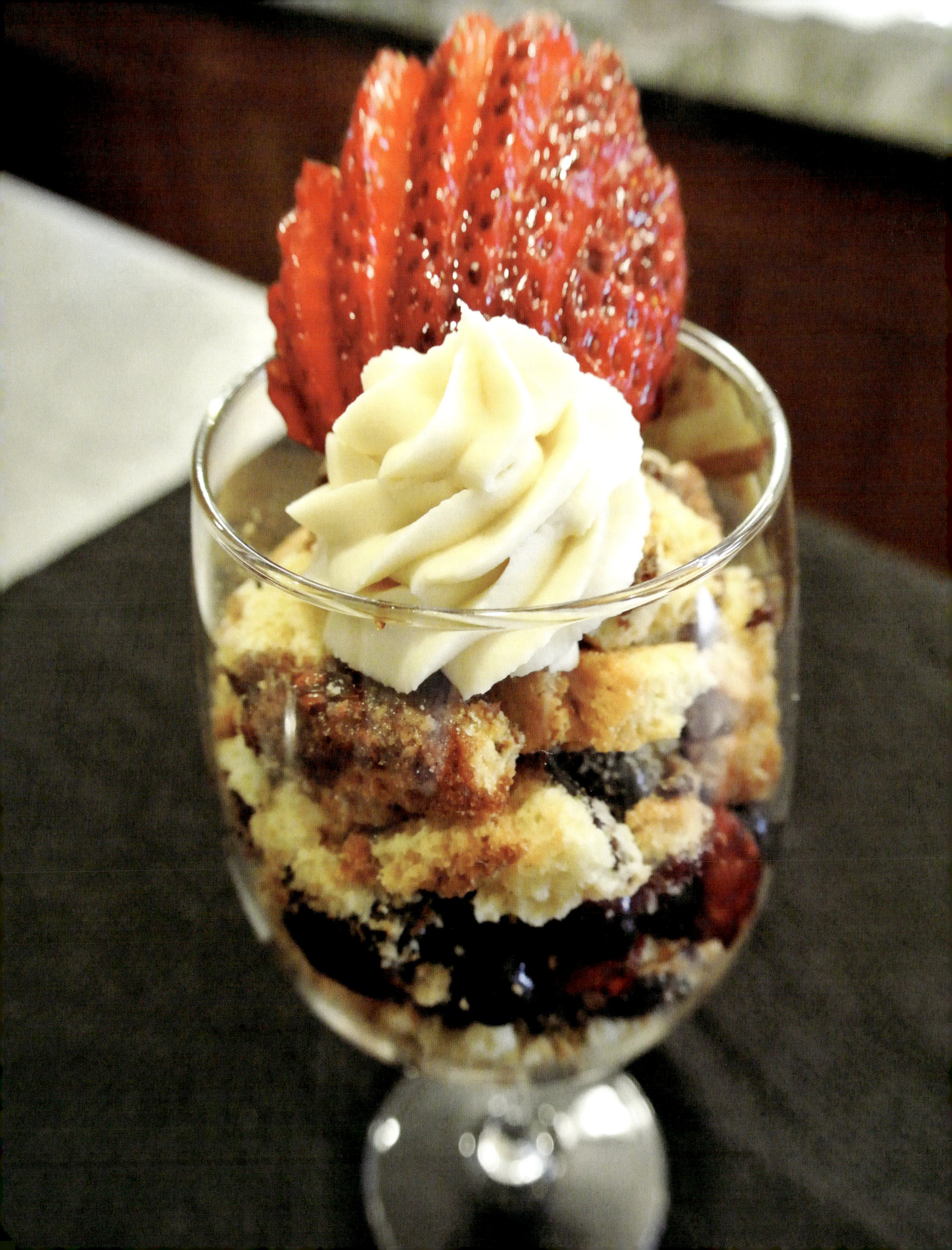

GRILLED POUND CAKE WITH WHITE BALSAMIC PEACHES

This is a great family dessert during the summertime. Grilling the pound cake creates a burnt sugar aroma, almost like burnt marshmallows over a campfire. If the pound cake gets too charred, don't worry, just call it extra crispy. Use a cookie cutter, ideally star shaped, in the middle of each slice to fill with ice cream and peaches. The peaches, having been marinated in White Peach Balsamic, bring some acidity and sweetness to the dish. We grate white and dark chocolate on top for an added presentation pop.

SERVES 8

INGREDIENTS:

8 slices pound cake, sliced 1-inch thick

3 cups White Balsamic Peaches

8 scoops Vanilla Bean ice cream

PREPARATION:

1. Grill slices of pound cake on the hot grill grates for 1 minute, rotate 45° for 1 minute until you have visible grill marks. Turn over and repeat grill process.
2. Cut out the middle of each slice of pound cake.
3. Scoop ice cream into cut-out center.
4. Top ice cream with white balsamic peaches.
5. Garnish the top of ice cream with peaches and cut out piece of pound cake.

POUND CAKE

INGREDIENTS:

1 ½ cups (3 sticks) unsalted butter, softened, plus more for pan

3 cups flour, sifted, plus more for pan

1 ½ cups sugar

¾ tsp salt

3 tsp vanilla extract

6 large eggs

PREPARATION:

1. Preheat oven to 350°F.
2. Butter and flour an 8½ x 4½ loaf pan. Set aside
3. With a mixer, cream butter and sugar on medium speed for about 5 minutes or until light and fluffy. Add eggs, one at a time, beating well after each addition. Mix in vanilla and salt.
4. With the mixer on low, add the sifted flour gradually until combined without overmixing.
5. Pour into loaf pan and bake for about 60-70 minutes, or until a toothpick inserted in the center of the cake comes out clean.
6. Let rest for 10 minutes, then invert onto a wire rack and let cool before slicing into 1-inch slices.

WHITE BALSAMIC PEACHES

INGREDIENTS:

¼ cup of superfine sugar

3 Tbsp White Peach Balsamic

Sea salt and black pepper, to taste

3 cups fresh peaches, sliced

PREPARATION:

1. In a bowl, whisk together the sugar, White Peach Balsamic, and a generous pinch of salt and pepper.
2. Add the peaches and toss gently until they are well coated.

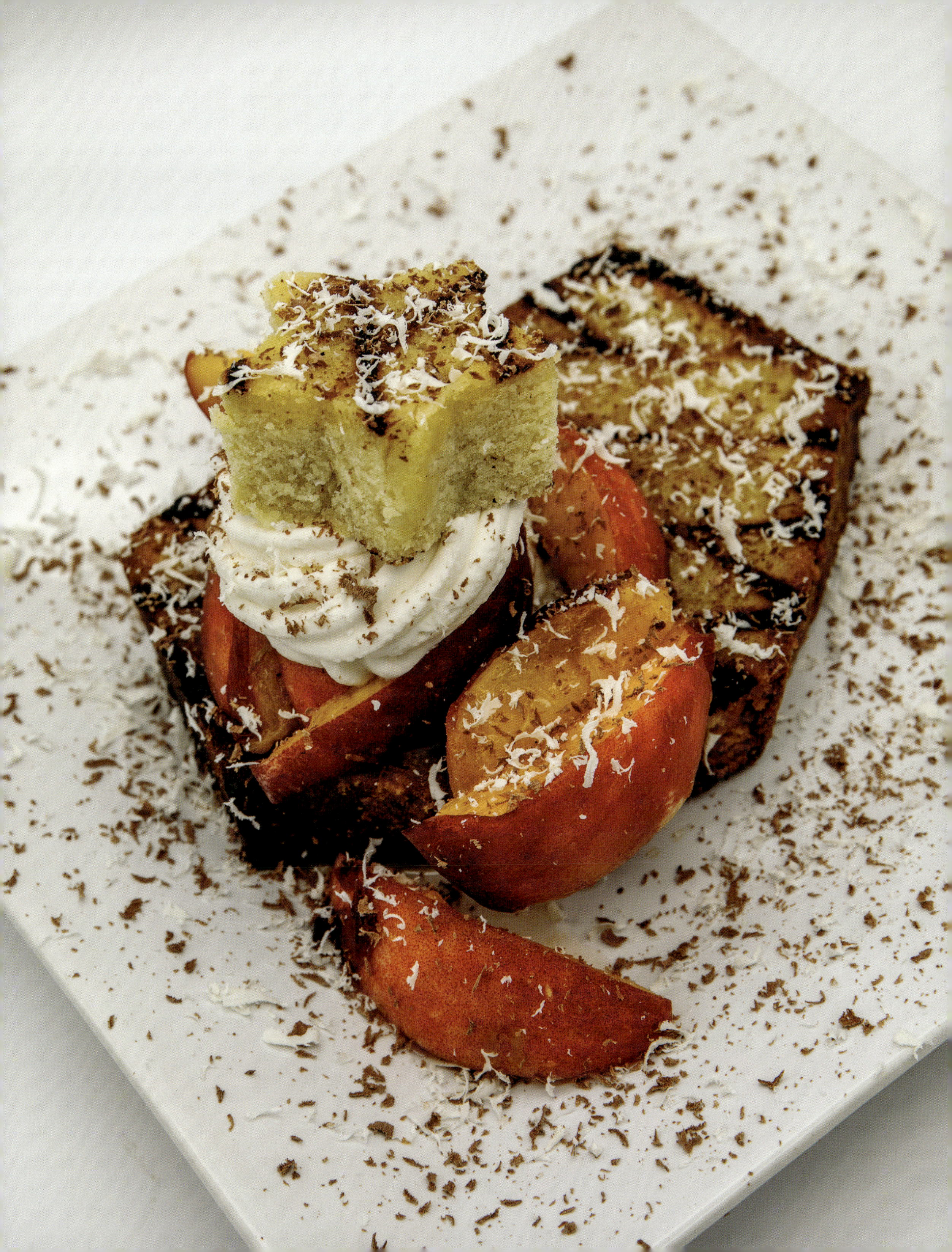

Grand Marnier Dark Chocolate Mousse

I love making this dessert several hours before a dinner party and letting it sit in the fridge to set up. The butter helps set the mousse, and the Grand Marnier and orange zest give this dish an intense flavor profile. This is a very rich dessert. While enjoying it, close your mouth and breathe up through your nose and you will enjoy a beautiful chocolate flavor. This mousse is a great way to finish off a summer meal.

SERVES 8

INGREDIENTS:

4 large egg yolks

¾ cup granulated sugar

¼ cup Grand Marnier

6 oz semisweet chocolate

4 Tbsp coffee

¾ cup unsalted butter, softened

4 large egg whites

Pinch of salt

1 tsp granulated sugar

1 orange, zested

PREPARATION:

1. Beat egg yolks and ¾ cup sugar together with mixer until mixture is thick and pale yellow and falls back upon itself forming a slowly dissolving ribbon (about 4 minutes). Beat in the Grand Marnier. Then set the mixing bowl over a hot water bath and continue beating (with wire whisk) for 3-4 minutes until the mixture is foamy and hot to the touch. Then beat over cold water for 3 to 4 minutes until the mixture is cool again and forms a ribbon.
2. Melt chocolate with coffee in a bowl over hot water.
3. Remove from heat, and beat in the butter 1 Tbsp at a time.
4. Add the egg yolks mixture to the chocolate mixture.
5. Beat the egg whites and salt with mixer until soft peaks are formed; add 1 tsp sugar, and beat until stiff, shining peaks are formed.
6. Stir ¼ of the egg whites into the chocolate mixture. Fold the remaining egg whites into the mixture in three additions.
7. Pour into individual serving glasses. Refrigerate until serving.
8. Top with Chantilly Cream (see recipe on page 195), berry of choice, and orange zest.

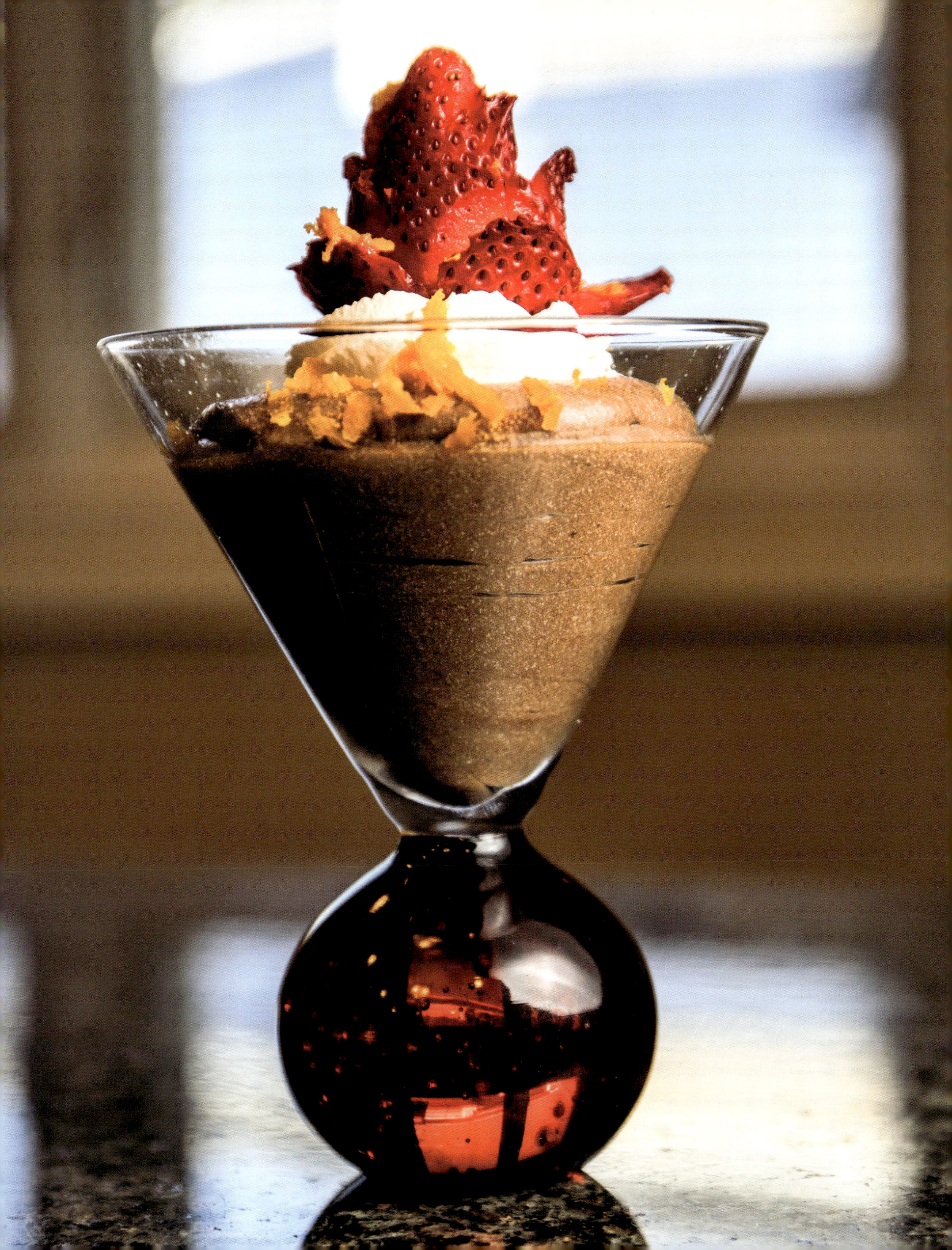

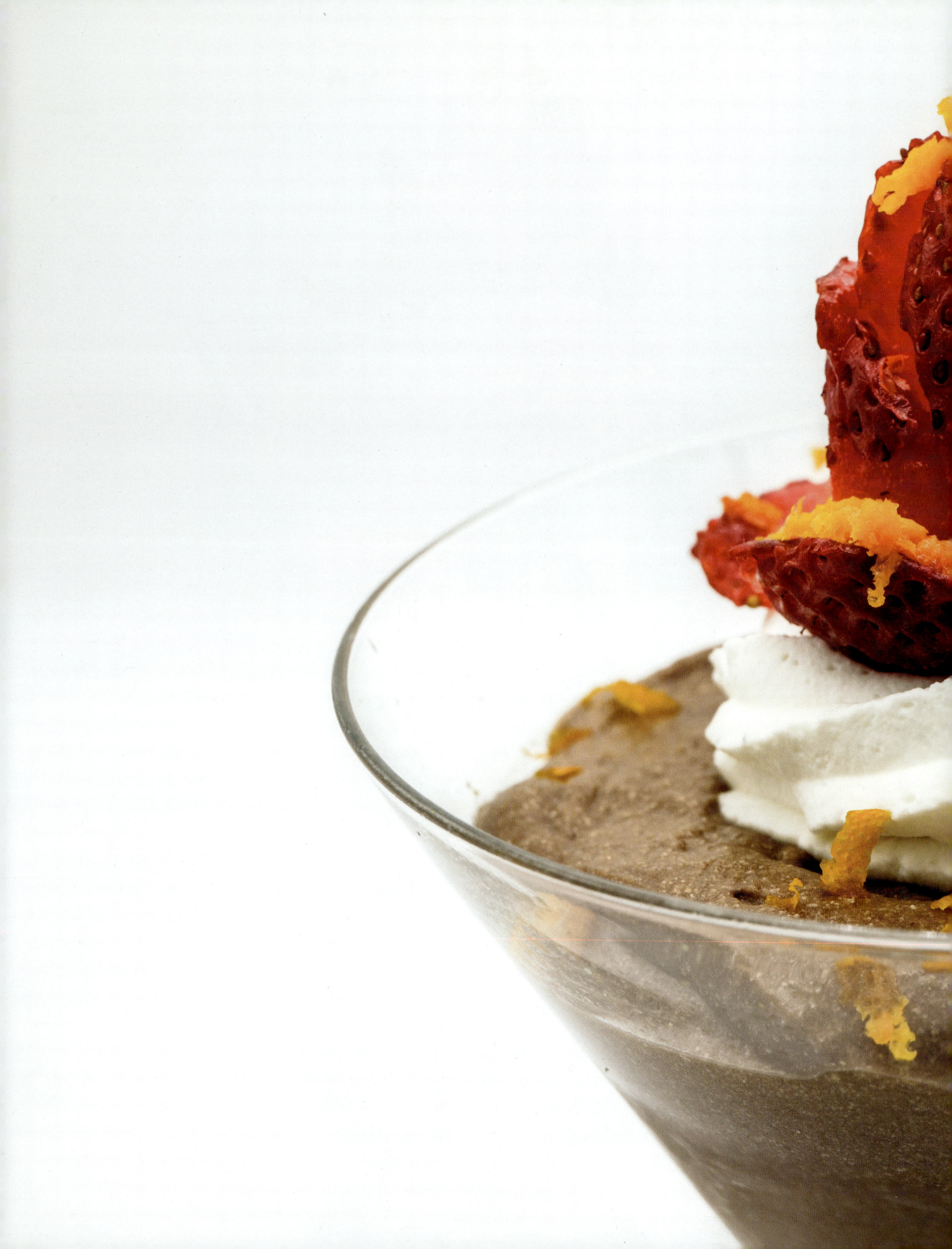

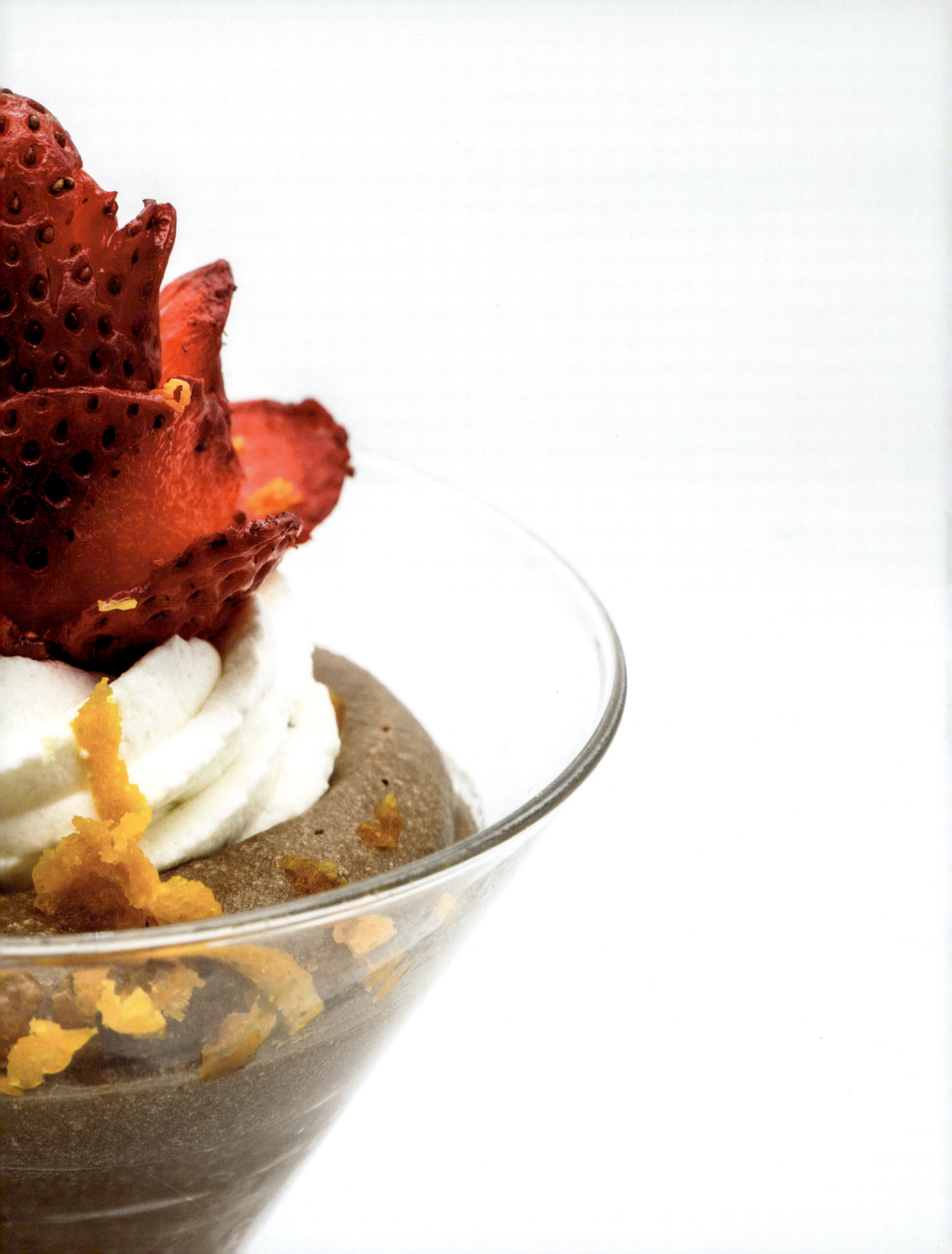

Pinn-Oak Ridge Farms
Rack of Lamb Dijonnaise

Farm Fresh

Growing up on my family farm in upstate New York, the Bogan Ranch, I have always understood the meaning of farm to table. It seems this has been a buzzword for a few years, but I have been following these ideals my whole life. My family used to raise our own pigs and chickens. We also had a fresh garden, and I had a roadside farm stand selling vegetables every summer. Here in Lake Geneva, we have access to so many amazing local farmers. Lake Geneva Country Meats provides standout product and is a staple in our community. Pinn-Oak Ridge Farms raises gorgeous lambs. River Valley Ranch Mushroom Farm is where all the mushrooms in this cookbook are from, and Yuppie Hill Poultry has an amazing, clean chicken farm where we source our eggs. In addition, Wilson Farm Meats has locally raised, superior Duroc pork products. I hope this chapter inspires you to support your local farmers and work with fresh, local ingredients.

Wilson Farm Bacon with Wisconsin Wedge Salad   106

Yuppie Hill Poached Eggs with Salad Lyonnaise   108

River Valley Ranch Mushroom Bisque   110

River Valley Ranch Portobellini   112

Pinn-Oak Ridge Farms Lamb Porterhouse   114

Pinn-Oak Ridge Farms Rack of Lamb Dijonnaise   116

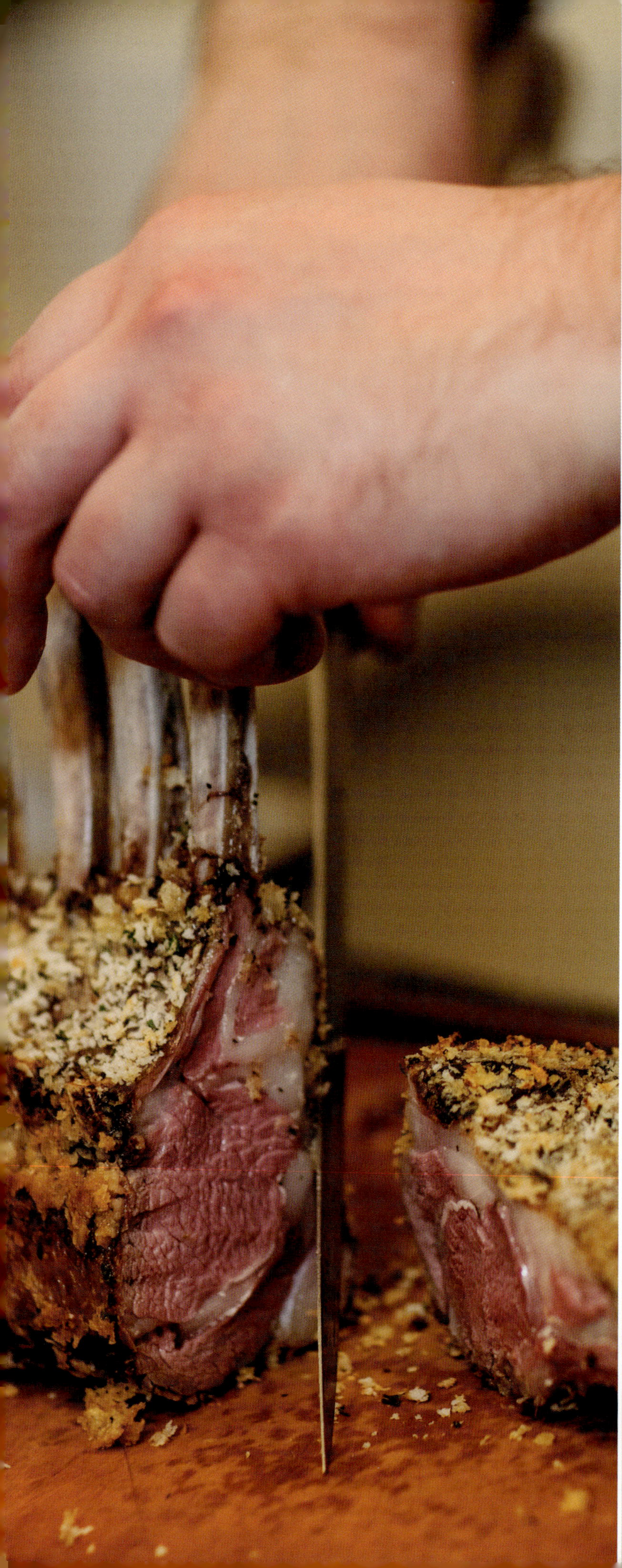

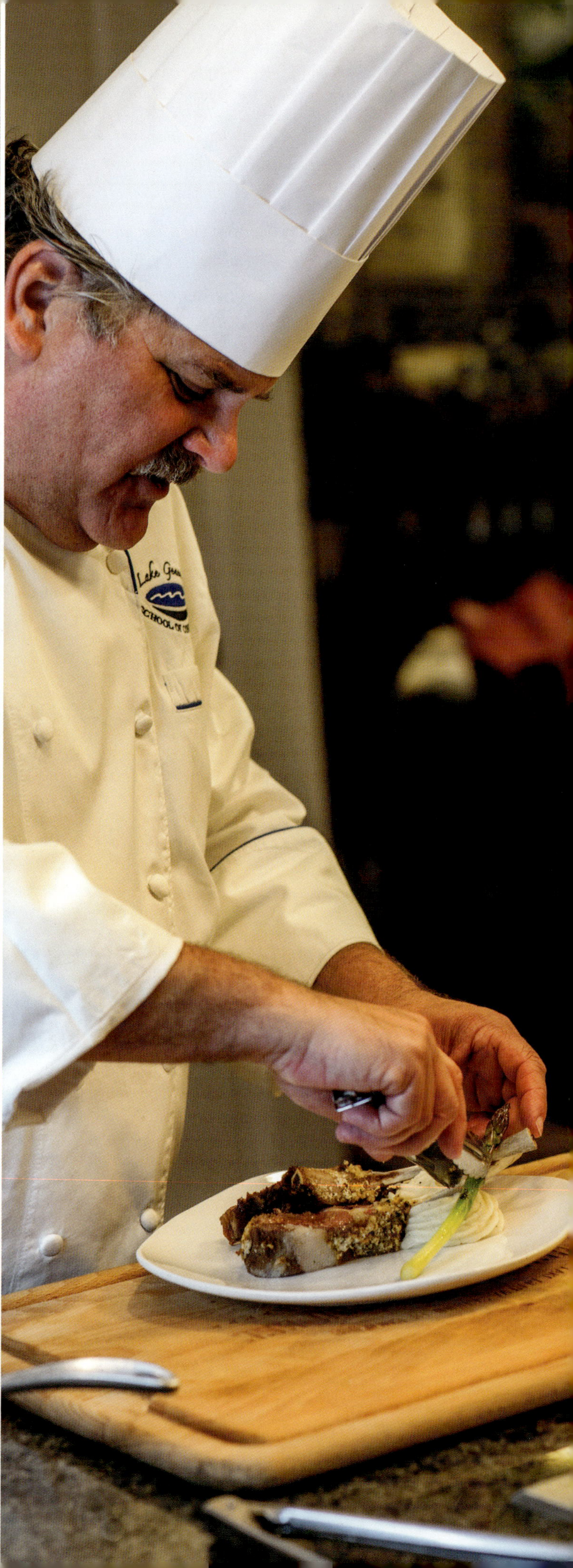

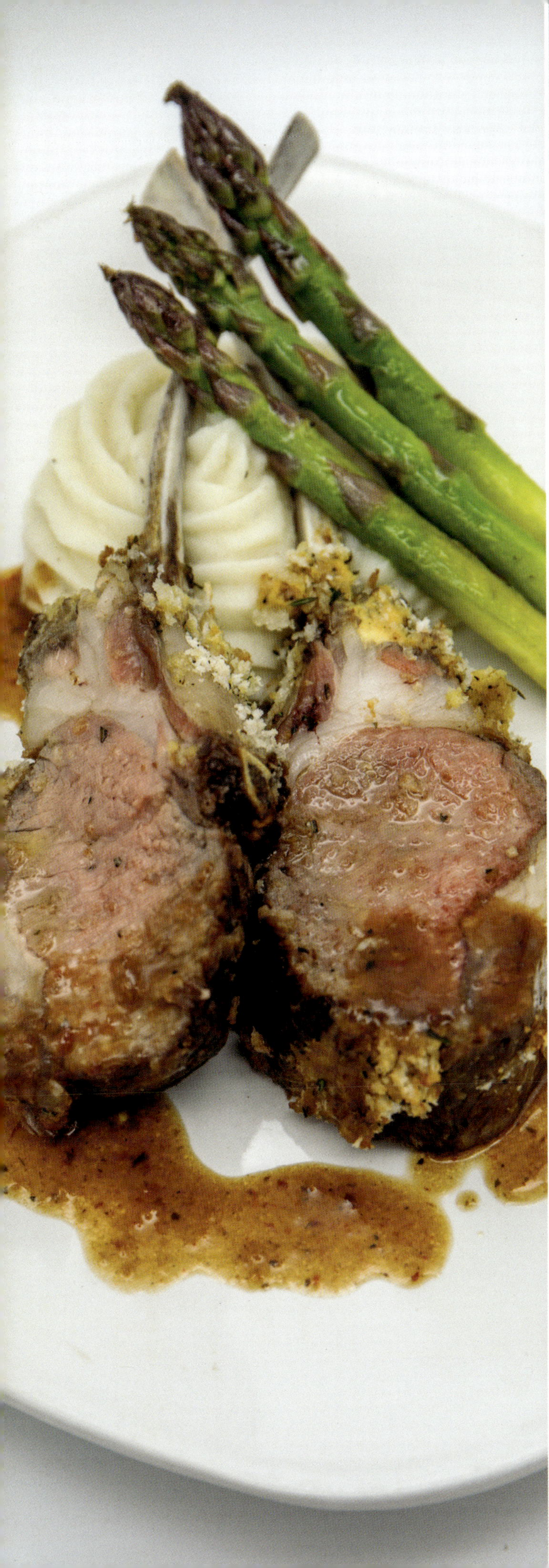

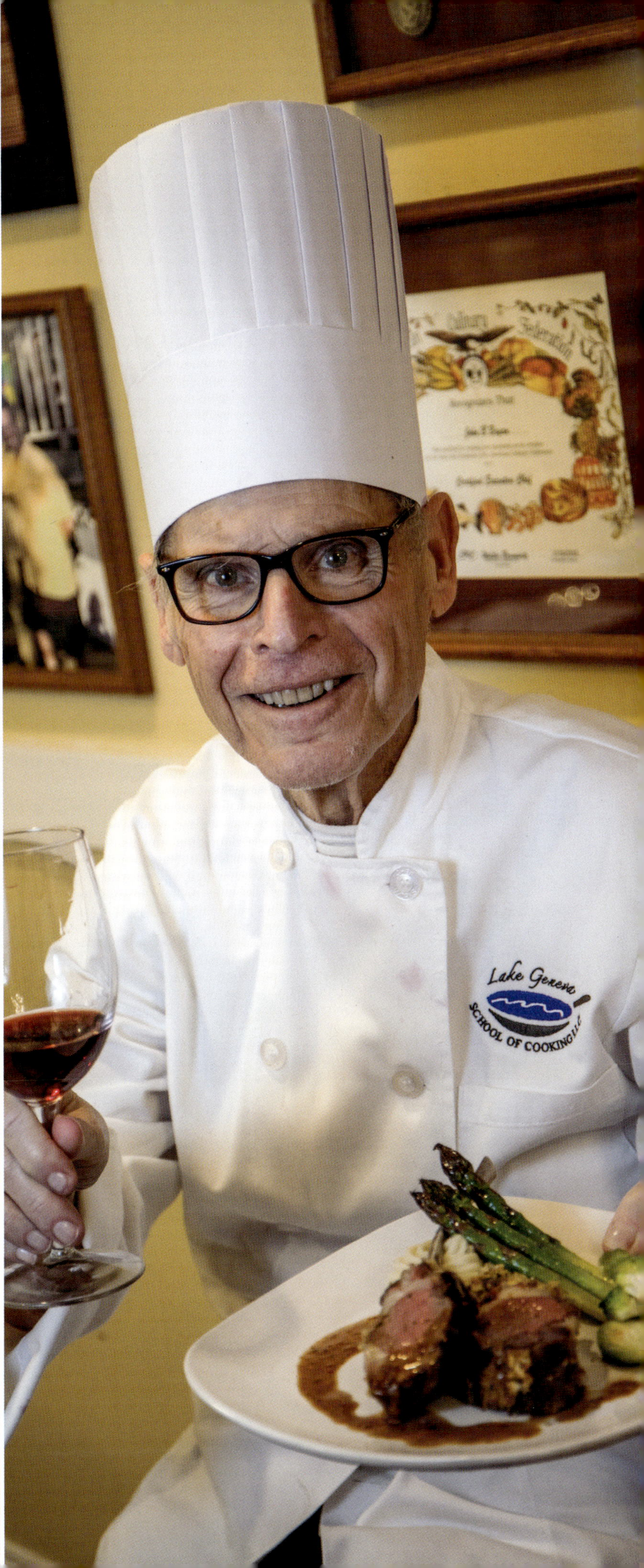
Lake Geneva
SCHOOL OF COOKING LLC

Wilson Farm Bacon
With Wisconsin Wedge Salad

Wilson Farm Meats is known for their award-winning pork products. Scott Wilson is a fifth generation farmer that raises his pigs locally and has a butcher shop in Elkhorn, Wisconsin. We feature their slab bacon cut into ¼-inch strips referred to as "Lardons" in this dish. Along with the bacon, we have a homemade buttermilk blue cheese dressing. A lot of people claim to not like blue cheese dressing, but they quickly change their minds after trying this dressing. When you work with quality ingredients, it makes cooking a lot easier.

SERVES 8
INGREDIENTS:

½ lb Wilson Farm Bacon slab

½ lb crumbled Blue Cheese

½ cup sour cream

⅓ cup buttermilk

½ cup mayonnaise

¼ cup red wine vinegar

1 Tbsp extra virgin olive oil

1 Tbsp sugar

1 clove garlic, minced

Chef John's Signature Seasoning, to taste

1 head iceberg, cut into 8 wedges

2 tomatoes, quartered in half (16 slices total)

1 red onion, halved and thinly sliced

4 hard-boiled large eggs (see note), shelled and coarsely chopped

Black pepper, freshly ground

PREPARATION:

1. Preheat oven to 375°F.
2. Slice bacon into ¼- inch strips "Lardons." Roast for 12-15 minutes.
3. Combine Blue Cheese, sour cream, buttermilk, mayonnaise, red wine vinegar, EVOO, sugar, garlic, and Chef John's Signature Seasoning in a bowl and blend together; chill until serving.
4. Build the salad by placing 1 lettuce wedge on each of 8 plates. Drizzle equal amounts of dressing over each wedge.
5. Scatter tomatoes, onion, egg, and bacon over each salad. Serve with fresh ground black pepper.

Note: Hard-boiled Egg Preparation

1. Place eggs in a 3- to 4-quart pan and cover with cold water.
2. Bring to a boil over high heat, reduce heat, and boil gently, uncovered, for about 15 minutes.
3. With a slotted spoon, lift eggs from water and immerse in cold water until cool.

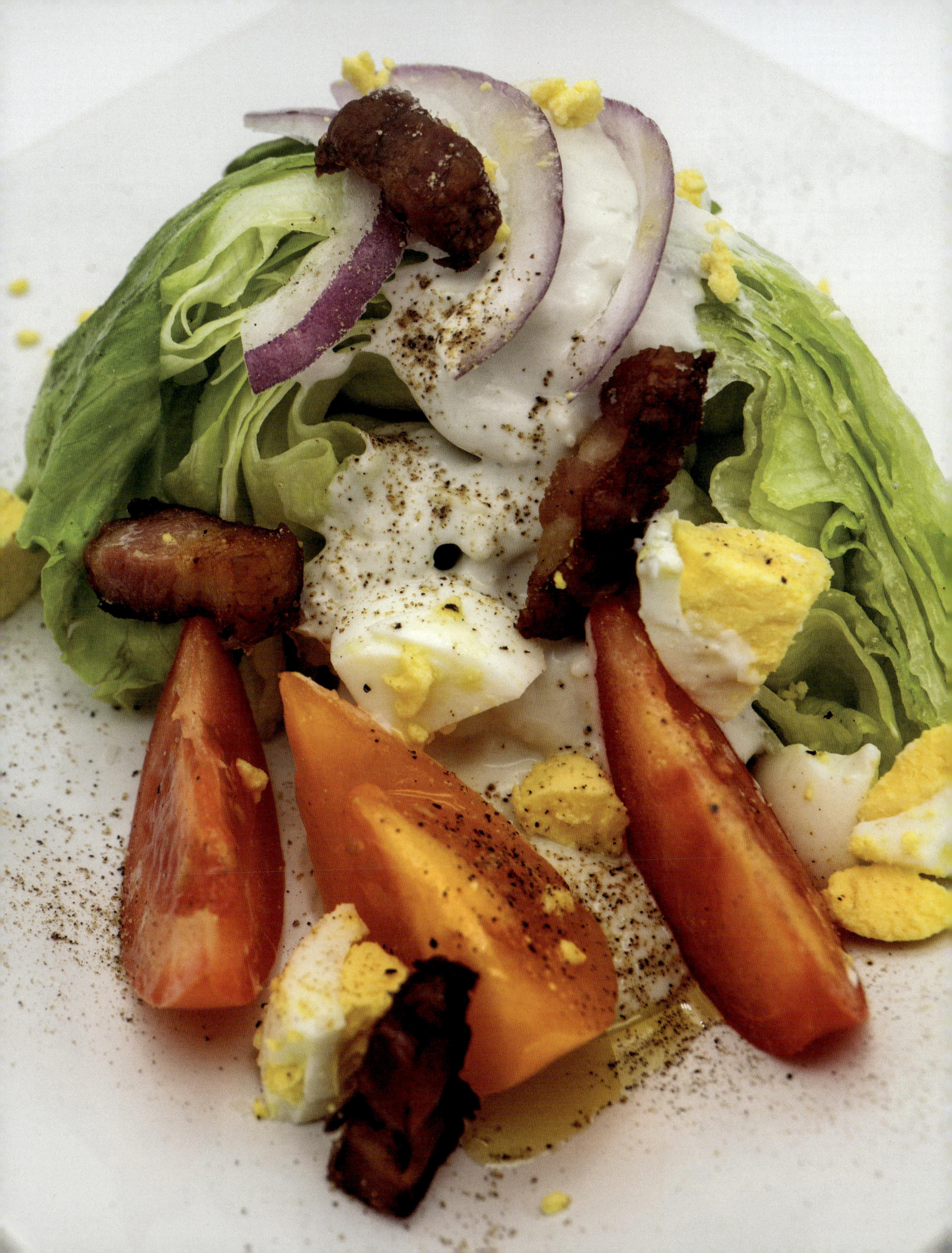

Yuppie Hill Poached Egg
With Salad Lyonnaise

This very popular salad was inspired by a trip to the Lyon region of France. With this dish we wanted to highlight our local Yuppie Hill Poultry Farm eggs. The owner, Lynn, does a great job creating a "yuppie" cage free environment for the chickens. We've taken these gorgeous cage free eggs, poached them, and put them on top of bacon "Lardons," croutons, and mixed greens. It is a beautiful, local take on a classic salad.

SERVES 8

INGREDIENTS:

8 Yuppie Hill large eggs

½ lb Wilson Farm Bacon slab

8 slices French bread

1 Tbsp extra virgin olive oil

1 Tbsp fresh herbs, chopped (parsley, thyme, and oregano)

3 quarts water, simmering

2 Tbsp white vinegar

1 tsp Black Truffle Oil

8 cups baby greens

DRESSING:

3 Tbsp extra virgin olive oil

1 Tbsp Aged Balsamic

1 Tbsp shallots, chopped

1 tsp Dijon mustard

Fresh herbs, to taste (parsley, thyme, and oregano)

Chef John's Signature Seasoning, to taste

PREPARATION:

1. Preheat oven to 350°F.
2. Cut bacon into ¼-inch "Lardons" and lay on sheet pan. Cook in oven for 12-15 minutes. Remove from heat, and let excess fat drain off on a paper towel.
3. Cut or tear slices of French bread into cubes. Toss with EVOO, Chef John's Signature Seasoning, and assorted fresh herbs. Toast in oven for 12-15 minutes.
4. In a small bowl, mix the EVOO, Aged Balsamic, shallots, mustard, fresh herbs, and Chef John's Signature Seasoning.
5. In a large shallow pan, bring 3 quarts of water to a simmer. Once simmering, add white vinegar and swirl water gently.
6. Add eggs one at a time, slowly, up to 4 in one pan. Poach eggs until whites are cooked and yolk is still soft, about 2-3 minutes. Repeat with remaining 4 eggs.
7. Remove from water and top each egg with drizzle of Black Truffle Oil and season with Chef John's Signature Seasoning. Reserve warm.
8. Toss greens with dressing, divide on to 8 plates.
9. Top with the poached egg, croutons, and bacon.

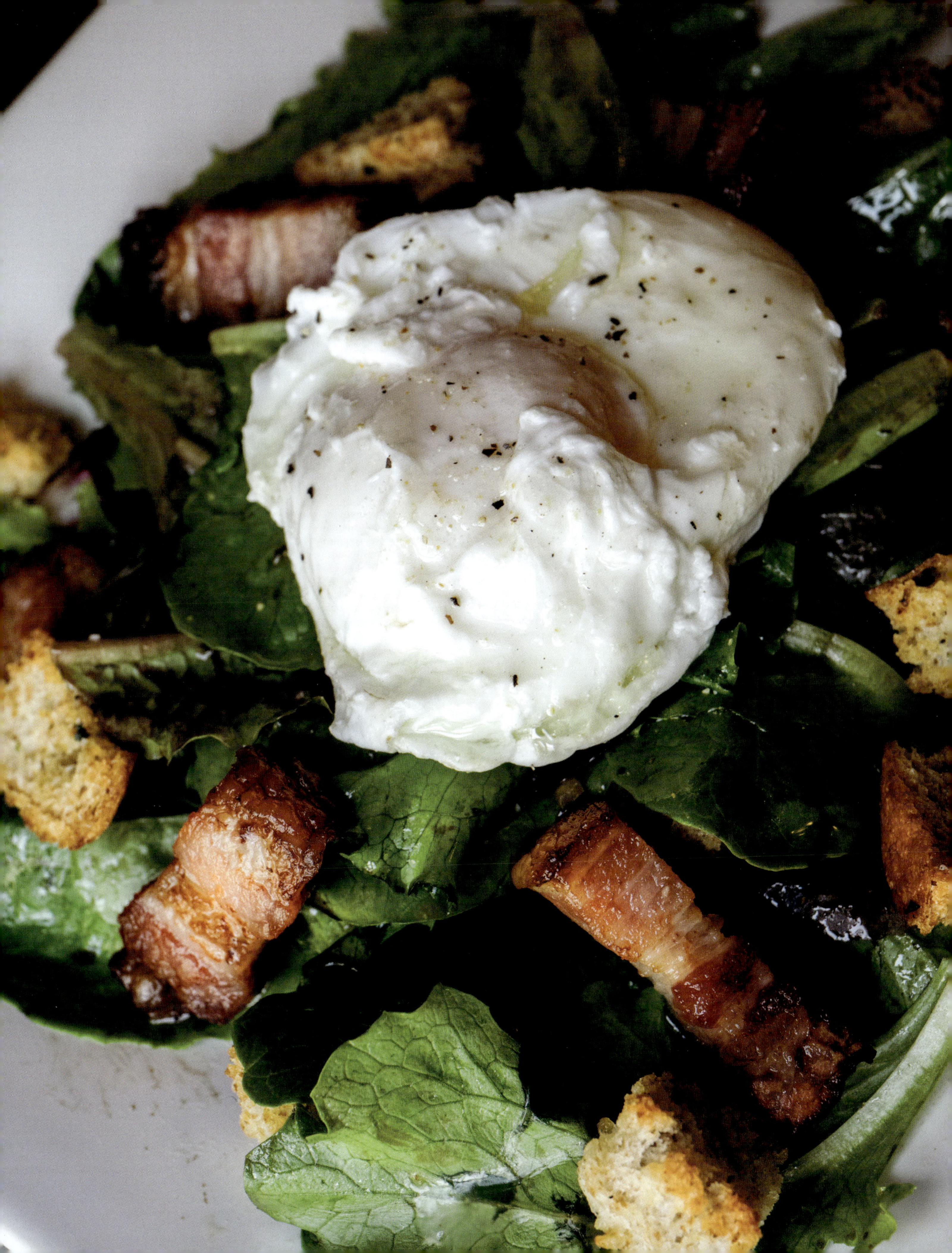

RIVER VALLEY RANCH MUSHROOM BISQUE

The great thing about this dish is that we use a plethora of mushrooms from the River Valley Ranch. Eric Rose and his father started this farm over 40 years ago and grow amazing food for us to enjoy. For this recipe, I like to use the widest variety of mushrooms possible. This bisque has a great presentation with the Wisconsin Cheddar Basket and grilled corn.

SERVES 12

INGREDIENTS:

1 lb fresh assorted mushrooms (morel, shitake, oyster, cremini)

½ cup additional whole mushrooms, for garnish

¼ cup butter

2 cloves garlic, chopped fine

4 stalks celery, chopped fine

2 medium onions, chopped fine

¼ cup flour

½ cup Cream Sherry

6 cups chicken stock

1 tsp Worcestershire sauce

½ tsp Tabasco

Chef John's Signature Seasoning, to taste

½ cup heavy cream

2 ears of corn, husked

1 Tbsp butter

Chili pepper puree, to taste

PREPARATION:

1. Clean mushrooms, remove stems (reserve for stock), and slice. Reserve ½ cup of smaller whole mushrooms for garnish.
2. Simmer the stems in chicken stock for 30 minutes, strain, and discard stems. Reserve stock.
3. In Dutch oven, melt butter and sauté onions, celery, and garlic until tender (5-6 minutes), add mushrooms. Sauté an additional 3-4 minutes.
4. Dust vegetables with flour (this is called "singer" and is a french culinary term), stir until thickened and blend (1-2 minutes). Deglaze with Cream Sherry. Stir to incorporate, trying to remove all lumps, then add stock and simmer for 20-30 minutes.
5. Season to taste with Worcestershire, Tabasco, and Chef John's Signature Seasoning.
6. Puree soup with immersion blender. Add cream and whisk.
7. Char grill corn cobs for 2 minutes per side for 8 minutes total. Slice kernels off the cob.
8. Sauté the reserved whole mushrooms in butter for 2 minutes, then add corn kernels, sauté for 1 minute more and season with Chef John's Signature Seasoning.
9. Garnish warm bowls of bisque with Wisconsin Cheddar Baskets filled with sautéed corn and whole mushrooms. Drizzle with chili pepper puree.

Serving Suggestion: *Top with Wisconsin Cheddar Basket (see recipe on page 202) with sautéed mushrooms and Grilled Corn (see recipe on page 199).*

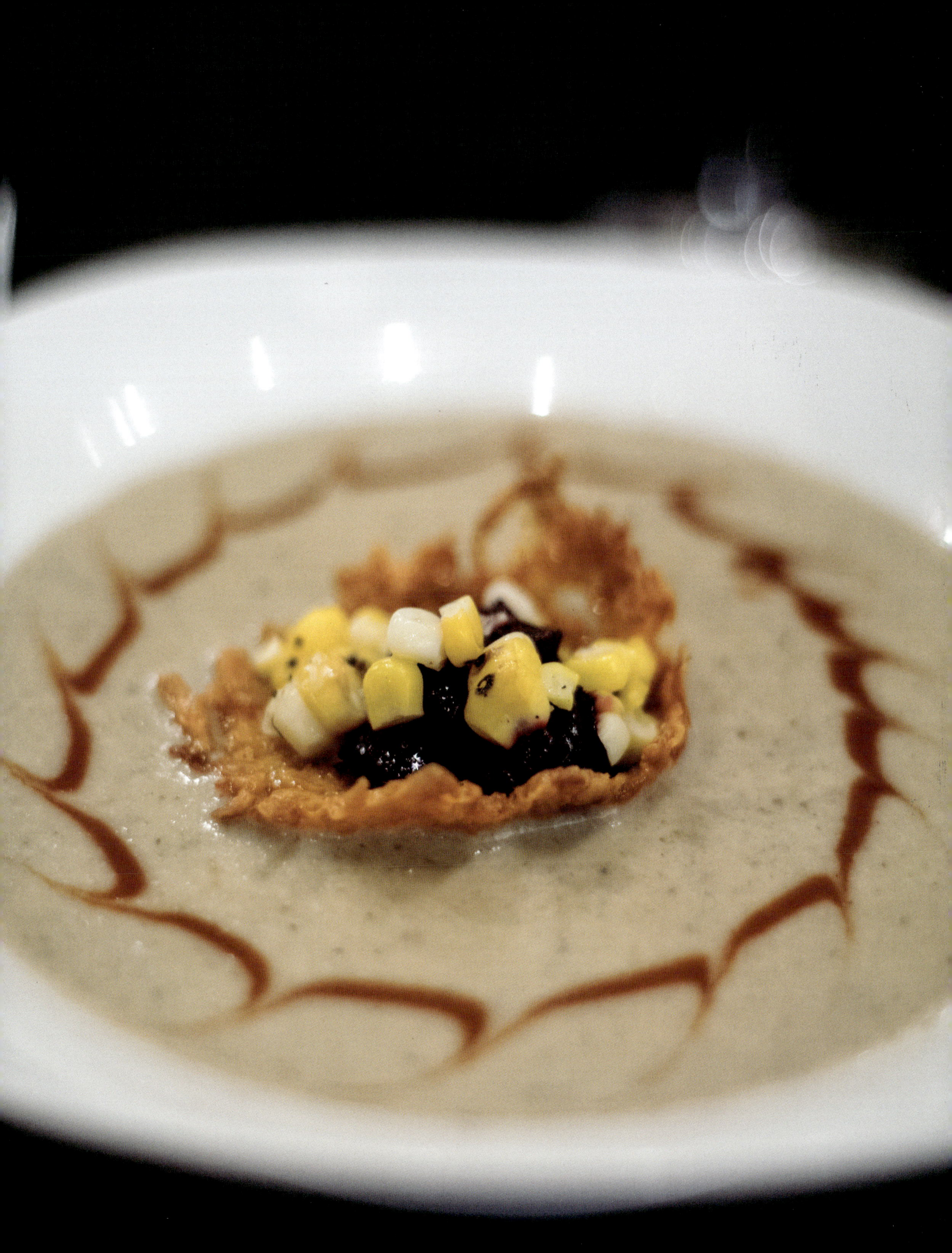

River Valley Ranch Portobellini
With Smokey Tomato-Chili Salsa

A Portobellini mushroom is described as a smaller Portabella mushroom. I like using the Portobellini as a starring role in this recipe as it is the perfect size to start off a meal. The Portobellini sits atop a puree of roasted tomatoes and Poblano chilies. It is then served on a bed of baby greens topped with Queso Fresco. This doesn't have to be a hot dish, just warm enough for a first course. This would pair very nicely with an ice cold margarita on the side.

SERVES 12

INGREDIENTS:

12 Portobellini mushrooms

1 onion, sliced ¼-inch rounds

2 cloves garlic, roughly chopped

3 Tbsp fresh lime juice

¼ tsp cumin

Chef John's Signature Seasoning, to taste

4 Tbsp extra virgin olive oil

3 ripe tomatoes, cut in half

2 fresh Poblano chilies

¼ Jalapeno pepper

½ cup white wine

2 Tbsp fresh cilantro, chopped

4 oz Queso Fresco, crumbled

1 Tbsp Aged Balsamic

4 oz baby greens

PREPARATION:

1. In a food processor, puree ⅓ of the onion and the garlic with 2 Tbsp EVOO until a very fine mince, add 1 Tbsp of the lime juice, the cumin, and 1 tsp Chef John's Signature Seasoning. Lay out the mushroom caps on sheet pan and rub the marinade over both sides of each mushroom cap. Let stand 10 minutes.
2. Heat grill to medium-high.
3. Season remaining ⅔ of onion slices and tomato halves with EVOO. Grill until slightly charred (7-9 minutes).
4. Set the Poblano chilies and Jalapeno over the hottest part of grill, char turning occasionally, until the chili skin is blistered and blackened all over. Remove them and place in pan and cover with plastic wrap. Let set for 10 minutes or until cooled.
5. Rub the blackened skin off the chilies, and then pull out the stems and seed pods. Rinse briefly to remove any stray seeds and bits of skin.
6. Puree grilled onions and tomatoes. Add Poblano and Jalapeno peppers and puree.
7. Add remaining 2 Tbsp lime juice, white wine, and the cilantro. Taste, season with Chef John's Signature Seasoning.
8. Brush the mushrooms with EVOO and lay gill side down on the grill. Cook until browned, about 2 minutes, then flip and continue grilling 2 more minutes. Remove from grill and fill mushroom cap with Queso Fresco, let rest.
9. Season baby greens with EVOO, Aged Balsamic, and Chef John's Signature Seasoning.
10. Ladle salsa onto center of plate and top with baby greens and Queso filled Portobellini.

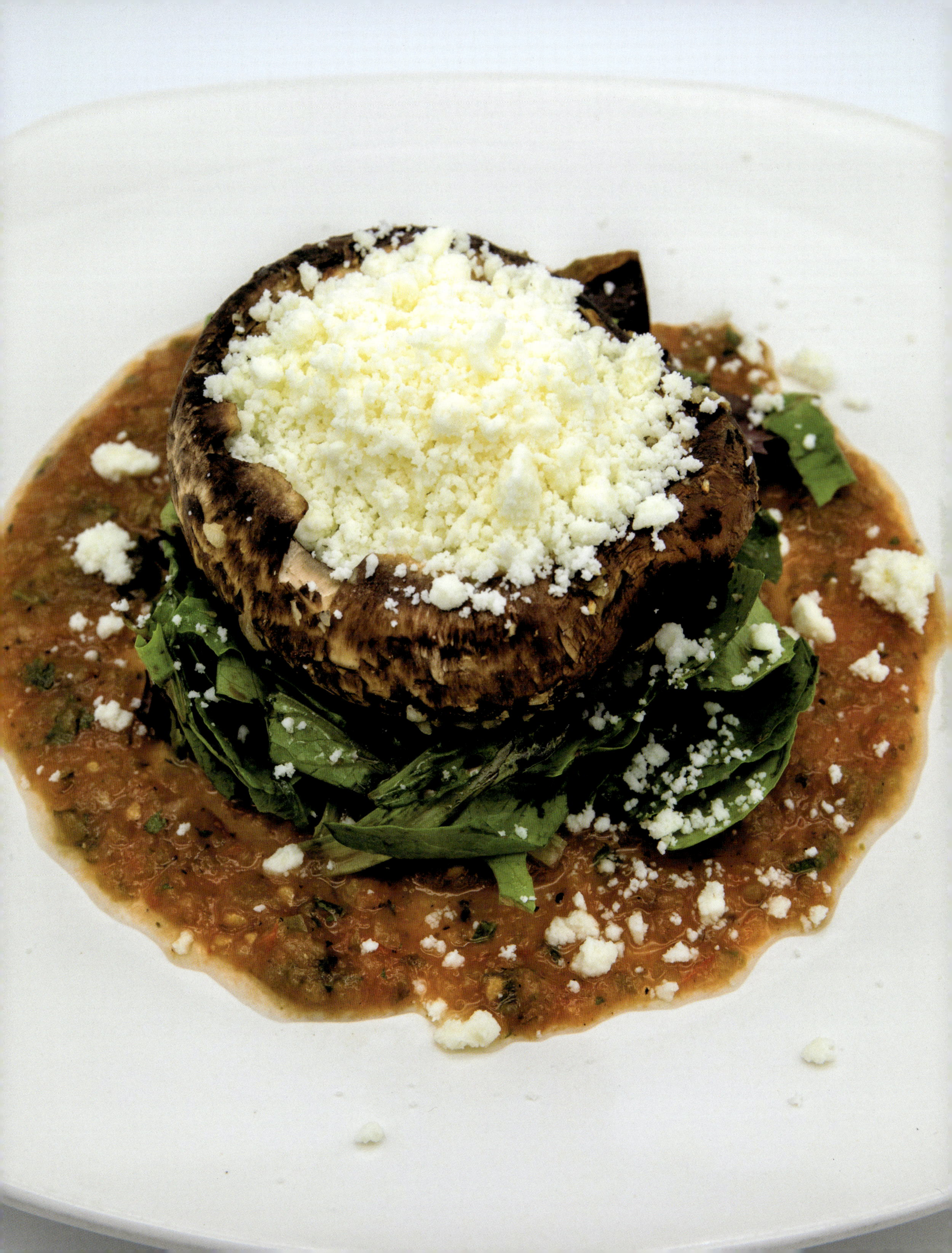

Pinn-Oak Ridge Farms Lamb Porterhouse

Once commonly referred to as a lamb loin chop, lamb porterhouses have the sirloin and the tenderloin together in a T-bone fashion. Steve and Darlene Pinnow of Pinn-Oak Ridge Farms do a great job raising beautiful, artisanal lamb on their Pin Oak Tree lined farm. Marinating these porterhouses with honey, fresh herbs, and red wine vinegar ensures that when you grill them, they char nicely and the honey helps to caramelize the lamb. This dish is a personal favorite.

SERVES 6

INGREDIENTS:

6 lamb loin chops, 8-10 oz each

2 Tbsp extra virgin olive oil

3 Tbsp honey

3 Tbsp red wine vinegar

2 cloves garlic, finely chopped

4 sprigs fresh herbs (parsley, thyme, and oregano)

Chef John's Signature Seasoning, to taste

PREPARATION:

1. Stir together EVOO, honey, red wine vinegar, garlic, fresh herbs, Chef John's Signature Seasoning; transfer to a sealable plastic bag.
2. Add lamb, then seal bag, pressing out excess air and turning to distribute marinade.
3. Marinate lamb, chilled, turning occasionally for 30 minutes to 1 hour. Bring lamb to room temperature.
4. Remove lamb from marinade and pat dry, reserve marinade.
5. Grill lamb chops on medium-high heat for 2 minutes, then rotate and grill an additional 2 minutes. Turn chops over and repeat this grilling process.
6. Heat marinade on low flame and drizzle over porterhouse.

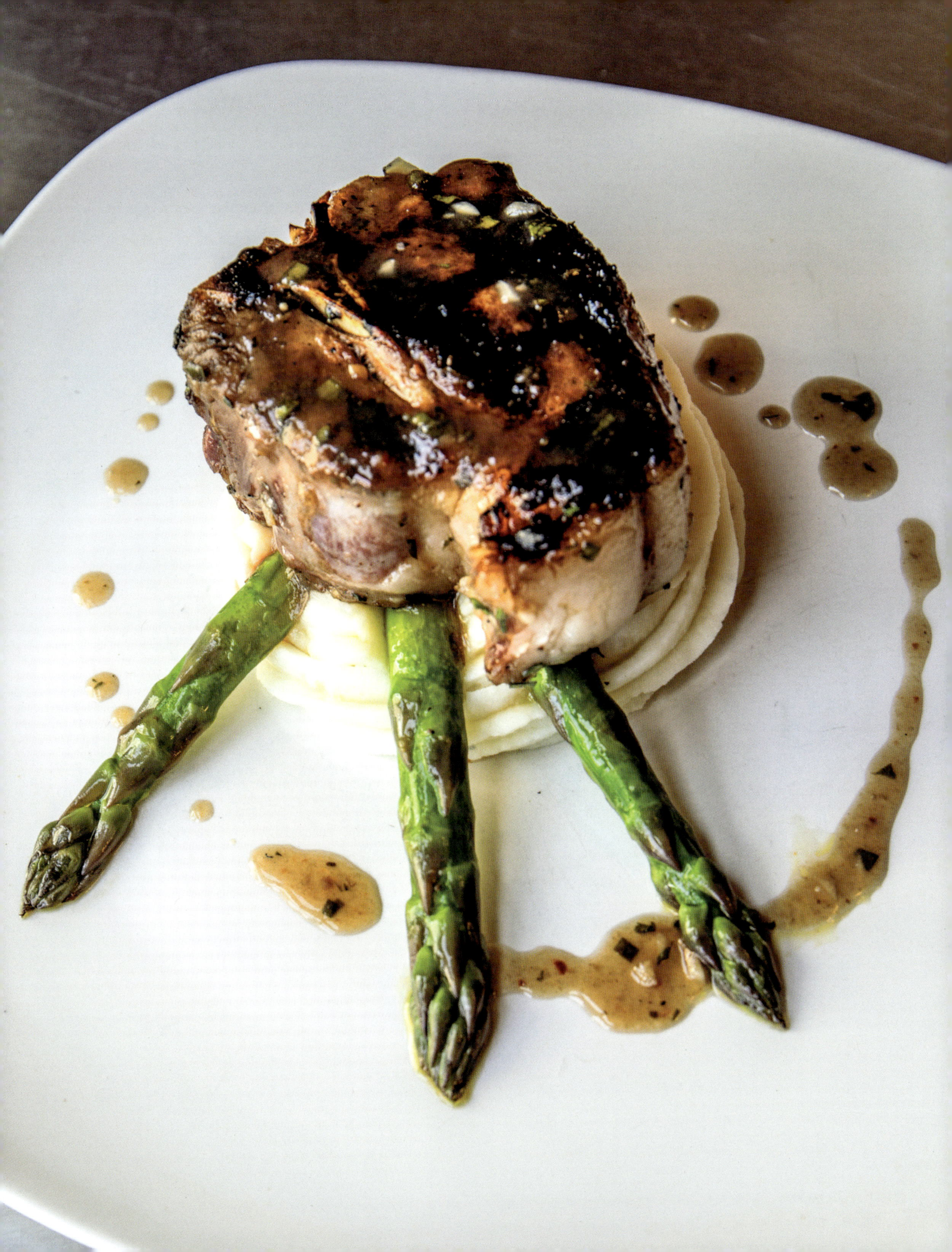

Pinn-Oak Ridge Farms Rack of Lamb Dijonnaise

This is a classic preparation in the style of Dijon, France. Searing the rack of lamb and coating it in Dijon mustard, fresh herbs, and bread crumbs finishes a classic preparation when roasted in the oven. The medium rare lamb melts just like butter and my mother-in-law, Nancy, would love to order this when she visited the French Country Inn. This is a classic dish that proves you don't always have to reinvent the wheel.

SERVES 6

INGREDIENTS:

2 rack of lamb (2-3 lbs each), frenched

3 Tbsp olive oil

¼ cup Dijon mustard

1 cup bread crumbs

2 cloves garlic, minced

1 Tbsp fresh parsley, chopped

1 Tbsp fresh rosemary, chopped

1 Tbsp fresh thyme, chopped

Chef John's Signature Seasoning, to taste

PREPARATION:

1. Preheat oven to 375°F.
2. Season rack of lamb with Chef John's Signature Seasoning. Sear lamb in olive oil in a roasting pan on medium-high heat for 10-12 minutes (making sure to sear all sides). Let cool to room temperature.
3. Brush on mustard generously.
4. Mix bread crumbs with garlic, parsley, rosemary, thyme, and Chef John's Signature Seasoning. Gently apply a coating of seasoned bread crumbs to the lamb.
5. Wrap exposed frenched lamb bones with aluminum foil. Place pan in oven and roast for 15-20 minutes. Lamb should be pink (medium rare) inside after about 15 minutes of cooking.
6. Let set for 10-15 minutes before slicing.

Note: "Frenching" is trimming the meat off the rib bones.

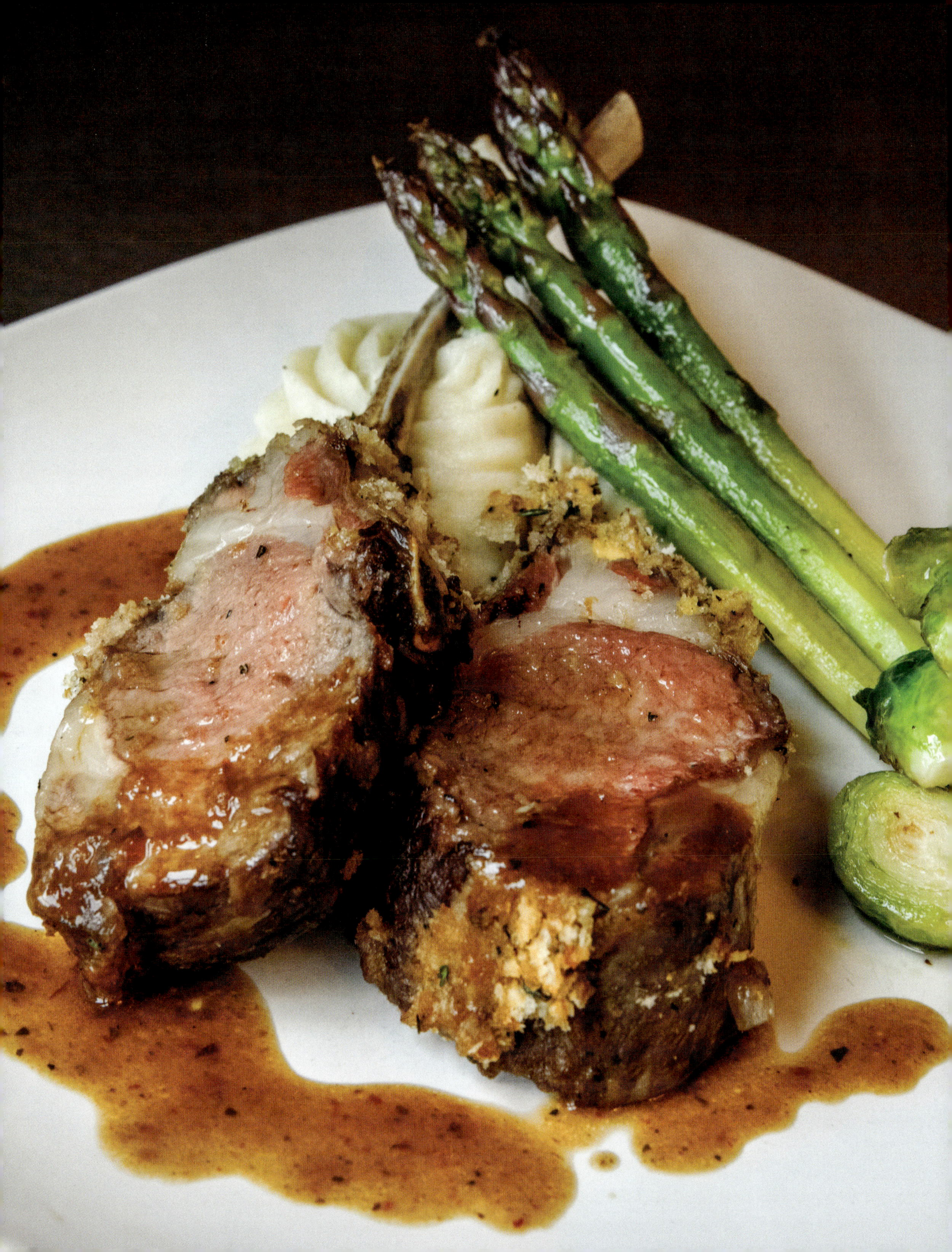

Hickory-smoked bacon "Lardons" from Wilson Farm Meats

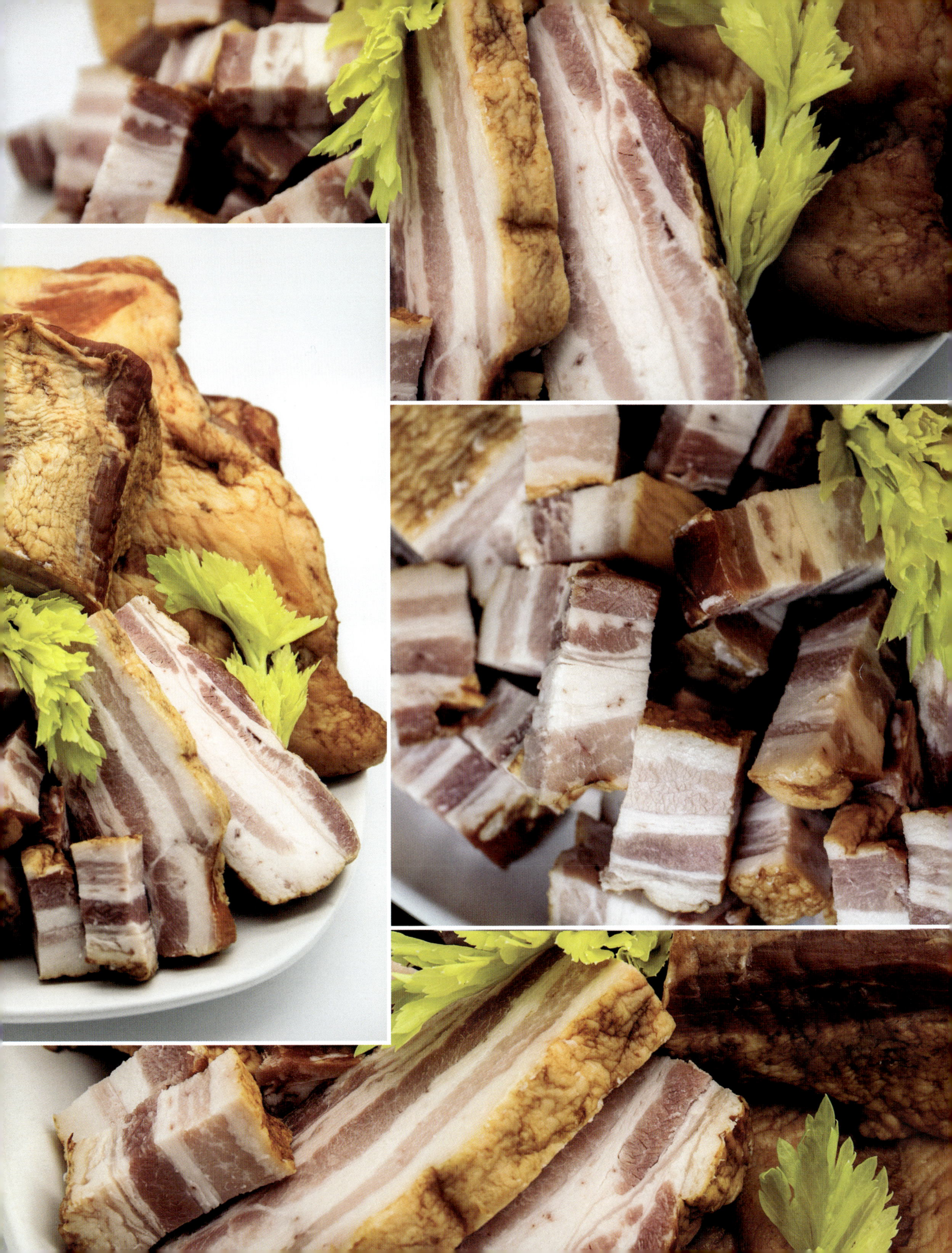

Baked Apples with Walnuts and Raisins

Fall

Fall is a wonderful transitional season and brings back many memories from the Bogan Ranch. My father, Larry, and I used to harvest our own potatoes and other root vegetables that we would use to prepare dinner for our entire family. There is an abundance of fall harvest produce such as beets, apples, squash, and those are showcased within this chapter. As the leaves are changing and the air becomes crisp, we start to bring the cooking inside the kitchen and create aromas that fill the entire home.

Acorn Squash and Sage Bisque   122

Spinach Stuffed Mushroom Caps   124

Beet and Goat Cheese En Croute Salad   126

Baby Greens with Pecans and Smoked Bacon   128

Chicken Medallions with Sage and Prosciutto   130

Potato Crusted Salmon Fillet   132

Chef Jake's Grilled Flat Iron Steak   134

Sautéed Pork Schnitzel with Spätzle   136

Grilled Pork Tenderloin with Apple Brandy   138

Baked Apples with Walnuts and Raisins   140

Gorgonzola Stuffed Pears   142

Bananas Foster   144

ACORN SQUASH AND SAGE BISQUE

This was a signature soup at the French Country Inn. Guests would call the restaurant at the end of summer wanting to know when we were going to release the fall classic Acorn Squash and Sage Bisque because they loved it so much. This bisque incorporates many fall ingredients and can be easily garnished with a cumin sour cream to make a beautiful presentation.

SERVES 8

INGREDIENTS:

2 acorn squashes

4 Tbsp brown sugar

4 tsp cinnamon

4 tsp nutmeg

4 Tbsp butter

1 small onion, chopped small

2 celery stalks, chopped small

2 Tbsp butter

2 Tbsp all-purpose flour

½ cup white wine

2 tsp fresh sage, chopped

1 tsp curry powder

1 tsp nutmeg

1 tsp cinnamon

4 cups chicken stock

½ cup brown sugar

Chef John's Signature Seasoning, to taste

1 cup heavy cream

8 Wisconsin Cheddar Baskets (see recipe on page 202)

PREPARATION:

1. Preheat oven to 400°F.
2. Split the acorn squash in half (horizontally). Scoop out seeds. Place the acorn squash halves in roasting pan. Sprinkle each of the four cavities with 1 Tbsp of brown sugar, 1 tsp of cinnamon, 1 tsp of nutmeg, and 1 Tbsp of butter.
3. Add 1 cup of water to roasting pan, cover with foil and bake for an hour, until fork tender.
4. Remove from the oven and let cool.
5. Scoop out the acorn squash and reserve. Discard the skins.
6. In a large Dutch oven, sauté the onion and celery in butter until translucent. Stir in flour, cook for 2 minutes. Deglaze with white wine.
7. Gradually add stock, while bringing to a boil; add sage, curry, nutmeg, cinnamon, brown sugar, acorn squash, Chef John's Signature Seasoning. Let simmer for 30-40 minutes.
8. Using an immersion blender puree the soup until smooth. Let simmer for 5 minutes and add heavy cream.
9. Pour into bowls; garnish with Wisconsin Cheddar Baskets and vegetable Brunoise.

Note: "Brunoise" very fine dice approximately ⅛-inch square.

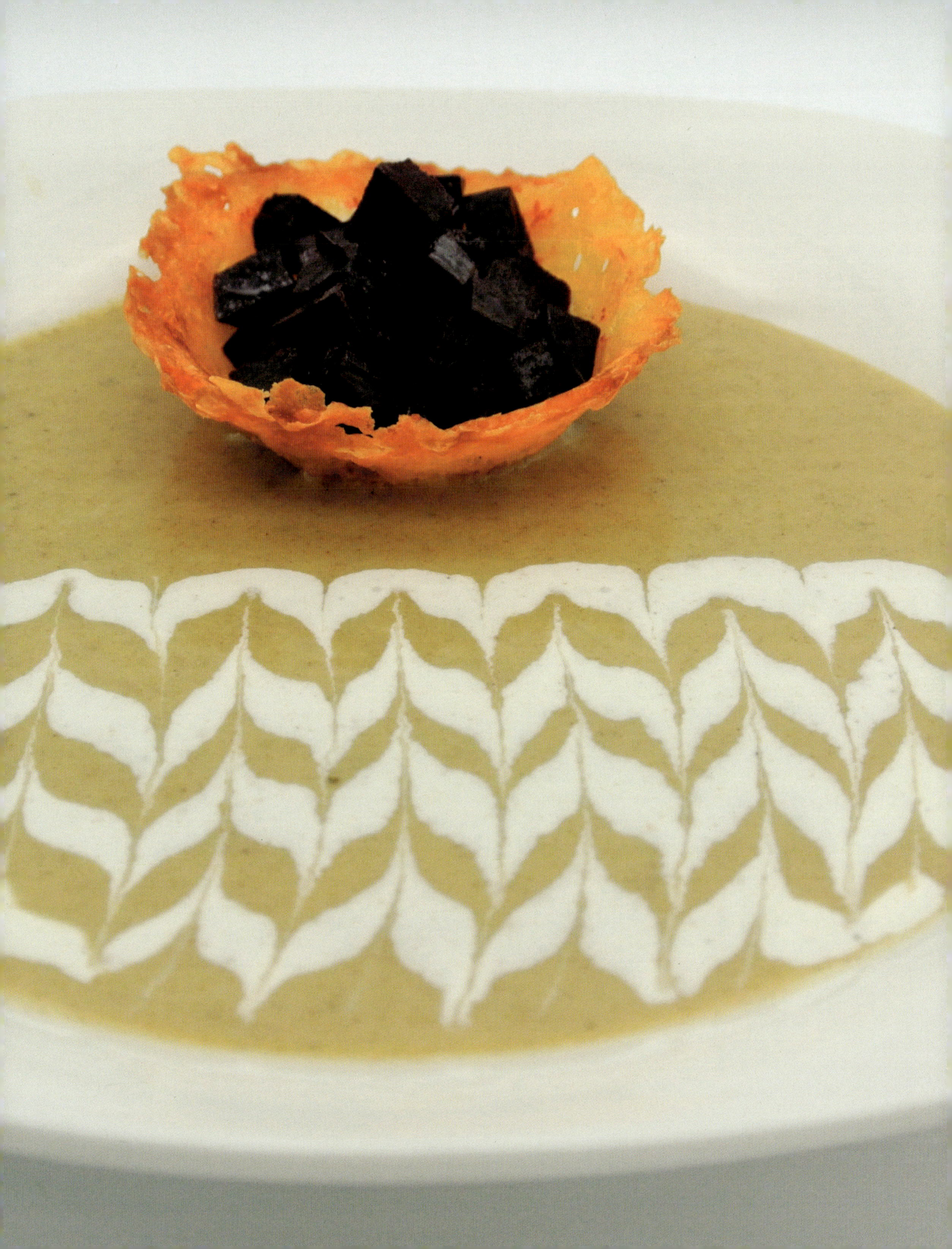

Spinach Stuffed Mushroom Caps

This dish is great to serve as an appetizer on a buffet reception or a plated first course. The spinach adds a luscious green color that really brightens the mushroom cap. We have served these spinach stuffed mushrooms as a plated first course at our Thanksgiving celebration for over 20 years.

SERVES 8

INGREDIENTS:

4 Tbsp butter, melted

20 large cremini mushrooms

3 Tbsp butter

2 Tbsp onion, finely chopped

2 cloves garlic, peeled and minced

1 package washed baby spinach, 5 oz

1 cup heavy cream

½ cup Parmesan cheese, grated

1 cup bread crumbs

Chef John's Signature Seasoning, to taste

PREPARATION:

1. Preheat oven to 350°F.
2. Melt 4 Tbsp of butter. Pour melted butter onto baking sheet and spread evenly.
3. Remove stems from mushrooms and reserve.
4. Arrange the mushroom caps on buttered baking sheet stem side up. Place in refrigerator.
5. Place stems in a food processor and blend for 30 seconds. Add spinach and pulse until finely chopped.
6. In a medium sauté pan over medium heat, melt 3 Tbsp butter. Sauté onions and garlic for 5 minutes or until translucent.
7. Add chopped spinach and mushroom stems, sauté about 2 minutes. Add heavy cream, bring to a boil, and let simmer for 3 minutes.
8. Remove from heat and mix in Parmesan, bread crumbs, and Chef John's Signature Seasoning.
9. Let cool to room temperature. Fill pastry bag with mixture and pipe into mushroom caps.
10. Bake in preheated oven for 12-15 minutes or until mushrooms are tender.

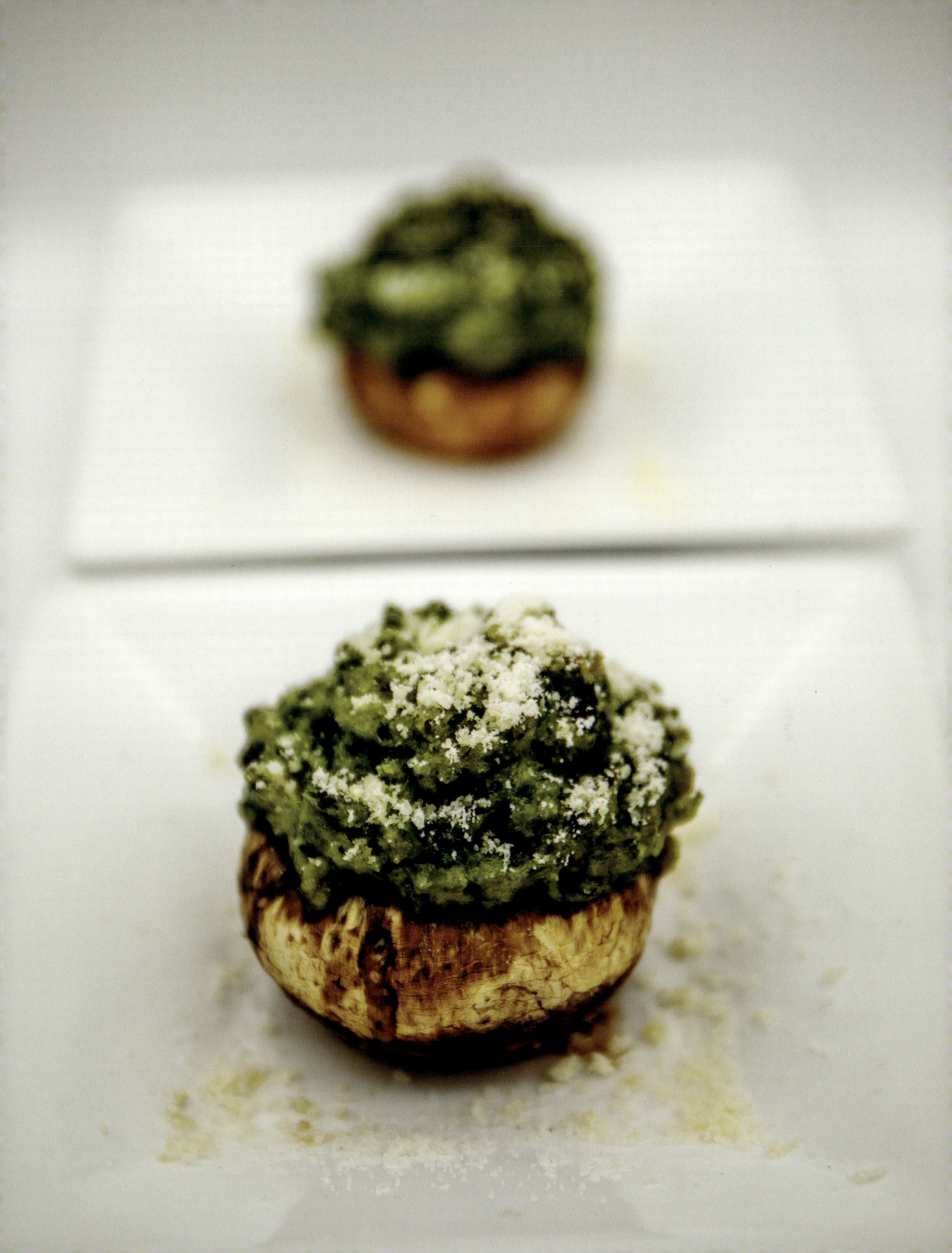

Beet and Goat Cheese En Croute Salad
With White Peach Orange Vinaigrette

It is great to pick up a variety of fresh beets from the farmers market for this salad. The colors from golden and red beets make this salad pop. The Panko breaded goat cheese, served warm, adds a wonderful creaminess to the salad. The greens are tossed with a white peach and orange vinaigrette creating a bright acidity.

SERVES 8

INGREDIENTS:

SALAD

- 4 medium beets, scrubbed and trimmed
- 2 Tbsp extra virgin olive oil
- ⅓ cup walnuts, chopped
- 3 Tbsp maple syrup
- 10 oz baby greens

WHITE PEACH ORANGE VINAIGRETTE

- 1 tsp orange, fresh squeezed
- 1 tsp lemon, fresh squeezed
- 1 Tbsp shallot, chopped finely
- 1 Tbsp assorted fresh herbs (parsley, thyme, and oregano)
- 2 Tbsp White Peach Balsamic
- ¼ cup orange extra virgin olive oil
- Chef John's Signature Seasoning, to taste

PREPARATION:

1. Preheat oven to 375°F.
2. Place beets into a roasting pan, and season with EVOO and Chef John's Signature Seasoning. Then roast for 45-60 minutes. Rinse under cold water to peel and cool.
3. While the beets are cooking, place the walnuts in a sauté pan over medium-low heat. Heat until warm and starting to toast, then stir in the maple syrup. Cook and stir until evenly coated, then remove from the heat and set aside to cool.
4. In a small bowl, whisk together the orange and lemon juice, shallots, fresh herbs, White Peach Balsamic, Orange EVOO, and Chef John's Signature Seasoning.
5. Toss baby greens in large bowl with ¾ of the White Peach Orange Vinaigrette. Place a large helping of greens onto each salad plate. Place equal amounts of beets over the greens, top with candied walnuts and Goat Cheese En Croute. Drizzle each plate with remaining vinaigrette.

Goat Cheese en Croute

INGREDIENTS:

- 8 oz Goat Cheese log
- ½ cup flour
- 3 large eggs, beaten
- ¾ cup Panko bread crumbs

- Chef John's Signature Seasoning, to taste
- 2 Tbsp olive oil
- 2 Tbsp butter

PREPARATION:

1. Slice Goat Cheese into 8 equal slices. Season flour with Chef John's Signature Seasoning.
2. Dredge Goat Cheese into flour, egg, and bread crumbs.
3. Sauté in fortified oil (mixture of olive oil and butter) for 1-2 minutes per side or until golden brown.

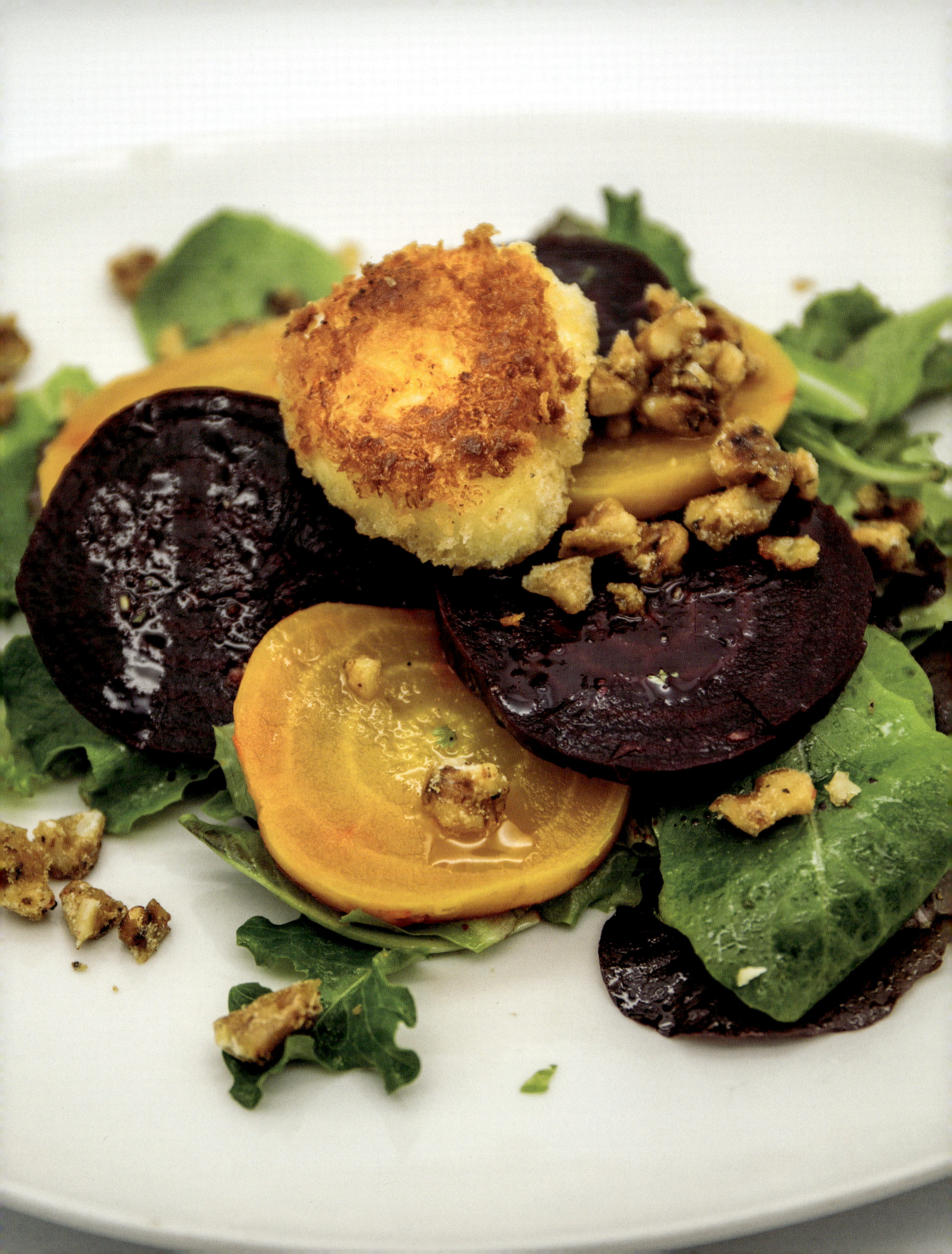

BABY GREENS WITH PECANS AND SMOKED BACON
WITH SHAVED GOAT CHEESE AND HONEY DIJON DRESSING

There are many components to this dish that bring this salad together. The caramelized spiced pecans, the bacon "Lardons" from Wilson Farm Meats, the pears, and the grated, frozen goat cheese. Freezing the goat cheese allows it to become light and airy when grated over the salad. This is much more than a salad, this is an amazing course.

SERVES 8

INGREDIENTS:

SPICED CANDIED PECANS

1½ tsp Chef John's Signature Seasoning

½ tsp cinnamon

¼ tsp Cayenne

2 cups pecan halves

½ cup powdered sugar

2 cups Canola oil

DRESSING

½ cup mayonnaise

2 Tbsp honey

2 Tbsp Dijon mustard

2 tsp white wine vinegar

2 tsp white wine

1 tsp fresh tarragon, chopped

Chef John's Signature Seasoning, to taste

SALAD

8 cups baby greens

1 pear, thinly sliced

1 lemon

1 lb smoked bacon slab

2 oz Goat Cheese, frozen

½ cup Spiced Candied Pecans

PREPARATION:

BACON

1. Preheat oven to 375°F.
2. Slice bacon into ¼-inch dice "Lardons."
3. Brown the bacon in oven for 12-15 minutes.

SPICED CANDIED PECANS

1. Combine the Chef John's Signature Seasoning, cinnamon, and Cayenne pepper into a small bowl and mix well.
2. Bring a 2-quart saucepan with 4 cups of water to a boil.
3. Holding the pecans in a sieve, dip them briefly into the boiling water, about 1 minute for large halves. Transfer to a large bowl with a little water clinging to them.
4. While the pecans are still hot and wet, add the powdered sugar and toss well until all the sugar has melted.
5. In a deep saucepan, add 2 cups of Canola oil and heat to 350°F.
6. Using a large slotted spoon, transfer a few nuts to the hot oil, allowing the foam to subside before adding another spoonful.
7. Fry in small batches until the nuts are medium brown, about 1 minute. Be careful not to overcook.
8. While pecans are warm, sprinkle with spice mix.

DRESSING

1. Add all ingredients in mixing bowl. Whisk gently, season to taste. Chill before serving.

PLATING:

1. Slice pear into wedges and squeeze fresh lemon over to prevent browning.
2. In a large bowl, toss the greens with dressing. Divide onto 8 plates. Top with three slices of pear.
3. Scatter the warm pecans and bacon on top.
4. Using a micro plainer, shave the frozen Goat Cheese over the salads, serve immediately.

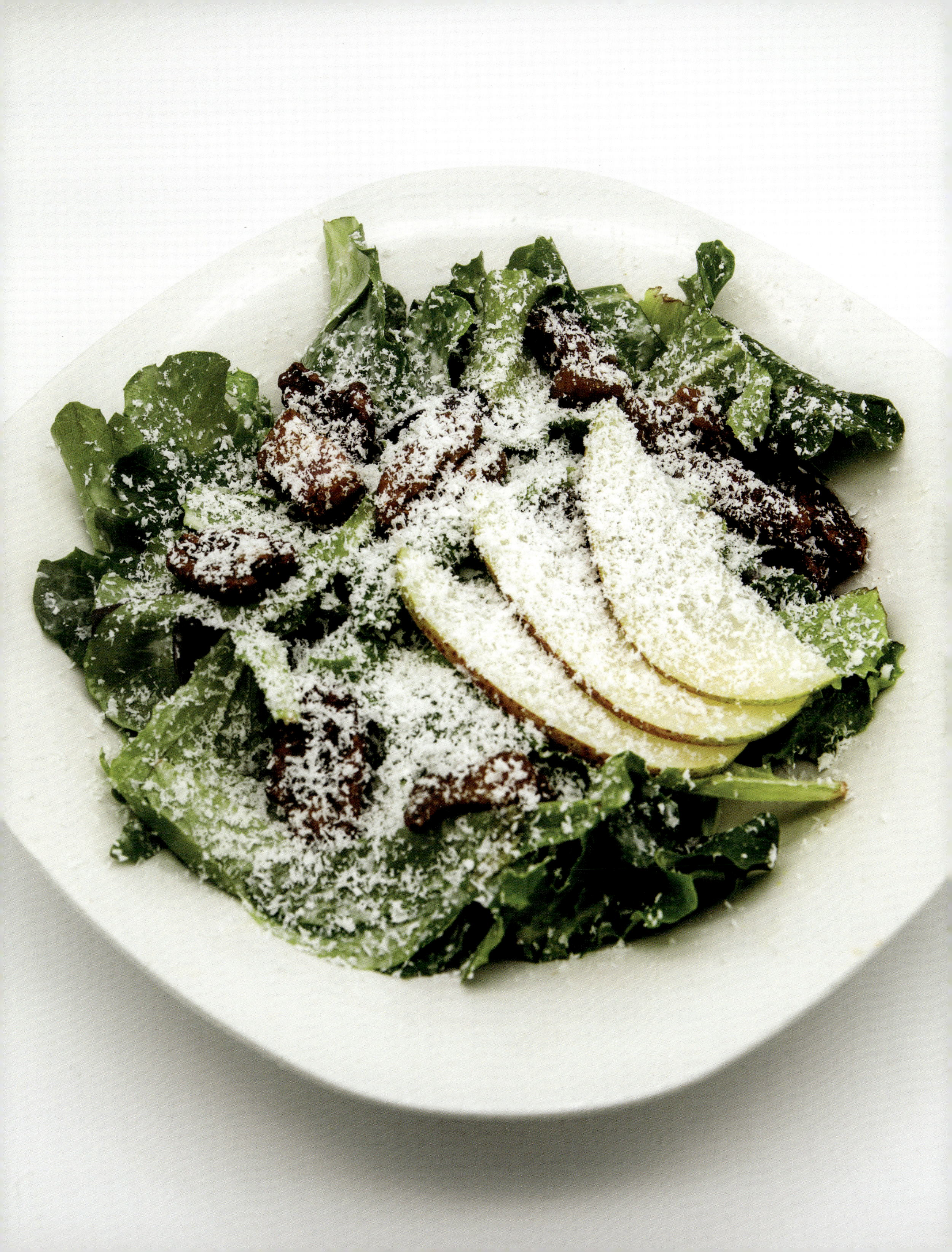

Chicken Medallions with Sage and Prosciutto
With Sherry Wine Reduction

Sage is a wonderful fall herb that adds a sense of warmth to this dish. In this recipe, the chicken medallions are pounded out, topped with sage and Prosciutto, and then sautéed to golden brown. The Sherry Wine Mushroom Reduction adds a little sweetness that brings this entrée together. This is a wonderful weeknight preparation as it is very simple to make.

SERVES 6
INGREDIENTS:

1 cup all-purpose flour

Chef John's Signature Seasoning, to taste

6 chicken breasts, 5 oz each

6 slices Prosciutto, 4-inch each

6 sage leaves

4 Tbsp olive oil

2 Tbsp butter

2 shallots, thinly sliced

2 cloves garlic, chopped

3 cups mushrooms, sliced

½ cup Cream Sherry

2 cups chicken stock

2 Tbsp fresh Italian parsley, chopped

PREPARATION:

1. Place plastic wrap on cutting board; lay out chicken breast with 1 piece of sage and 1 slice of Prosciutto. Cover with plastic wrap and pound chicken with a meat tenderizer until ½-inch thick.
2. Season flour with Chef John's Signature Seasoning and dredge each chicken medallion in flour.
3. In a 12-inch sauté pan, heat the olive oil until medium hot. Add the chicken and sauté until golden brown on both sides (about 3 minutes per side); remove and let rest. Remove remaining oil left in pan.
4. Add butter to the pan and sauté the shallots and garlic for 2 minutes, then add mushrooms and cook until the mushrooms are browned, about 4-5 minutes.
5. Deglaze with Cream Sherry and reduce in half, then add chicken stock and cook over medium heat until reduced by half. Add the parsley and season with Chef John's Signature Seasoning.

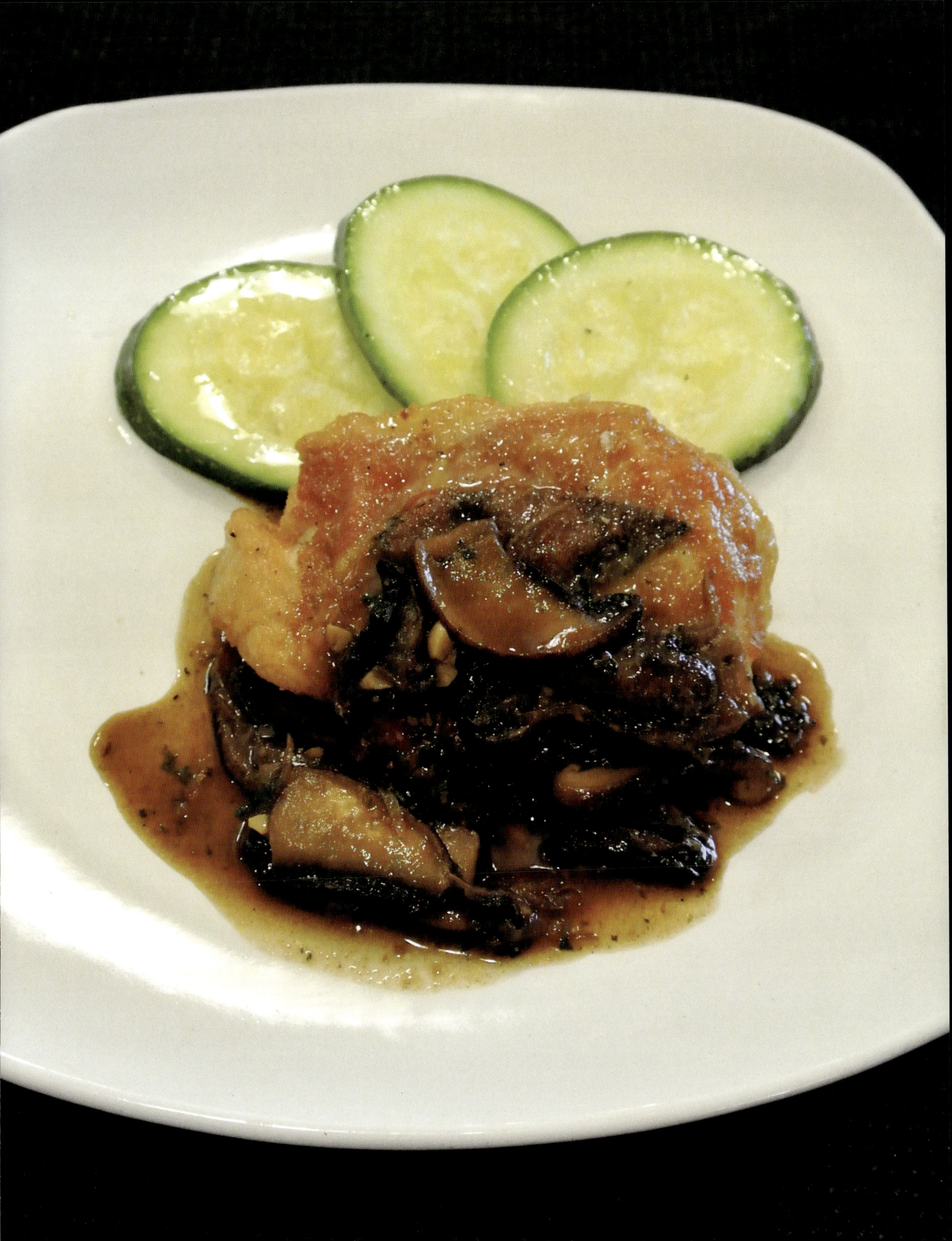

Potato Crusted Salmon Fillet
With Duet of Three Mustard Sauce and Berry Coulis

This is my personal favorite preparation of salmon. I love the crispy hash browns encrusted around the salmon fillet. The salmon is then served on a Three Mustard Sauce with Berry Coulis to create a beautiful plate design. The Three Mustard Sauce has delicate flavors that pair well with seafood and chicken. This is a great dish to serve all through Fall and the holidays as it can be a first course or an entrée preparation.

SERVES 10

INGREDIENTS:

10 salmon fillets, 2 oz each

1 cup fortified oil (½ cup oil and ½ cup butter)

6 russet potatoes, peeled

2 large egg yolks

¼ cup flour

4 Tbsp Dijon mustard

Chef John's Signature Seasoning, to taste

3-inch round ramekins (5)

2 cups Three Mustard Sauce (see recipe on page 194)

¼ cup Berry Coulis (see recipe on page 197)

PREPARATION:

1. Shred peeled potatoes in cold water, rinse, drain, and dry. In an additional bowl, add potatoes, egg yolks, flour, and Chef John's Signature Seasoning. Toss to incorporate.

2. Season salmon with Chef John's Signature Seasoning.

3. Fill lower ⅓ of ramekin with shredded potato, while allowing some potato to come up the sides. Add salmon fillet and ½ Tbsp of Dijon mustard. Top exposed salmon with additional potato.

4. Bring fortified oil to medium-hot temperature.

5. Invert salmon and potato ramekin onto spatula. Gently slide into hot fortified oil, cook 3-4 minutes on each side, and remove onto sheet pan.

6. Finish in 335°F oven for 5-6 minutes, making sure potato crust is warm.

7. Ladle 2 oz of Three Mustard Sauce on the center of the plate. Drizzle Berry Coulis around outer edge of mustard sauce and pull through with toothpick in an attractive design.

8. Place potato crusted salmon in center of plate.

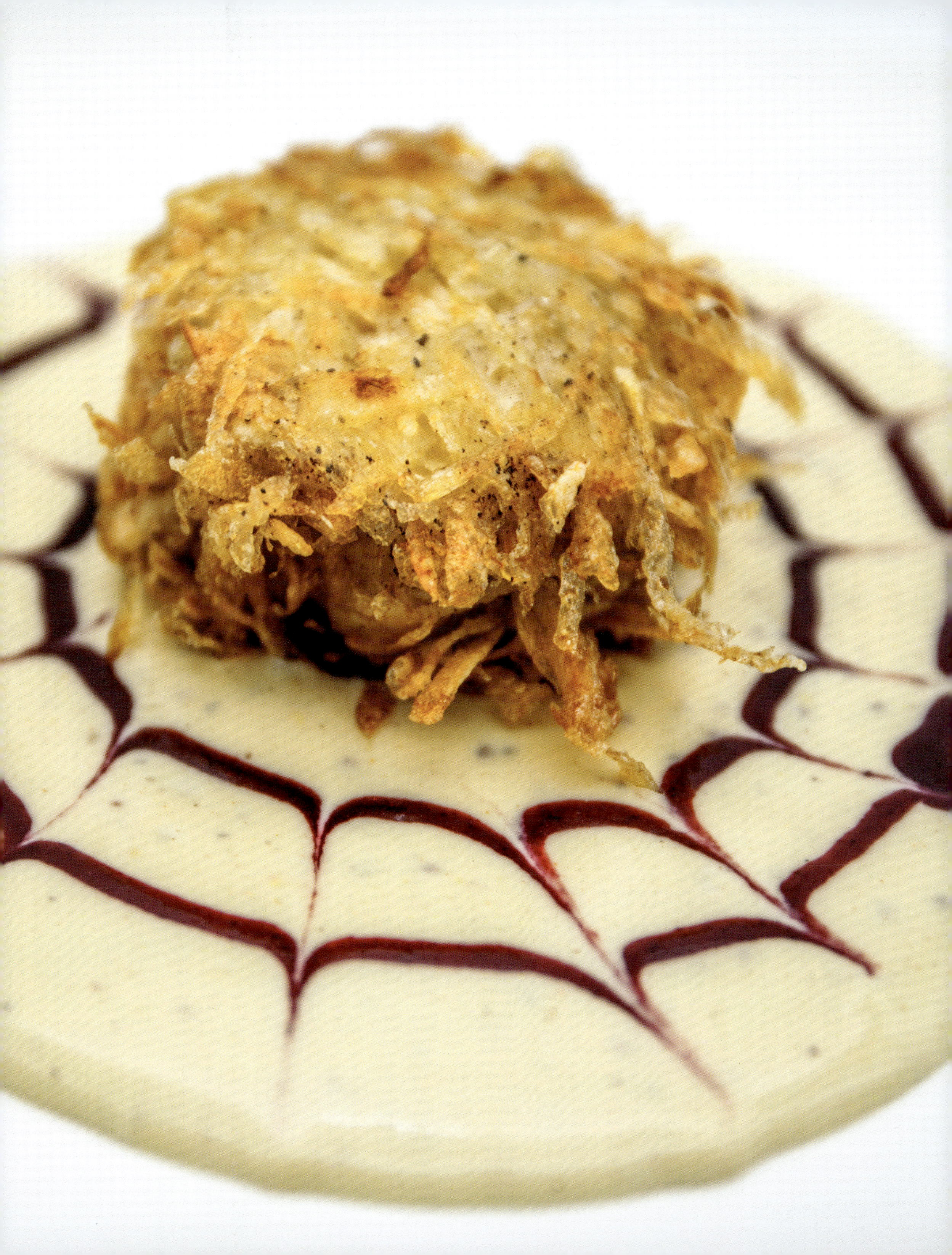

Chef Jake's Grilled Flat Iron Steak
With Merlot Marinade and Roasted Balsamic Vegetables

Through the years at the Lake Geneva School of Cooking, this has become a signature dish of Chef Jake. We created this dish by marinating the Flat Iron Steak in Merlot wine. This cut of beef accepts a marinade very well and adds great flavor to the meat. Once the steak is marinated, it is then grilled and sliced on the bias to see the beautiful, medium rare inside. The steak pairs wonderfully with roasted balsamic Fall vegetables.

SERVES 8
INGREDIENTS:

- 6 Prime Flat Iron Steaks, 10 oz each
- ¼ cup extra virgin olive oil
- 2 cloves garlic, minced
- 2 Tbsp fresh parsley, chopped
- 1 Tbsp fresh rosemary, chopped
- ¼ cup fresh chives, chopped
- 1 cup Merlot wine
- 1 Tbsp dry mustard powder
- Chef John's Signature Seasoning, to taste
- 1 Tbsp extra virgin olive oil

MARINADE:

1. Place the steak inside of a large bag.
2. In a small bowl, stir together ¼ cup EVOO, garlic, parsley, rosemary, chives, Merlot, Chef John's Signature Seasoning, and mustard powder. Pour over and coat all steaks.
3. Marinate in the refrigerator for 1-2 hours.
4. Rotate steaks in marinade every 20 minutes.

PREPARATION:

1. Heat grill over medium-high heat.
2. Pat steaks dry with paper towel. Discard the marinade. Season with Chef John's Signature Seasoning and EVOO.
3. Grill the steaks for 2 minutes, rotate and grill 2 minutes on the same side, turn steaks over and repeat grilling process until your desired degree of doneness.
4. These steaks taste best at medium rare. Allow them to rest for about 8 minutes before serving.
5. Slice each steak on the bias into 6 slices.

Roasted Balsamic Vegetables

INGREDIENTS:

- 2 cups broccoli, large dice
- 2 cups cauliflower, large dice
- 2 cups zucchini, large dice
- 2 cups peppers, large dice
- Chef John's Signature Seasoning, to taste
- ¼ cup balsamic vinegar
- ¼ cup extra virgin olive oil

PREPARATION:

1. Preheat oven to 375°F.
2. Whisk together the balsamic vinegar and Chef John's Signature Seasoning in a small bowl. Slowly incorporate EVOO until a dressing is formed.
3. Prepare vegetables into 1-inch pieces. Place the vegetables in a single layer on a baking sheet, drizzle with balsamic mixture, and gently toss to coat.
4. Bake for 20-25 minutes, turning once, until vegetables are lightly browned.

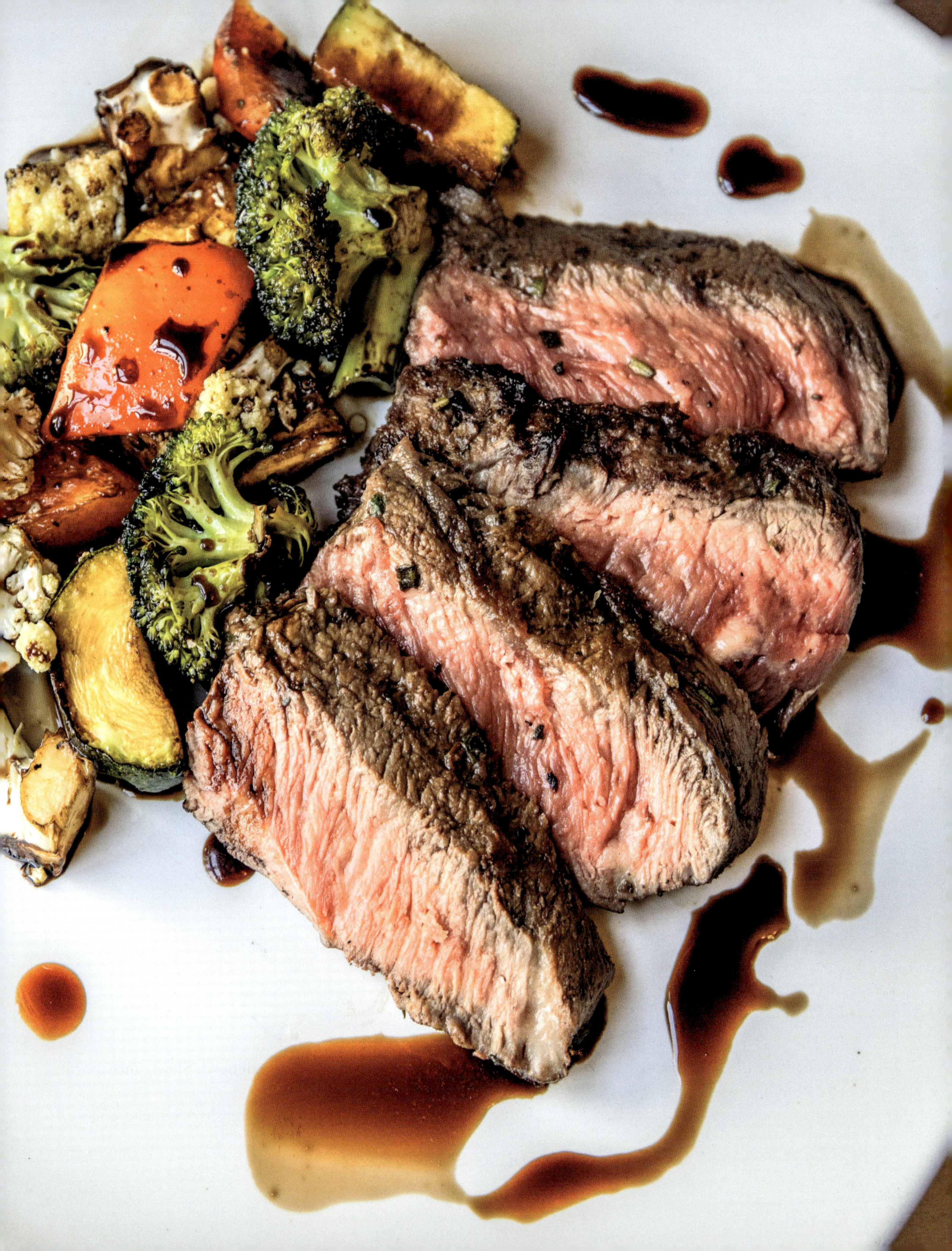

Sautéed Pork Schnitzel
With Spätzel

Lake Geneva does a wonderful job celebrating Oktoberfest. The streets are closed off in front of the Lake Geneva School of Cooking with live entertainment and fall activities. We love serving this dish during this time of year to celebrate German culture and cuisine. This recipe prepares a beautiful pork tenderloin in Schnitzel style and is paired with homemade spätzel.

SERVES 6

INGREDIENTS:

2 pork tenderloins, 1½ lbs each

3 large eggs, lightly beaten

½ cup all-purpose flour

¼ cup butter plus 2 Tbsp

¼ cup olive oil

2 cloves garlic, chopped

2 medium leeks, thinly sliced

4 cups mushrooms, sliced

½ cup white wine

2 cups chicken stock

1 Tbsp fresh parsley, chopped

Chef John's Signature Seasoning, to taste

PREPARATION:

1. Trim tenderloin, removing any visible fat. Slice into 1-inch medallions. Pound each medallion to ¼-inch thickness.
2. Season eggs and flour with Chef John's Signature Seasoning, dip each cutlet into egg, coat with flour, and shake off excess.
3. In a sauté pan over medium heat, add butter and olive oil; add tenderloin and sauté until lightly browned, about 3-4 minutes. Remove and keep warm.
4. Sauté garlic and leeks in 2 Tbsp butter for 2 minutes, then add mushrooms; cook an additional 3-4 minutes or until tender.
5. Deglaze with wine. Stir in the stock, parsley, and season with Chef John's Signature Seasoning; let reduce. Serve over the Schnitzel.

Spätzel

INGREDIENTS:

2 cups all-purpose flour

¾ cup milk

4 large eggs

1 tsp nutmeg

Chef John's Signature Seasoning, to taste

2 gallons hot water

4 Tbsp butter

4 Tbsp fresh parsley, chopped

PREPARATION:

1. Mix together flour, 2 tsp Chef John's Signature Seasoning, and nutmeg. Beat eggs well, and add alternately with the milk to the dry ingredients. Mix until smooth.
2. Spoon batter onto small cutting board and slice batter into simmering water.
3. Cook 1-2 minutes or until Spätzel floats to the top of the boiling water; remove and drain well.
4. In a large sauté pan, melt butter and add cooked Spätzel.
5. Sprinkle chopped fresh parsley on top and serve.

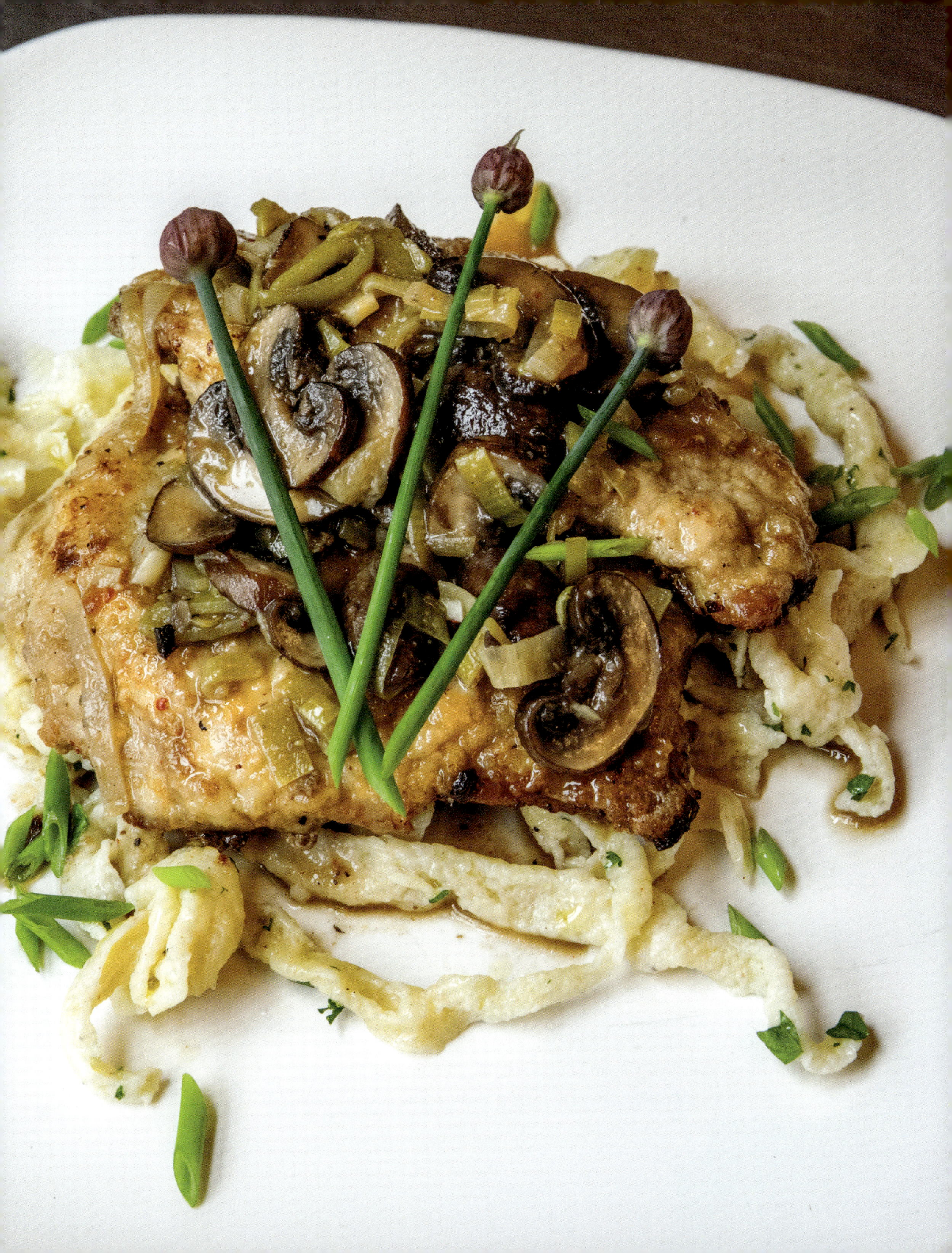

GRILLED PORK TENDERLOIN WITH APPLE BRANDY

This entree is a great way to highlight Fall apples. The apple brandy reduction combines tart apples, like a Granny Smith or McIntosh, with leeks and mushrooms, and is reduced with cream to pair with grilled pork tenderloin. I also like to serve this with Dijon Whipped Potatoes that adds a subtle complexity to this dish.

SERVES 8

INGREDIENTS:

16 pork medallions, 2-3 oz each
2 Tbsp extra virgin olive oil
¼ cup butter
1 garlic clove, chopped
1 leek, sliced ¼ inch

2 cups mushrooms, sliced ¼ inch
¼ cup Apple Brandy
1 cup chicken stock
1 cup heavy cream
2 apples, peeled, cored, sliced into ¼-inch wedges
Chef John's Signature Seasoning, to taste

PREPARATION:

1. Heat the grill plate over medium-high heat. Season medallions with EVOO and Chef John's Signature Seasoning.
2. Cook until charred on the first side, about 2 minutes, rotate and cook another 2 minutes. Turn over and grill for 2 more minutes, then remove from grill and let rest. Finish in 335°F oven for 7-8 minutes just before plating.
3. Meanwhile, in a saucepan over medium heat, sauté the leeks and garlic in butter to soften, 2-3 minutes.
4. Add mushrooms and sauté an additional 4-5 minutes.
5. Add apples and sauté for 2-3 minutes. Deglaze with Apple Brandy (being careful that the Brandy's alcohol vapors burn off), add stock to sauté pan, simmer, and let reduce by half.
6. Add cream, and let gently simmer for about 10 minutes until reduced to about half again and thickened.

Serving Suggestions: *We use Dijon Whipped Potatoes (see recipe on page 200) with Blanched and Sautéed Asparagus (see recipe on page 198).*

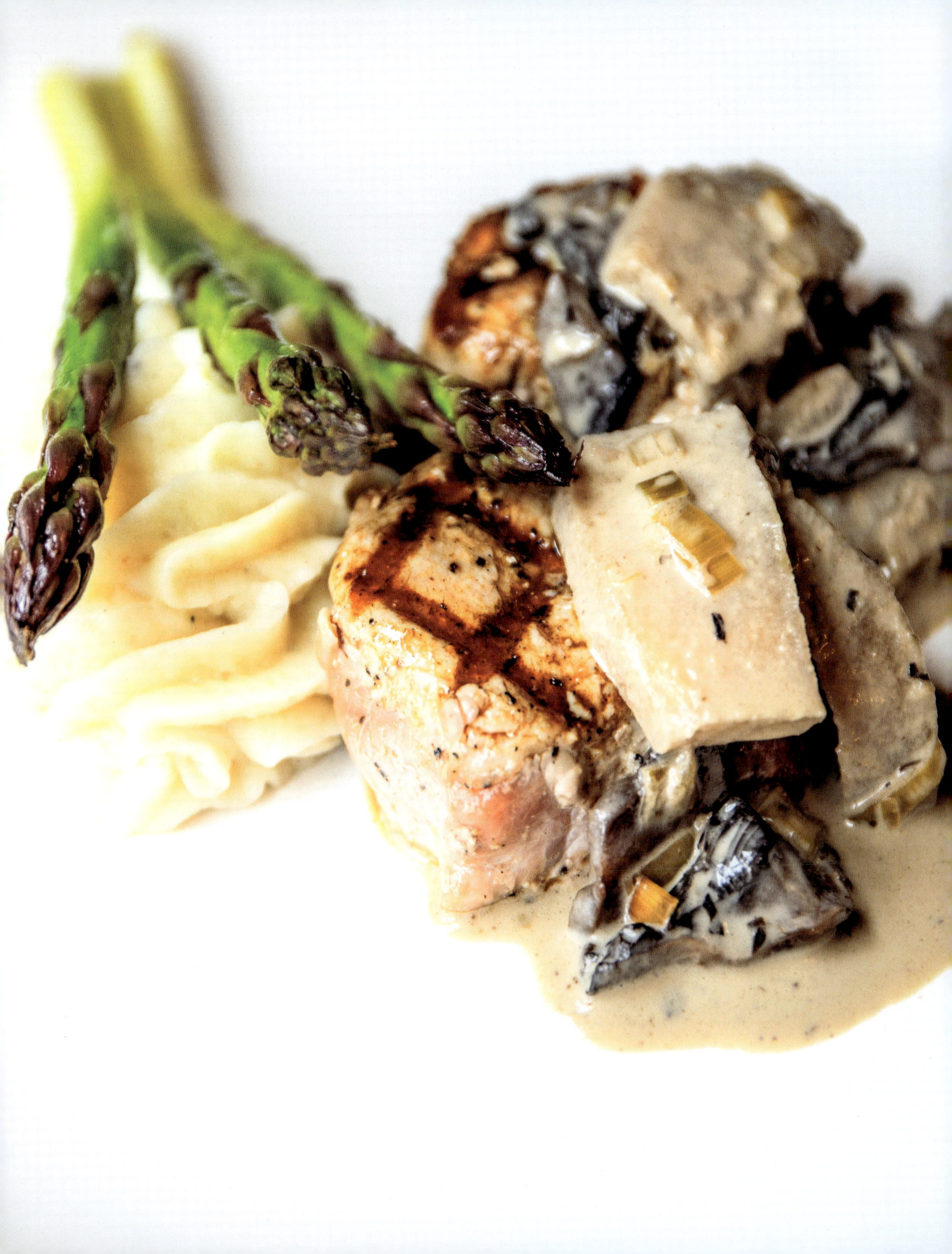

Baked Apples with Walnuts and Raisins

This is a warm dessert for a Fall dinner party. With this dish, you can create your proper "mise en place" ahead of time. The apples are filled with walnuts, raisins, brown sugar, and maple syrup, then topped with a chocolate truffle and Vanilla Bean ice cream. The ice cream melts slowly over the top and seeps into the filled apple. Slicing the apple in half and letting it gently fall open, you can identify all the morsels of awesomeness inside.

SERVES 8

INGREDIENTS:

8 apples, Gala or Granny Smith

1 fresh orange, halved

½ cup brown sugar

1 tsp cinnamon

1 tsp nutmeg

⅓ cup walnuts, chopped

⅓ cup raisins, chopped

4 Tbsp butter

4 Tbsp maple syrup

2 cups boiling water

PREPARATION:

1. Preheat oven to 375°F.
2. Wash apples and peel. Remove cores to the bottom of the apples. It helps if you have an apple corer, but if not, you can use a paring knife to first cut out the stem area, and then the core. Use a spoon to dig out the seeds.
3. Make the holes about ¾-inch to 1-inch wide. Rub apples with fresh orange juice to prevent oxidation. Place in baking dish.
4. In a small bowl, combine the brown sugar, cinnamon, nutmeg, chopped walnuts, and chopped raisins. Stuff each apple with this mixture. Top with ½ Tbsp of butter.
5. Add boiling water into baking pan ¼ inch up the side. Drizzle apples with maple syrup.
6. Bake 30-40 minutes, until tender, but not mushy.
7. Remove from the oven and baste the apples several times with the pan juices. Top with chocolate truffle and let soften.
8. Serve warm with Vanilla Bean ice cream on top.

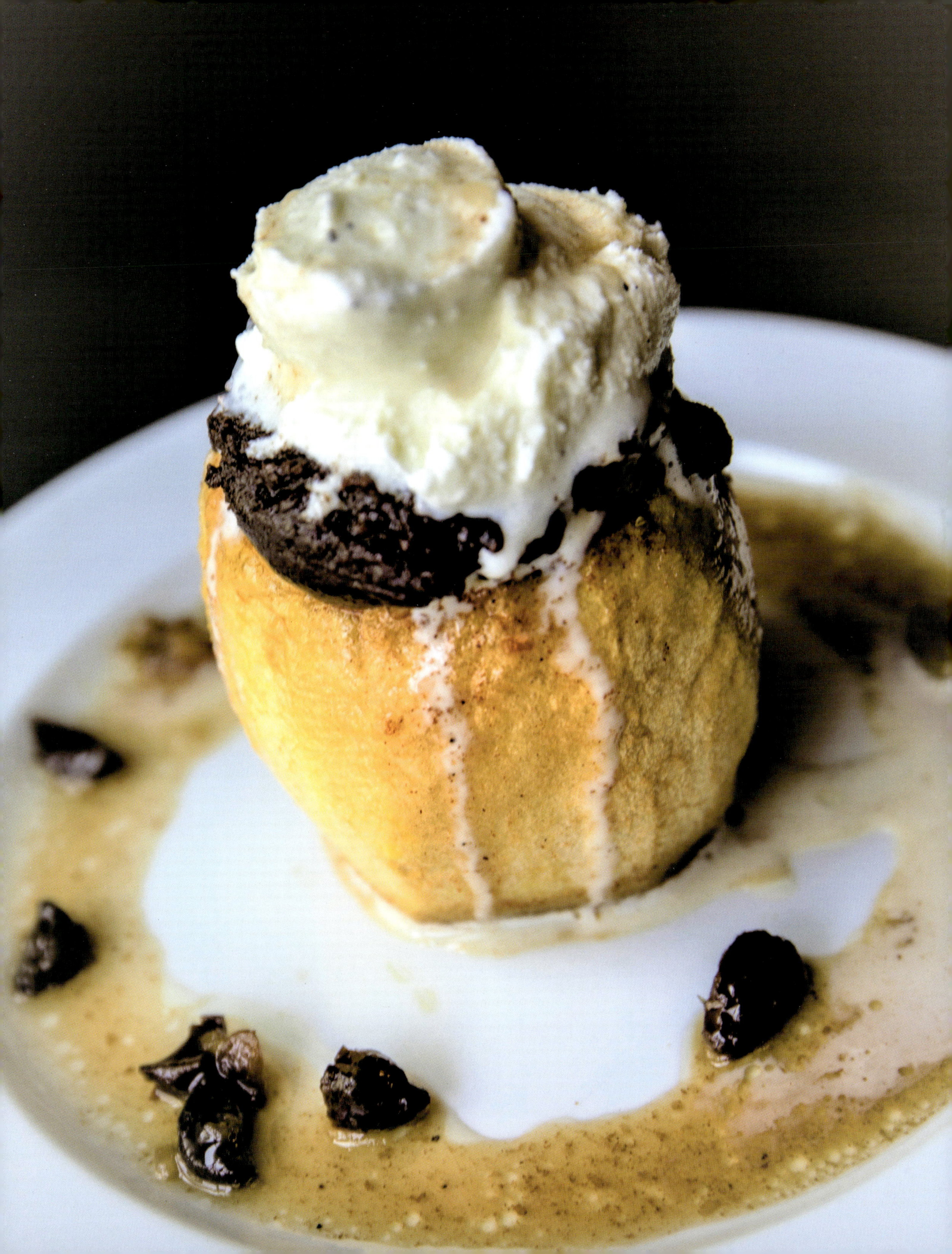

Gorgonzola Stuffed Pears

This dessert was inspired by a pear tree that we had in our front yard in Williams Bay, Wisconsin. The pears are baked with Italian Gorgonzola cheese and a Port wine reduction. Port wine and Gorgonzola cheese "pear" wonderfully together.

SERVES 8

INGREDIENTS:

8 pears, peeled and cored

½ cup brown sugar

2 Tbsp butter, softened

½ cup (2 oz) crumbled Gorgonzola cheese

¼ cup dried cranberries

¼ cup pecans, chopped

¼ cup apple juice

½ cup Port wine

2 Tbsp butter

1 cup flourless chocolate pâté (see recipe on page 48)

¼ cup Smoked Gouda cheese, grated

PREPARATION:

1. Preheat oven to 375°F.
2. Cut 1 inch off stem end of pear; reserve top.
3. Cut about ¼ inch from base of pears to square off so they will sit flat. Peel pears.
4. Remove core from pear and slice about ⅛ inch off the bottom of the core and place back into pear to form a well.
5. Place the pears in a 13 x 9 inch baking dish. Rub gently with an orange. This keeps pear from browning.
6. Combine brown sugar and butter in a small bowl and stir until well blended. Add Gorgonzola, cranberries, and pecans; stir well.
7. Fill each pear with about 2 Tbsp nut mixture and place tops back on pears.
8. Combine the apple juice and Port wine and pour over pears into baking dish. Dot baking dish with butter. Baste pears 20 minutes into cooking.
9. Bake for 30 minutes or until tender. Let cool for 20 minutes. Reserve Port wine/apple juice mixture.
10. Center baked pear on a plate. Remove tops of pears.
11. Place a 1 oz scoop of flourless chocolate pâté on each pear and press top of pear down on top of pâté.
12. Drizzle with reduced Port wine/apple juice mixture and sprinkle with grated Smoked Gouda.

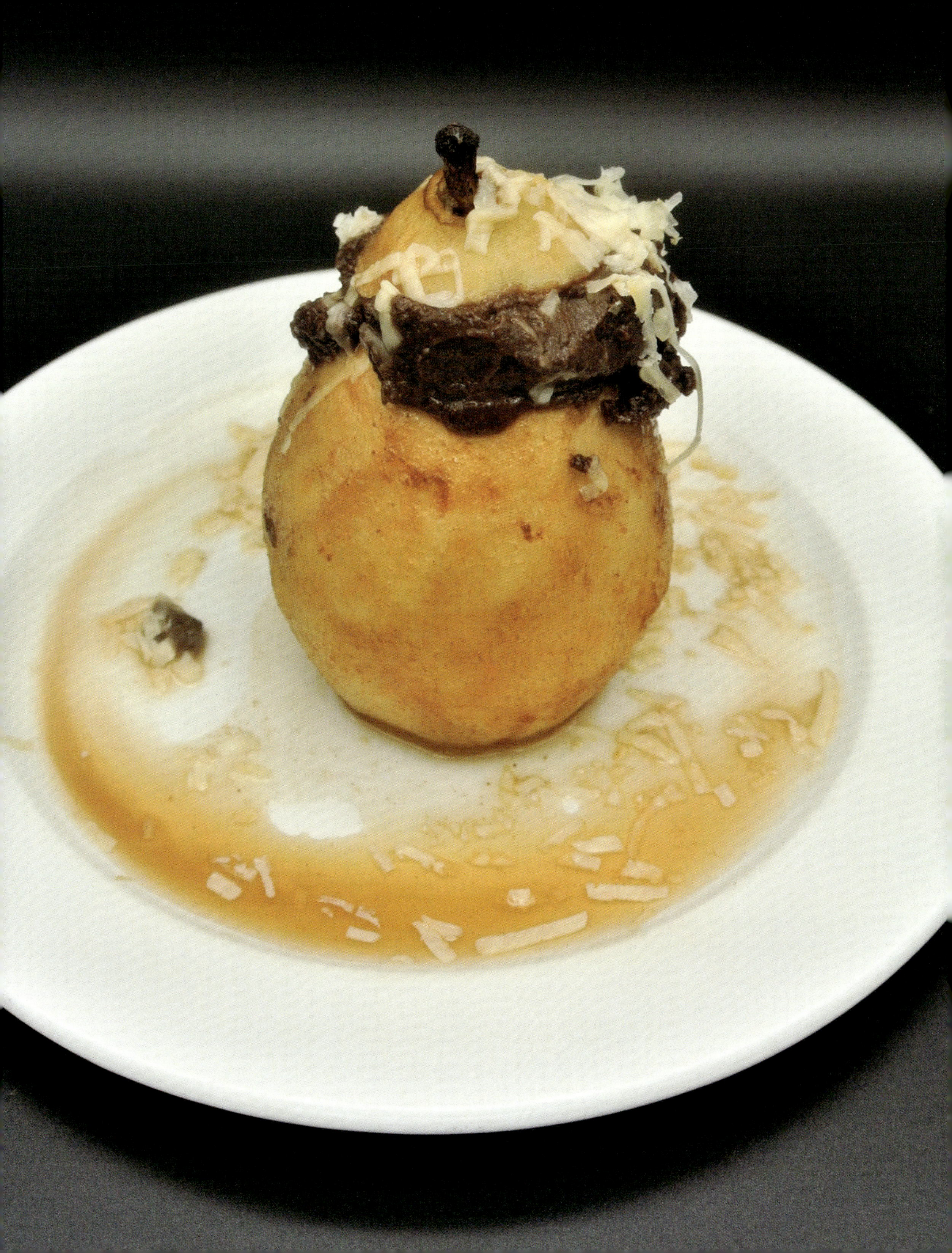

BANANAS FOSTER

I have been fortunate enough to travel to New Orleans many times. New Orleans cuisine always inspires me and Bananas Foster is no exception. This is a fantastic dessert to make for celebrations as the flambéing creates quite a phenomenal tableside presentation. The orange zest is a personal, unique addition to this classic dessert. The aromatic of the orange lightens up the rich caramel sauce.

SERVES 10

INGREDIENTS:

½ cup butter

2 cups brown sugar

10 bananas, 1-inch slices on the bias

2 oz banana liqueur

2 oz dark rum

2 oz 151 rum

1 tsp cinnamon

2 Tbsp granulated sugar

10 scoops Vanilla Bean ice cream

1 Tbsp orange zest

PREPARATION:

1. Combine the butter and brown sugar in a large sauté pan. Place the pan over low heat on top of the stove and cook, stirring until the brown sugar dissolves, creating a caramel sauce.

2. Place the bananas in the pan. When the banana sections soften and begin to brown, carefully add the banana liqueur, dark rum, and 151, making sure your hand is not over the pan. Continue to cook the sauce until the rum is hot, and then tip the pan slightly to ignite the rum, while being very careful, as this will ignite.

3. Mix cinnamon with granulated sugar and sprinkle over top of pan to create a dramatic sparkle effect. When the flames subside, lift the bananas out of the pan and place bananas over scooped out portion of ice cream.

4. Generously spoon warm sauce over the top of the ice cream and garnish with orange zest; serve immediately.

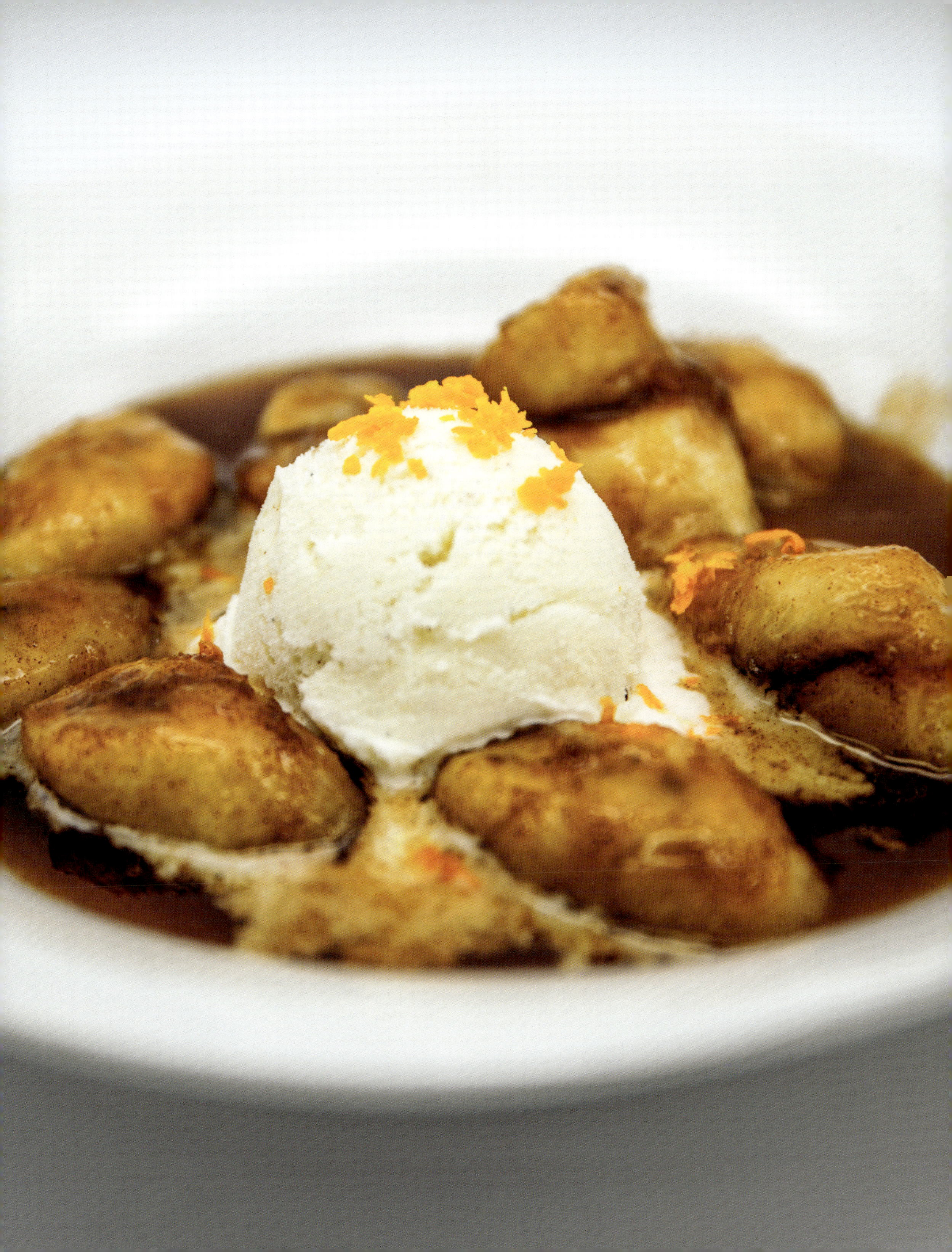

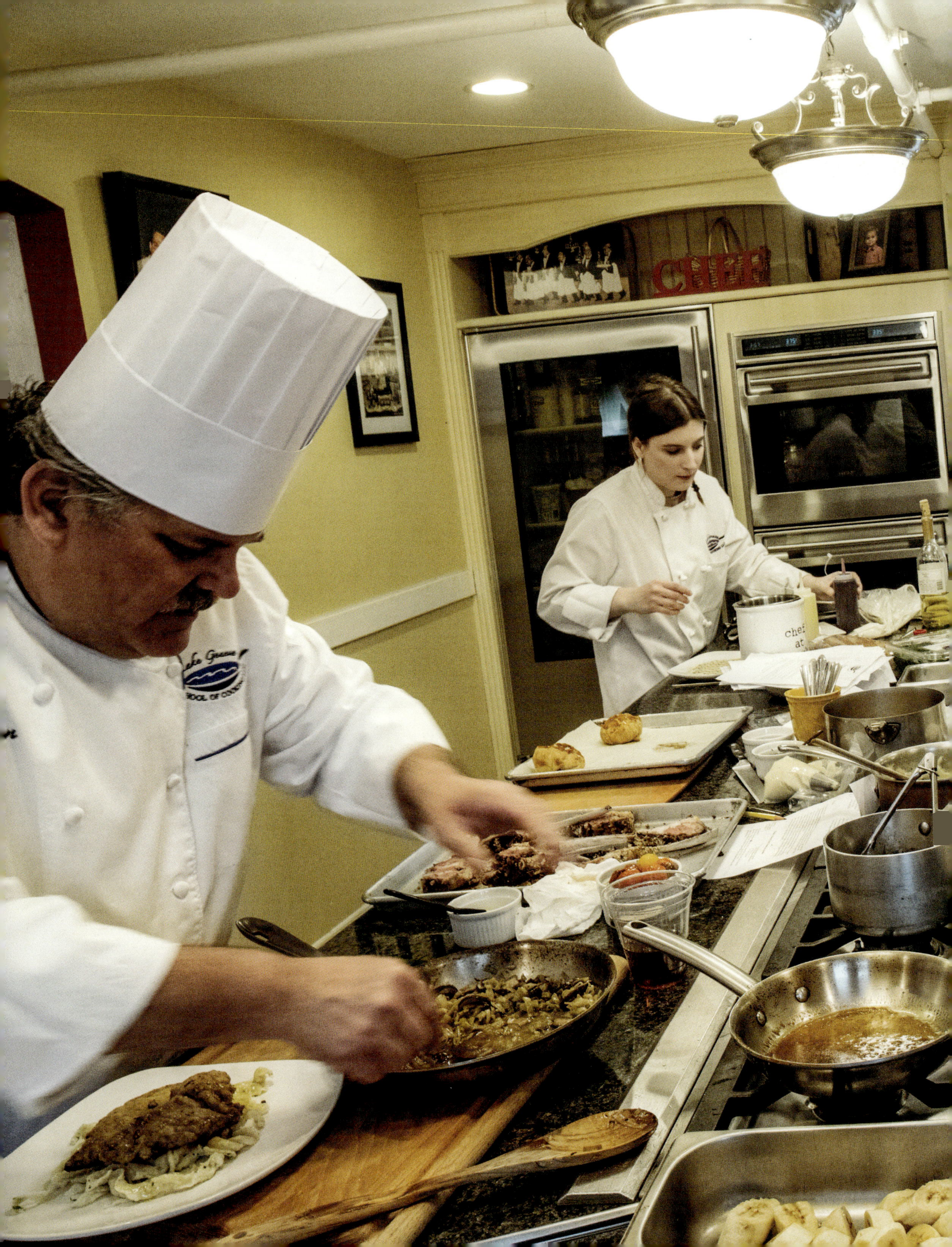
CHEF

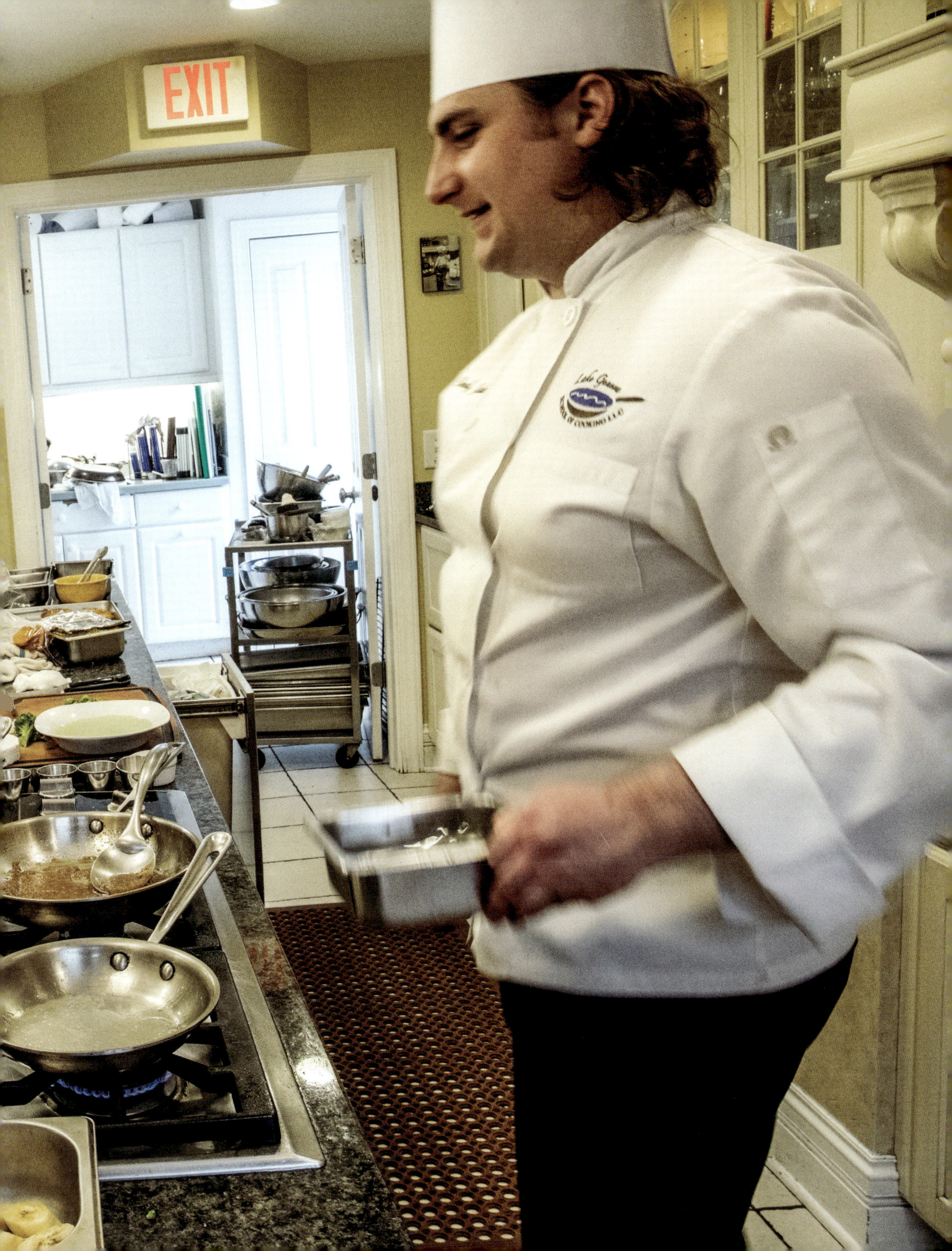
EXIT

Chef John's Classic Italian Sausage

Signature Sausage Making

Sausage making classes are very busy days at the Lake Geneva School of Cooking. We generally make 100 pounds of sausage at a time with natural hog casings and a 70/30 blend of coarse ground pork. My father, Larry, used to bring out 20 pounds of our favorite Italian sausage from Dino's in upstate New York. He would bring the sausage in his suitcase, on a train, all the way to Lake Geneva, Wisconsin. My friend, Dominic Trumfio, saw this and asked, "Why don't we just make our own sausage?" And this is how we created our Signature Italian Sausage. Our perfected recipe is not too hot, meaning no Cayenne pepper, but it is not too mild either, because of the chili pepper flakes. We call this Chef John's Classic Italian Sausage. Dominic likes to incorporate his personal red wine, the Triumvirate, in his sausage. This is another personal chapter for me and includes unique ways to incorporate Italian sausage in our dishes.

Homemade Italian Sausage   150

Toad in the Hole   152

Grilled Caesar Salad   154

New England Clam Chowder   156

Pasta Shells Stuffed with Three Cheeses   158

Lake Geneva Giambotta   160

Homemade Italian Sausage
Chef John's Classic Italian Sausage

This is my ideal Italian sausage recipe. We start with coarse ground pork shoulder and toss it with black pepper, chili pepper flakes, whole fennel, paprika, and a little water to help it move through the stuffer. We use natural hog intestines for casing. The sausage has great color and no unnatural additives or ingredients so you know exactly what you are incorporating into your sausage.

INGREDIENTS:

10 lbs coarsely ground pork

4 tsp ground black pepper

3 Tbsp chili pepper flakes

3 Tbsp fennel, whole

4 Tbsp paprika

4 Tbsp kosher salt

10 oz water

Hog intestines for casing

PREPARATION:

1. Mix all ingredients in large bowl thoroughly, reserve casings for stuffing.
2. Load stuffer with sausage mix and fill casings.

DOMINIC'S SAUSAGE MAKING TIPS:

1. Grind all pork coarse.
2. Be sure to get meat with a ratio of 30% fat/70% lean.
3. Water is added for texture, so you decide how much you like.
4. Wine can also be added; you may use a dry red (any type).
5. Mix together ⅓ of the seasonings and pork in large plastic tub.
6. Cut back on ingredients at first, mix-fry-taste. Add seasoning according to desired taste.
7. Fry in lightly oiled frying pan.
8. Stuff only after you're satisfied with taste.
9. Hog intestines are used as casing and can be purchased at your local butcher shop. A Hank of hog casings will stuff 100-125 lbs of meat.

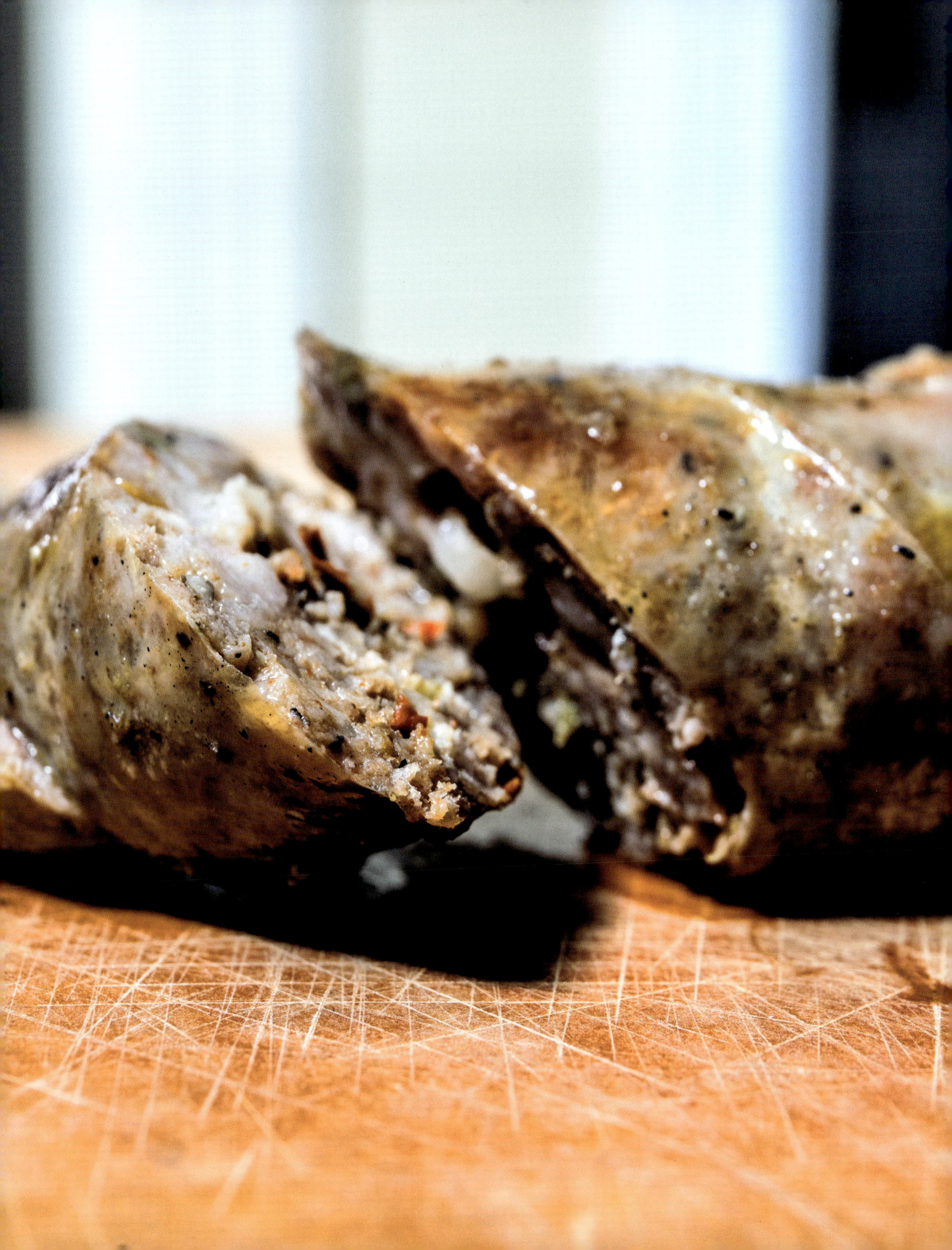

Toad in the Hole
With Caramelized Onions and Italian Sausage

A toad in the hole is traditionally a baked Yorkshire pudding stuffed with sausage. Our twist on this traditional dish is to take caramelized onions and grilled Italian sausage, and stuff them into our signature Parmigiano Popover. The popovers are hollow in the center, so this allows a great vessel. We like to position our sliced sausage atop the caramelized onion in the popover to resemble a "toad in the hole."

SERVES 12

INGREDIENTS:

1 ½ cups milk

4 large eggs

1 ½ cups all-purpose flour

1 tsp kosher salt

Nonstick spray

4 oz Parmigiano-Reggiano cheese, grated

PREPARATION:

1. Heat oven to 400°F.
2. Place a popover or muffin pan with 24 cups in the oven.
3. In a small saucepan, heat the milk until just simmering.
4. In a large bowl, whisk the eggs until frothy. Slowly whisk in the hot milk so as not to cook the eggs. Gradually whisk the dry ingredients into the egg mixture, stirring until almost smooth.
5. Remove the popover pan from the oven and spray it with nonstick spray. While the batter is still slightly warm, fill each cup level to the top.
6. Top each popover with half of the Parmigiano-Reggiano. Bake for 15 minutes. Rotate the pan 180° so that the popovers will rise evenly.
7. Turn down oven to 350°F. Bake for 20 minutes more, or until golden brown.
8. Let cool for 10 minutes and slice tops in half, fill with caramelized onions and Italian sausage, top with remaining Parmigiano-Reggiano.

Caramelized Onions and Grilled Italian Sausage

INGREDIENTS:

16 oz Italian sausage, rope or links

2 sweet onions, sliced ¼-inch rounds

¼ cup extra virgin olive oil

1 cup Parmigiano-Reggiano shavings

Chef John's Signature Seasoning, to taste

PREPARATION:

1. Season sausage and onion with EVOO and Chef John's Signature Seasoning.
2. Grill Italian sausage 12-15 minutes or until lightly charred.
3. Grill onion 9-10 minutes or until lightly charred.
4. Let sausage rest 10 minutes, and then slice on the bias.
5. Stuff popovers with sausage and onions, top with Parmigiano-Reggiano shavings.

SIGNATURE SAUSAGE MAKING

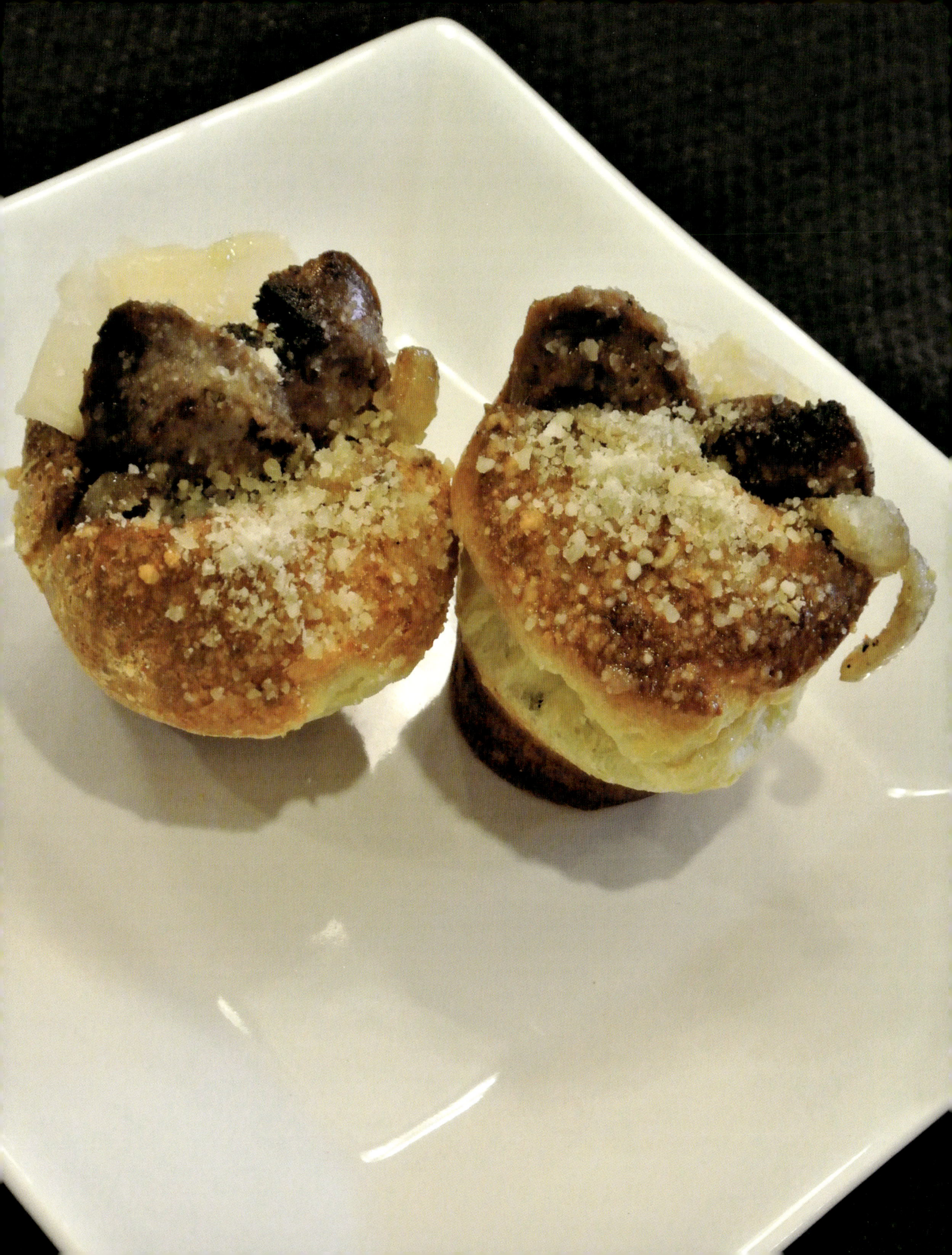

Grilled Caesar Salad
With Caramelized Onion and Crispy Italian Sausage

This is the one dish that I get the most phone calls asking how to remake. The key to this salad is leaving the core of the romaine lettuce intact so it does not fall apart on the grill. It is topped with caramelized onions, crispy Italian sausage, and a thicker-style Caesar dressing. This salad is perfect for grilling season.

SERVES 8

INGREDIENTS:

4 romaine hearts, halved lengthwise

8 oz Italian sausage

1 sweet onion, sliced ¼-inch rounds

¼ cup extra virgin olive oil

1 cup Parmigiano-Reggiano shavings

Chef John's Signature Seasoning, to taste

½ cup Caesar dressing

PREPARATION:

1. Season romaine hearts with EVOO and Chef John's Signature Seasoning.
2. Grill over medium-high heat, cut side down for 15 seconds; rotate at 45° angle and grill 15 more seconds, then turn over and grill 15 more seconds.
3. Chill in refrigerator until cold.
4. Just before plating, remove lettuce core from heart by cutting ½-inch above the core; slice on an angle as you cut down into the core.
5. Season sausage and onions with EVOO and Chef John's Signature Seasoning.
6. Grill Italian sausage (12-15 minutes) and onion (9-10 minutes) until lightly charred.
7. Let sausage rest 10 minutes, then slice on the bias and pan sear with grilled onions just before plating.

PLATING:

1. Place romaine heart intact, cut side up.
2. Brush with Caesar dressing.
3. Garnish with sausage and onions, Parmigiano-Reggiano shavings, and fresh cracked black pepper.

Caesar Dressing

INGREDIENTS:

3 coddled eggs

2 cloves garlic, peeled

1 Tbsp anchovy paste

1 Tbsp Dijon mustard

1 tsp Tabasco

½ cup Parmigiano-Reggiano cheese, grated

1 tsp Worcestershire sauce

2 Tbsp lemon juice

1 cup extra virgin olive oil

Chef John's Signature Seasoning, to taste

CODDLED EGG PREPARATION:

1. Place 4 cups water in medium saucepan.
2. Bring the water to a boil and reduce the heat to low, add eggs.
3. Cook for 2 minutes.
4. Cool in ice water for 3 minutes.

DRESSING PREPARATION:

1. Crack the coddled eggs and scoop yolk into food processor.
2. Add garlic, anchovy paste, Dijon mustard, Tabasco, cheese, Worcestershire, and lemon juice.
3. Process or blend until smooth.
4. IMPORTANT: With the motor running, lastly add the EVOO in a slow, thin stream to combine well.
5. Add Chef John's Signature Seasoning.

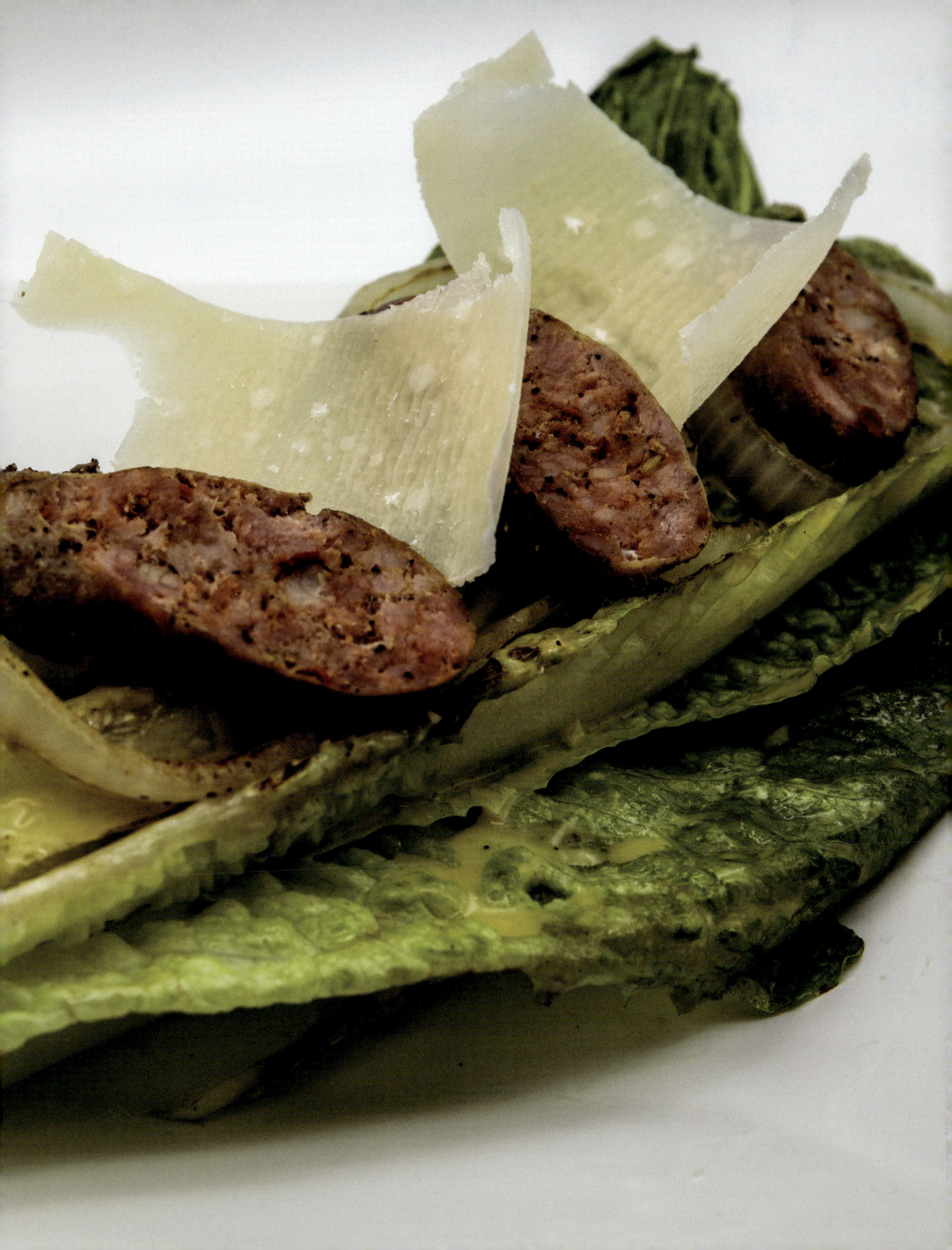

New England Clam Chowder
With Italian Sausage

This recipe goes back to my history of working in Boston at the Top of the Hub restaurant and my friend Chef Mark Sapienza. Traditionally, a clam chowder recipe would call for a pork product like bacon, but we like to jazz it up with our "wicked" Homemade Italian Sausage. Rendering the sausage leaves pork fat to sauté the "Mirepoix." From there, it is a classic clam chowder recipe.

SERVES 10

INGREDIENTS:

1 lb Italian sausage, links
1 cup butter
2 sweet onions, medium dice
4 celery stalks, medium dice
2 carrots, medium dice
1 cup flour
1 cup white wine
8 sprigs fresh thyme

2 bay leaves
2 quarts clam juice
3 potatoes, medium dice
1 tsp Worcestershire sauce
¼ tsp Tabasco
1 cup half and half
1 cup heavy cream
4 cans (6½ oz) of clams
Chef John's Signature Seasoning, to taste

PREPARATION:

1. In large pot over medium heat, sauté and render the sausage and remove after browning.
2. Let cool and slice into the size of small coins.
3. Pour off half the drippings and add the butter and melt.
4. Bring to medium heat and add onion, celery, and carrots; cook covered until soft, about 7 minutes. Dust the vegetables with flour and cook for 3-4 minutes.
5. Add the wine and cook until flour has absorbed the wine.
6. Add the clam juice and potatoes to the vegetables and simmer, covered.
7. Tie the thyme and bay leaves together (herb bouquet) with string so they can be easily removed from the pot after cooking. Let simmer for 30-40 minutes.
8. Remove the herb bouquet from the pot. Add the clams, sausage, Worcestershire, Tabasco, half and half, and heavy cream.
9. Season with Chef John's Signature Seasoning.
10. Let simmer for 15 minutes.
11. Remove the soup from the heat. Garnish finished chowder with Tabasco.

Note: "Mirepoix" is a blend of diced onion, carrots, and celery.

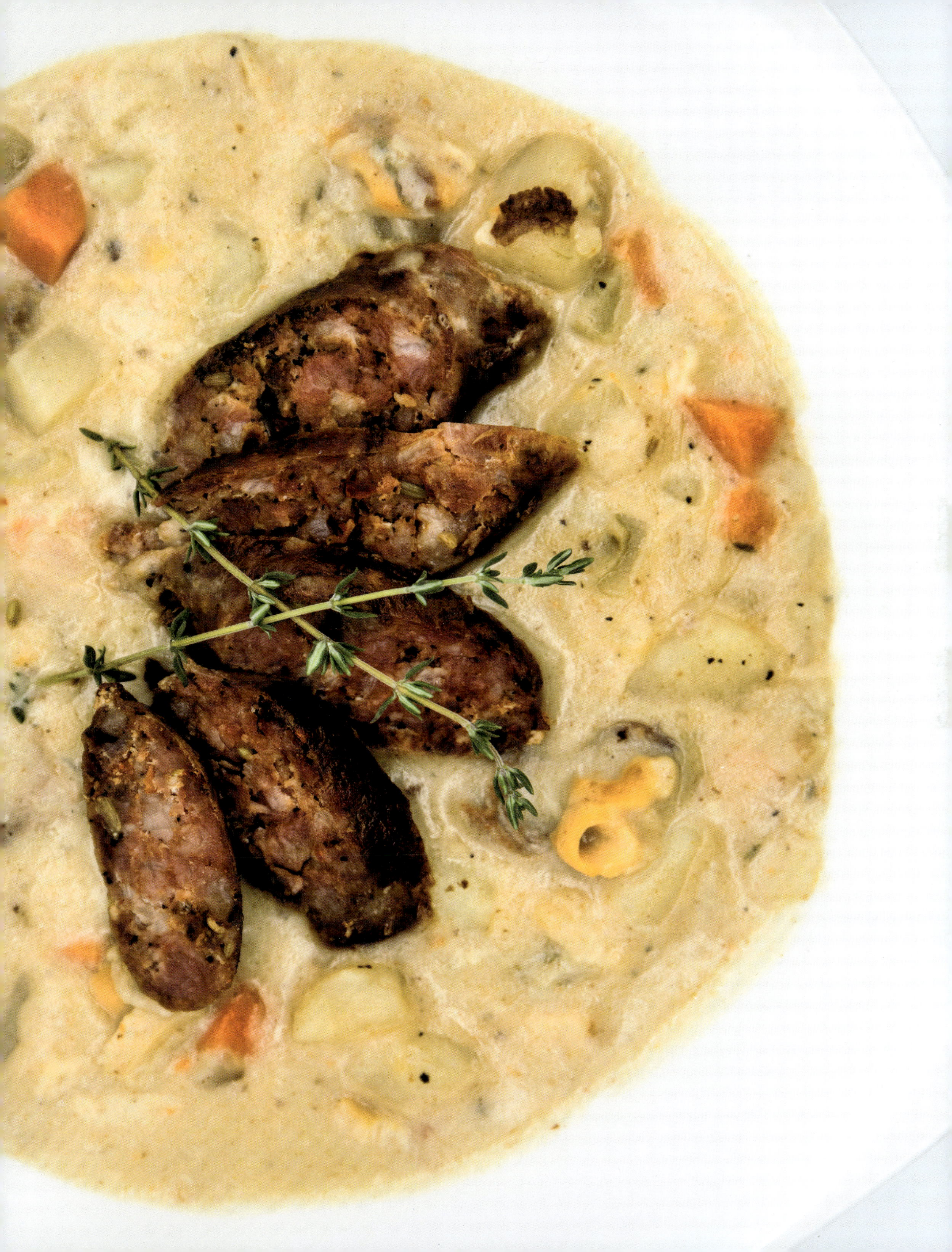

Pasta Shells Stuffed with Three Cheeses
With Cloe's Italian Sausage Gravy

We mentored Cloe when she was in the Badger High School Pro Start program and she has since become a standout chef for us at the Lake Geneva School of Cooking. I wanted to feature a recipe that we created with her. Cloe's Italian Sausage Gravy starts with a marinara base and is elevated with our homemade Italian sausage. This is an ideal dish to feature for a Sunday family supper.

SERVES 12

INGREDIENTS:

2 Tbsp kosher salt

1 box (12 oz) jumbo pasta shells

1 ½ lbs Ricotta cheese

1 cup Mozzarella cheese, grated

½ cup Parmigiano-Reggiano cheese, grated

½ cup Asiago cheese, grated

¼ cup fresh parsley, chopped

CLOE'S ITALIAN SAUSAGE GRAVY:

2 Tbsp extra virgin olive oil

2 lb Italian sausage, ground

3 cloves garlic, chopped

2 small onions, finely chopped

1 cup red wine

2 cans (28 oz) crushed tomatoes

1 Tbsp sugar

Chef John's Signature Seasoning, to taste

6-7 fresh basil leaves, chiffonade

3-4 sprigs fresh oregano

PREPARATION:

1. Preheat oven to 350°F.
2. Bring a large pot of water to a boil. Salt water and add pasta. Cook shells 10-12 minutes; they should be softened but still undercooked at the center. Drain pasta and cool.
3. Combine Ricotta, ½ of the grated Mozzarella, ½ of the Parmigiano-Reggiano, and ½ of the Asiago. Add parsley to the cheeses and stir to combine.
4. In a small saucepot over moderate heat add EVOO and Italian Sausage, brown for 6-8 minutes, then add garlic and onions.
5. Sauté for an additional 5-6 minutes. Deglaze with red wine, tomatoes, sugar, and Chef John's Signature Seasoning. Simmer sauce for 20 minutes and stir in basil and oregano leaves.
6. Pour a little sauce into the bottom of a shallow medium size casserole dish. Fill shells with rounded spoonfuls of cheese mixture and arrange them seam side up in casserole dish.
7. Top shells with remaining sauce, Mozzarella, and Asiago cheeses. Place shells in hot oven and cook 12-15 minutes, until the cheeses melt and sauce bubbles.

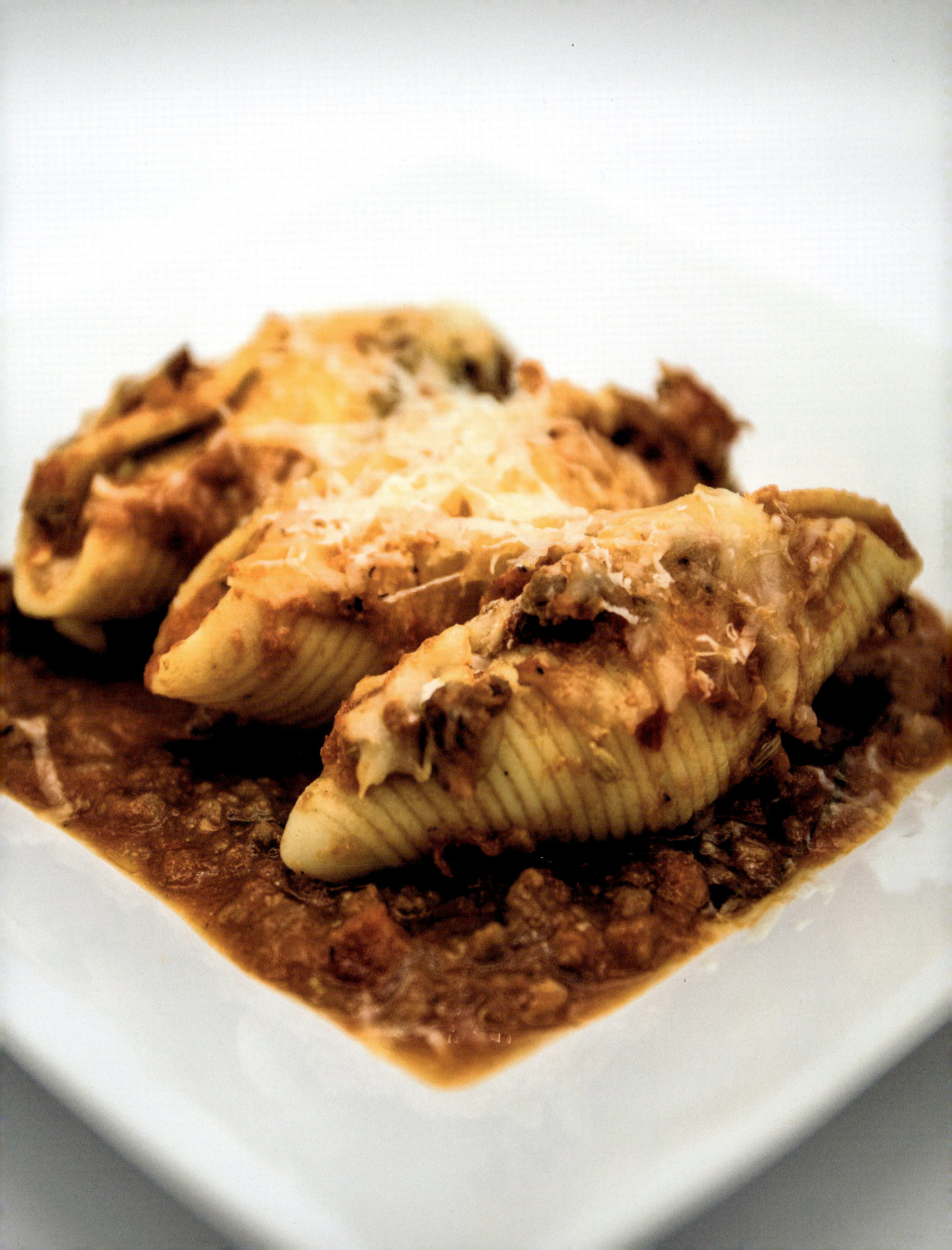

Lake Geneva Giambotta

Giambotta is an old school Italian dish with peppers, vegetables, and potatoes that we took to another level with Italian sausage and beef filet medallions. I have very fond memories of sharing this dish with my family over the years. I learned to cook from my grandmother, Tid, and loved being in the kitchen with her. On the day she passed away, our family gathered in her home and I cooked Giambotta for everyone. There were over 25 of us that celebrated her life that day. I filled all of her burners and ovens while preparing this dish and I know she was cooking with me in spirit. 'Til we meet again...

SERVES 8

INGREDIENTS:

- 3 potatoes, each peeled and wedge cut into 8 pieces
- ½ cup plus 2 Tbsp extra virgin olive oil
- 2 Tbsp butter, melted
- 1 Tbsp Italian seasoning
- ¼ cup Parmesan cheese
- 1 lb Italian sausage, links
- 8 chicken breasts, 4 oz each
- 8 beef filet medallions, 2 oz each
- 2 onions, 1-inch dice
- 4 stalks celery, 1-inch slices
- 1 red pepper, 1-inch dice
- 2 cups mushrooms, large dice
- 4 cloves garlic, whole
- ¼ cup flour
- 1 cup red wine
- 2 cups chicken stock
- 1 tbsp fresh sage, chopped
- 1 tbsp fresh thyme, chopped
- 1 tbsp fresh basil, chopped
- 4 sprigs parsley, chopped
- Chef John's Signature Seasoning, to taste

PREPARATION:

1. Preheat oven to 395°F.
2. Toss potato wedges in ¼ cup EVOO and 2 Tbsp melted butter, 1 Tbsp Italian seasoning, Parmesan, and Chef John's Signature Seasoning.
3. Roast in oven until browned (30-40 minutes).
4. Season sausage, chicken, and beef filets with 2 Tbsp EVOO and Chef John's Signature Seasoning.
5. Sear over medium-hot grill until charred (beef 2-3 minutes per side, chicken and sausage 7-8 minutes). Let rest on platter.
6. In large roasting pan with ¼ cup EVOO, sauté celery, onions, peppers, mushrooms, and garlic until slightly caramelized.
7. Dust with ¼ cup flour and cook out flour for 2-3 minutes more.
8. Deglaze pan with wine. Add chicken stock.
9. Portion sausage and chicken into 1-inch pieces. Add these pieces and beef medallions to vegetable mixture. Season with herbs and Chef John's Signature Seasoning.
10. Bring to a simmer and cook for 5 minutes. Pull off heat and let rest.
11. Just before plating, finish off roasting in oven for 8-10 minutes.

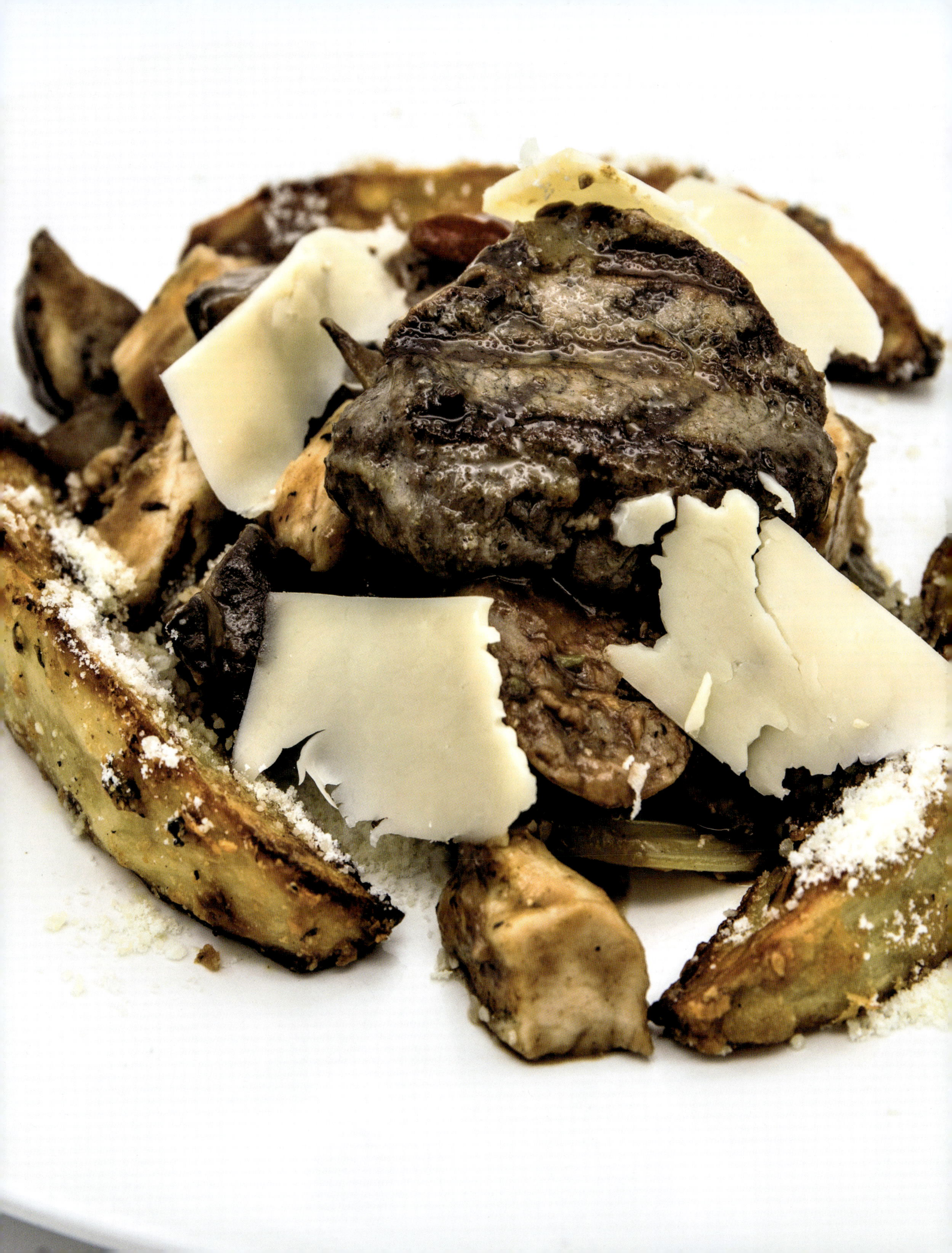

Triumvirate
Vineyards
2016
Zinfandel
Buon Cibo • Boun Vino • Buoni Amici
Triumvirate
Syrah
2014
Buon Cibo • Boun Vino • Buoni Amici
2013
Triumvirate
Cabernet Sauvignon

Triumvirate Red Wine Verticle

Chef John's catered meals are a highlight for many U.S. National Snow Sculpting teams each year at Winterfest.

Winter

What an exciting time of year for chefs and restaurateurs. As we head into the holiday season, this is a great time to share your family traditions and celebrations. These recipes feature baking, broiling, and sautéing to stay warm in your kitchen. I have been involved with the Lake Geneva Winterfest celebration for the last 25 years. As we welcome snow sculptors from all over the United States, I have had the pleasure to share some of the dishes that are featured in this chapter. It is beautiful when culinary arts and the fine arts support each other.

Classic French Onion Soup 166

Broccoli and Brie Bisque 168

Mardi Gras Gumbo 170

Jerry Pawlak's Caesar Salad 172

Colossal Sea Scallops Au Gratin 174

Roast Turkey Breast Wellington 176

Crispy Duck and Mushroom Napoleon 178

Steak Diane with Brandy Mushroom Reduction 180

Stout Braised Prime Beef Short Ribs 182

Chocolate Midnight Truffle Cake 184

Chocolate Grand Marnier Tart 186

Kahlúa Espresso Brownie 188

CLASSIC FRENCH ONION SOUP

This Classic French Onion Soup was inspired by the many steakhouses I have been to over the years. Caramelize and "Singer" onions with Cream Sherry gives the dish a complex and sublime aromatic. Traditionally this soup would be topped with Gruyére cheese, but we like to take it to another level and add Smoked Gouda cheese as well. One non-negotiable step of this dish is that it has to be gratinéed under the broiler. The cheese must develop character and be bubbling for an amazing, Classic French Onion Soup.

SERVES 8
INGREDIENTS:

2 Tbsp butter

2 Tbsp extra virgin olive oil

4 onions, halved and sliced thin

2 cloves garlic, chopped

1 Tbsp granulated sugar

3 Tbsp flour

½ cup Cream Sherry

6 cups chicken and beef stock, combined

Chef John's Signature Seasoning, to taste

16 baguette slices, ¼-inch thick, toasted

2 cups Gruyére cheese, grated

2 cups Smoked Gouda cheese, grated

PREPARATION:

1. In a large saucepan over medium heat, melt the butter and add the EVOO.
2. Add the onions, garlic, and sugar. Sauté until slightly browned, stirring occasionally (don't stir too much — you want them to brown), for 20 minutes.
3. Dust with flour (singer) and sauté 2 minutes more, add Cream Sherry, stir to incorporate.
4. Add the stock, bring to a boil then simmer uncovered for 20-30 minutes; add Chef John's Signature Seasoning.

PLATING:

1. Preheat the broiler. Ladle the soup into the oven-proof soup ramekins.
2. Place two slices of toasted baguette on top of each soup.
3. Mix the grated Gruyére and Smoked Gouda together; top each soup with ½ cup of mixture.
4. Place soup ramekins onto a baking sheet and place in oven under preheated broiler. Broil until the cheese melts (watch them carefully—depending on your broiler, it can take anywhere from 45-90 seconds or so).
5. Serve immediately.

Note: *"Singer" is a French term that refers to the dusting of flour over vegetables cooked in fat to create a roux.*

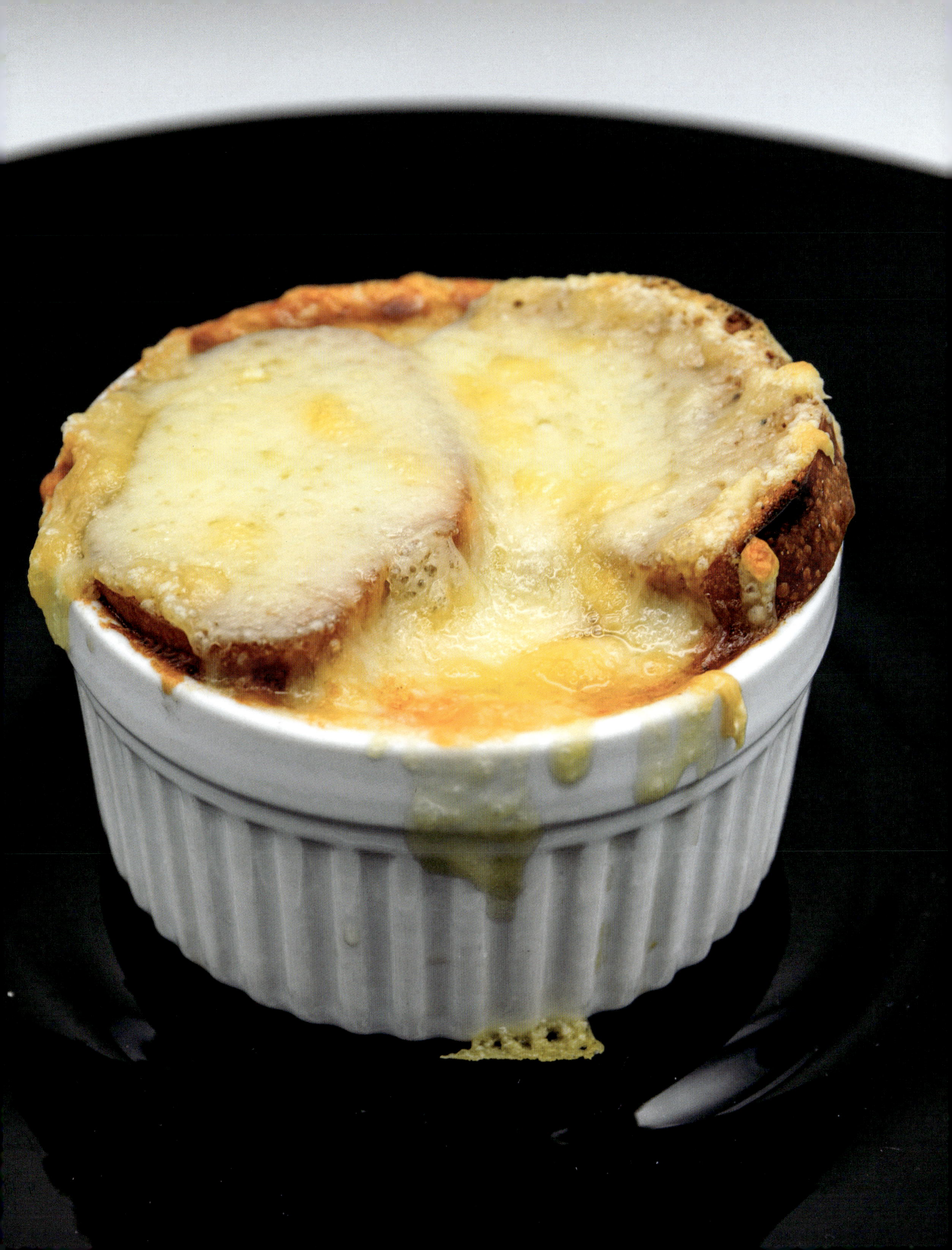

BROCCOLI AND BRIE BISQUE

This bisque was created to elevate Broccoli and Cheddar soup to another level. The Brie cheese gives this bisque a beautiful silkiness and a very svelte mouth feel. I love the color this preparation provides with the bright green broccoli florets. The stems are also simmered in the stock, as that adds a depth of flavor. This dish would be well accompanied with a little hot sauce as this is a rich bisque.

SERVES 12

INGREDIENTS:

3 bunches broccoli

½ cup butter

½ cup onion, medium dice

½ cup celery, medium dice

½ cup flour

¼ cup white wine

6 cups chicken stock

1 cup half and half

½ cup heavy cream

2 tsp Worcestershire sauce

Chef John's Signature Seasoning, to taste

12 oz Brie cheese, rind removed, 8 oz diced; reserve 12 slices for garnish

PREPARATION:

1. Simmer broccoli heads and stems in chicken stock. Reserve about ⅓ of the uncooked florets (needing 36 for garnish).
2. In large soup pot, sauté onions and celery in butter.
3. Dust with flour (singer) and cook for 2 minutes. Add white wine and whisk into sautéed vegetables.
4. Remove brocolli stems and add brocolli/chicken stock to soup pot. Add 8 oz diced Brie, Worcestershire and Chef John's Signature Seasoning. Let simmer for 15- 20 minutes.
5. Puree mixture with immersion blender.
6. Add half and half, heavy cream, and Chef John's Signature Seasoning.
7. Blanch reserved broccoli florets in salted, boiling water for 2 minutes and shock in ice bath.

PLATING:

1. Pour bisque into bowls.
2. Place broccoli florets in center of bisque and top with a slice of Brie.

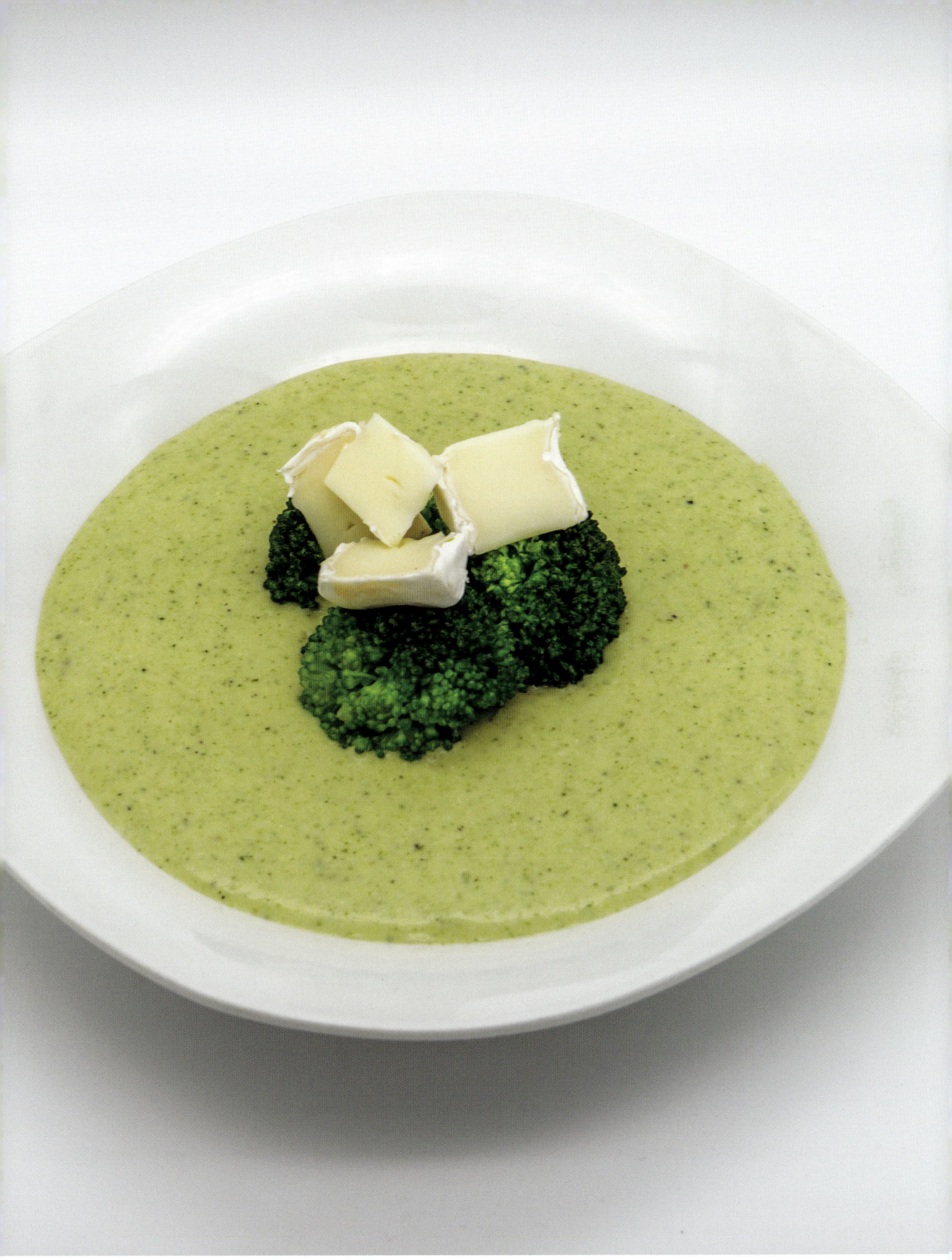

Mardi Gras Gumbo
With Chef John's Classic Italian Sausage and Chicken

New Orleans is an amazing food town. Mardi Gras usually falls in late winter, but Gumbo is available in New Orleans year-round. The key to a classic gumbo is influenced by a dark roux. There are many different ways to create a dark roux, but in this preparation we have toasted the flour in the oven. We add our classic Italian sausage, chicken breast, andouille sausage, and Gumbo File, which is another key component to this N'awlins specialty. We top this dish with Saffron rice for an added pop of color. When enjoying, close your mouth and breathe up through your nose to experience all the deep flavors.

SERVES 8
INGREDIENTS:

½ cup flour

3 Tbsp extra virgin olive oil

2 Tbsp butter

2 cups onion, medium dice

2 cups bell pepper, medium dice

4 ribs celery, medium dice

3 cloves garlic, chopped

1 lb Chef John's Classic Italian Sausage, links

1 lb chicken breast, ¼-inch dice

1 lb andouille sausage

5 cups chicken stock

1 Tbsp Cajun blend spice mix

1 tsp dried thyme

2 large bay leaves

2 cups okra, sliced

1 can (28 oz) diced tomatoes

1 Tbsp Gumbo File

Chef John's Signature Seasoning, to taste

PREPARATION:

1. Preheat oven to 425°F.
2. Place flour on sheet pan and cook in oven, shaking and stirring once until flour is the color of peanut butter (15-20 minutes). The flour can be cooked longer if desired to intensify the flavor.
3. Heat EVOO over medium-high heat. Brown sausages and chicken in Dutch oven (8-10 minutes). Remove from pan and reserve. Slice Italian sausage into ¼-inch slices. Slice andouille sausage in ¼-inch slices.
4. Add butter and sauté onion, peppers, celery, and garlic. Cook until tender, about 4-5 minutes.
5. Sprinkle toasted flour (singer) over top and stir until blended. Cook for 1-2 minutes, deglaze with white wine.
6. Stir in chicken stock and bring to boil, stirring until thickened.
7. Add sausage, chicken, and spices. Lower heat, cover, and simmer for 15 minutes.
8. Add okra and tomatoes. Stir and simmer additional 15 minutes.
9. Stir in Gumbo File and adjust flavor with Chef John's Signature Seasoning before serving.

Serving Suggestion: *Serve with Saffron Basmati Rice (see recipe on page 202). Place a ladle of Gumbo in bowl and top with a 2 oz scoop of Saffron Basmati Rice in center of the bowl.*

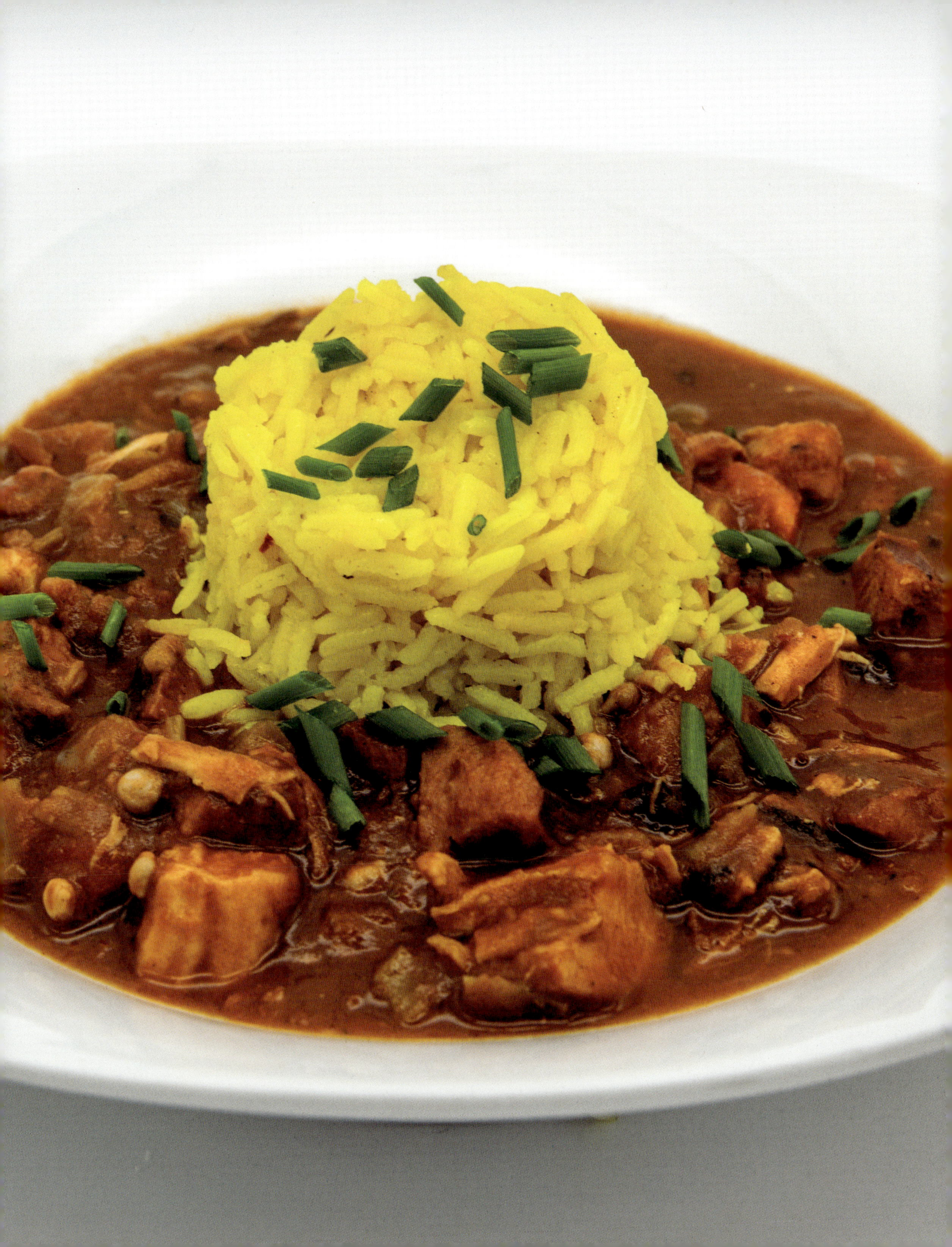

Jerry Pawlak's Tableside Caesar Salad

Jerry Pawlak is recognized as Maitre D' Extraordinaire. I've worked with Jerry for many years through the French Country Inn and the Lake Geneva School of Cooking, and he is a great friend. Jerry began his Maitre D' career years ago when Hugh Hefner hired him to work at the Playboy Club here in Lake Geneva. Jerry would work in the VIP room with all the stars and celebrities that were visiting and prepare tableside Caesar Salad and Bananas Foster. Jerry loves sharing all the stories of this bygone era along with this Caesar Salad recipe.

SERVES 8

INGREDIENTS:

- 1 tsp kosher salt
- 1 garlic clove, peeled
- 2 anchovy fillets
- 1 Tbsp Dijon mustard
- 1 tsp Worcestershire sauce
- ½ tsp Tabasco
- 1 large egg yolk, coddled
- ¼ cup plus 1 Tbsp extra virgin olive oil
- 1 half fresh lemon, juiced
- Chef John's Signature Seasoning, to taste
- 4 heads of romaine lettuce, large pieces
- ½ cup plus 2 Tbsp Parmigiano-Reggiano cheese
- ½ baguette, torn into ½ x ½ pieces (approximately 2 cups croutons)

PREPARATION:

1. In a large wooden bowl, crush garlic with kosher salt.
2. Remove garlic and salt from the bowl. Add two anchovy fillets and Dijon mustard, while incorporating this into a paste.
3. Mix in Worcestershire and Tabasco.
4. Add one coddled egg yolk and drizzle EVOO into bowl while constantly whisking all together. Add fresh lemon juice.
5. Toss Romaine lettuce with Caesar dressing.
6. Add Parmigiano-Reggiano and croutons.
7. Place tossed Caesar salad on chilled plate and serve with chilled salad fork.

CROUTONS:

1. To flavor the baguette croutons, crush a garlic clove with the flat of a chef's knife, then sprinkle on ¼ tsp of kosher salt, and mince well.
2. Scrape the garlic into the frying pan, add 1 Tbsp of EVOO, and warm over low-medium heat.
3. Preheat oven to 375°F.
4. Mix garlic infused olive oil and Chef John's Signature Seasoning onto croutons, place onto baking sheet.
5. Bake 10-12 minutes, until golden brown.
6. While croutons are still warm, toss with 2 Tbsp of Parmigiano-Reggiano.

CODDLED EGG:

1. To coddle the egg, bring a small saucepan of water to a boil, drop an egg in the shell, and simmer for exactly 2 minutes.
2. Shock in an ice bath.

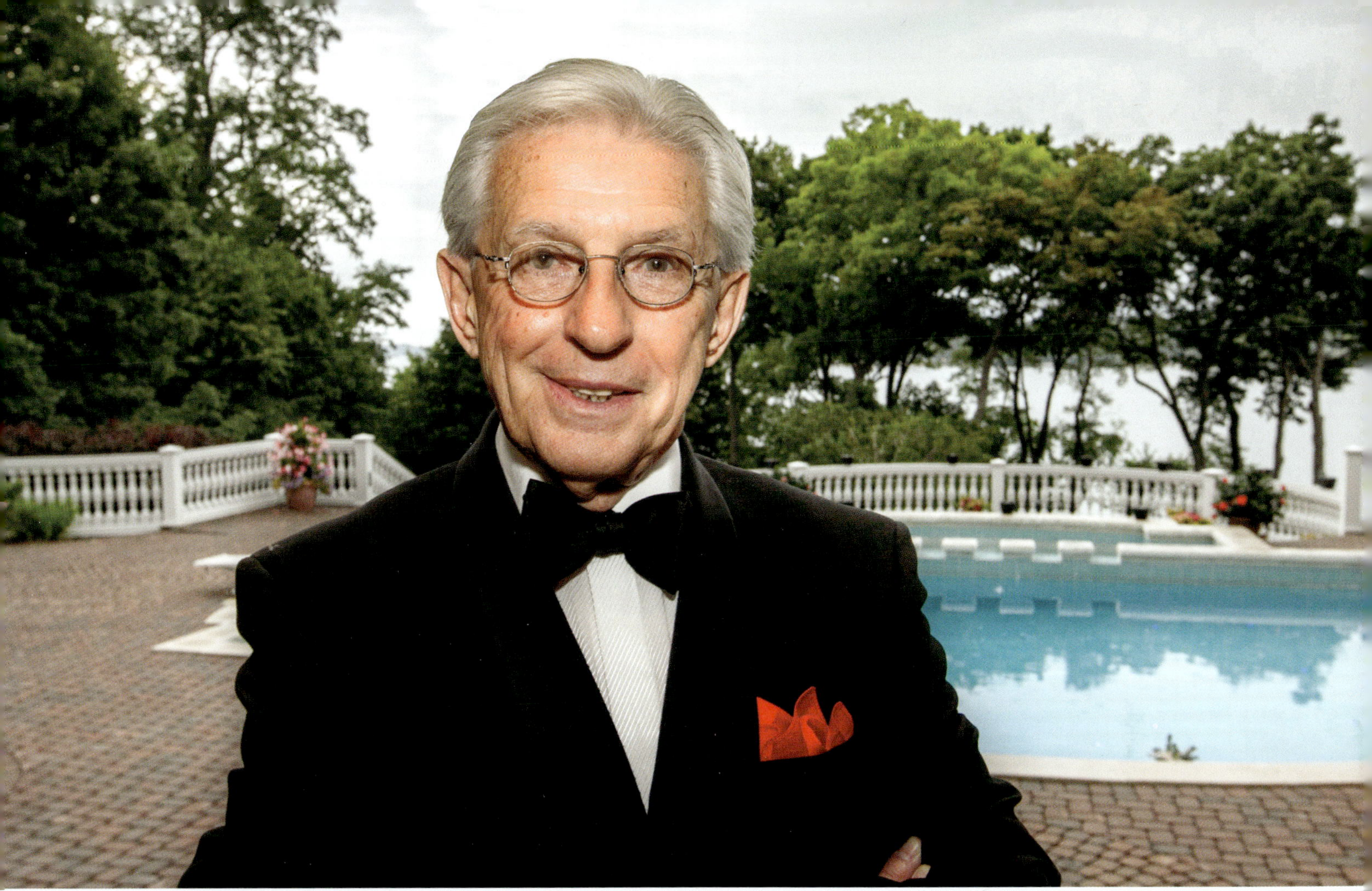

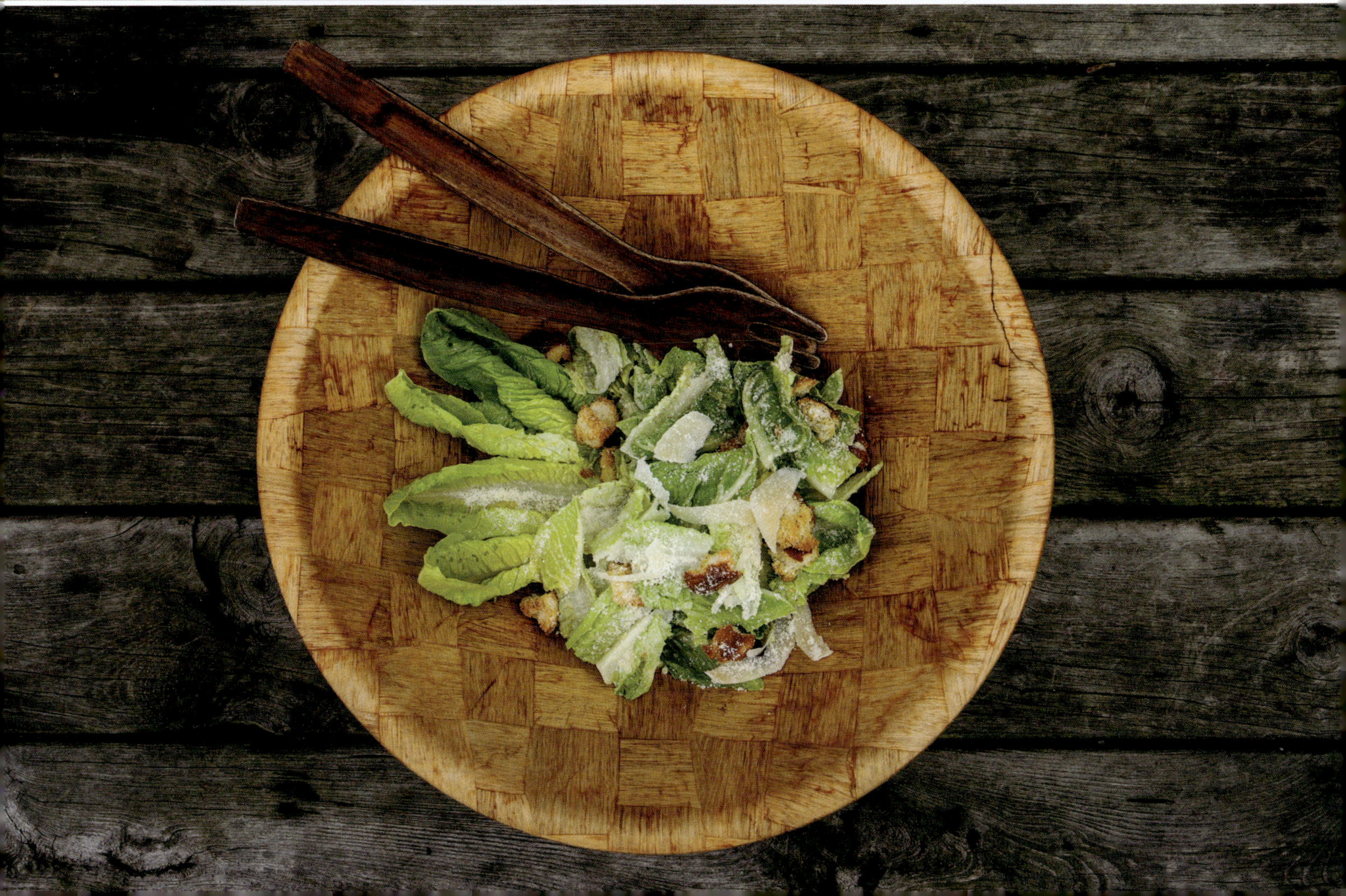

Colossal Sea Scallops Au Gratin
With Mushrooms and Gruyére Cheese

I love the sweet, beautiful aroma of colossal sea scallops sautéing in a pan. You want to use a nice, jumbo scallop, we use U-10 count, meaning under 10 scallops to a pound. They are then gently sautéed and served with mushrooms, deglazed with Cognac, and topped with grated Gruyére cheese and gratinéed under the broiler.

SERVES 8

INGREDIENTS:

16 sea scallops, (U-10 ct.)

½ cup all-purpose flour

Chef John's Signature Seasoning, to taste

½ tsp curry powder

⅛ Cayenne pepper

4 Tbsp butter

4 Tbsp olive oil

1 lemon

1 cup onion, chopped

2 cups mushrooms, quartered

¼ cup Cognac

⅔ cup white wine

¼ cup bread crumbs

2 Tbsp butter, melted

½ cup Gruyére cheese, grated

PREPARATION:

1. Mix the flour, Chef John's Signature Seasoning, curry powder, and Cayenne pepper together in a pan.
2. Dredge the scallops in the seasoned flour mixture.
3. Melt the butter and olive oil in a large sauté pan over medium-high heat. Add the scallops to the butter and olive oil and sauté them, turning once, until they are golden brown on both sides, about 2 minutes each side. Transfer to a platter, squeeze fresh lemon over scallops and set aside.
4. Add the onions to the sauté pan and sauté over medium-high heat for 2-3 minutes. Then add the mushrooms and sauté an additional 3-4 minutes.
5. Deglaze the pan with Cognac, being careful to ignite the alcohol vapors; let vapors burn out and add white wine and reduce by half. Add Chef John's Signature Seasoning.
6. Divide the scallops and mushroom sauce between 8 scallop shells or small ovenproof serving dishes.
7. Mix together the bread crumbs, melted butter, and Gruyére cheese; divide and spoon the mixture evenly over each dish of scallops.
8. Place the dishes under the broiler and cook until the scallop mixture is hot, bubbly, and browned on top.

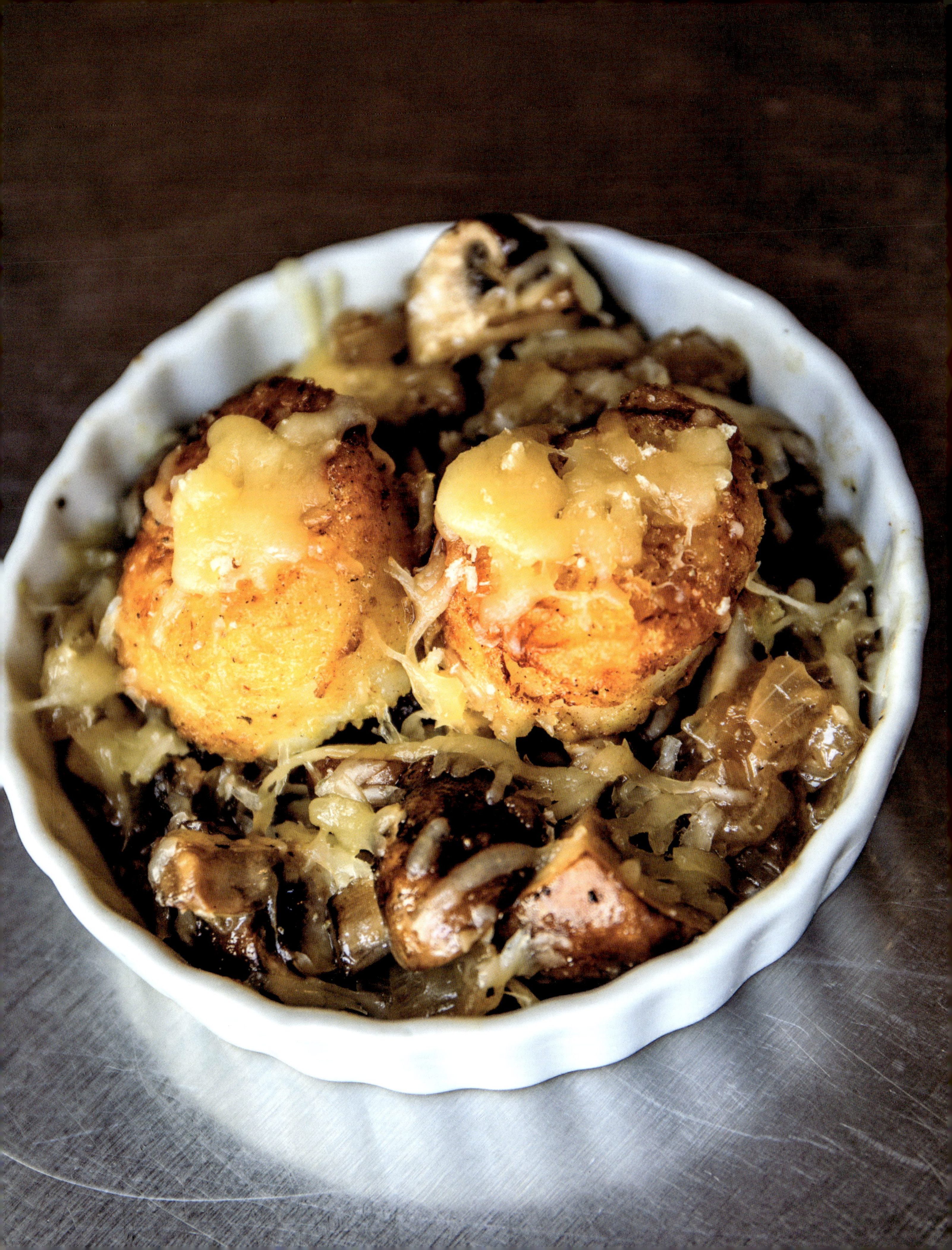

Roast Turkey Breast Wellington

Years ago, the classic rendition of this dish would be to use roast tenderloin of beef, but we wanted to update this and make it a lighter style using boneless, skinless turkey breast. The great thing about this dish is, if you are having a holiday dinner party, you can prepare the individual Wellington ahead of time and then bake them while you are enjoying time with your guests. The turkey stays very moist within the puff pastry, and the honey mustard and mushroom duxelle adds a wonderful complexity to this classic dish.

SERVES 12

INGREDIENTS:

2 puff pastry sheets

12 turkey breast medallions, 4 oz each

Chef John's Signature Seasoning, to taste

2 Tbsp olive oil

2 whole eggs, beaten

1 Tbsp water

2 large egg yolks, beaten

2 Tbsp butter

1 medium onion, finely chopped

2 cups mushrooms, sliced ⅛ inch

1 Tbsp fresh herbs, chopped (parsley, thyme and oregano)

¼ cup honey mustard

PREPARATION:

1. Preheat oven to 375°F.
2. Thaw the pastry sheet at room temperature for 40 minutes or until it's easy to handle.
3. Slice roasted turkey breasts into 4 oz pieces. Season turkey breasts with Chef John's Signature Seasoning.
4. In a medium sauté pan, heat 2 Tbsp olive oil. Sear turkey breasts 3-4 minutes until golden brown on both sides. Let rest.
5. In large sauté pan, heat the butter over medium-high heat. Add the onion and sauté for 2 minutes; add mushrooms and cook until tender. Add the fresh herbs and cook until the liquid is evaporated, stirring often.
6. Mix whole eggs and water together in small bowl.
7. Unfold the pastry sheets on a lightly floured surface. Roll out pastry and flip over to make sure it is not sticking. Cut each sheet of pastry into six even squares. Brush the edges of pastry sheet with egg and water mixture.
8. Place turkey in center of puff pastry square. Spoon tsp of honey mustard on top of the turkey breast. Spoon the mushroom mixture over top of the honey mustard on turkey breasts making sure it is flat.
9. Starting at the long sides, fold the pastry over the turkey.
10. Place seam side down on a baking sheet. Tuck the ends under to seal. Brush the pastry with egg yolks.
11. Bake for 25 minutes or until pastry is golden brown.

Serving Suggestion: Serve with fresh Sautéed Vegetables (see recipe on page 198) and Beef Stock Reduction (see recipe on page 197).

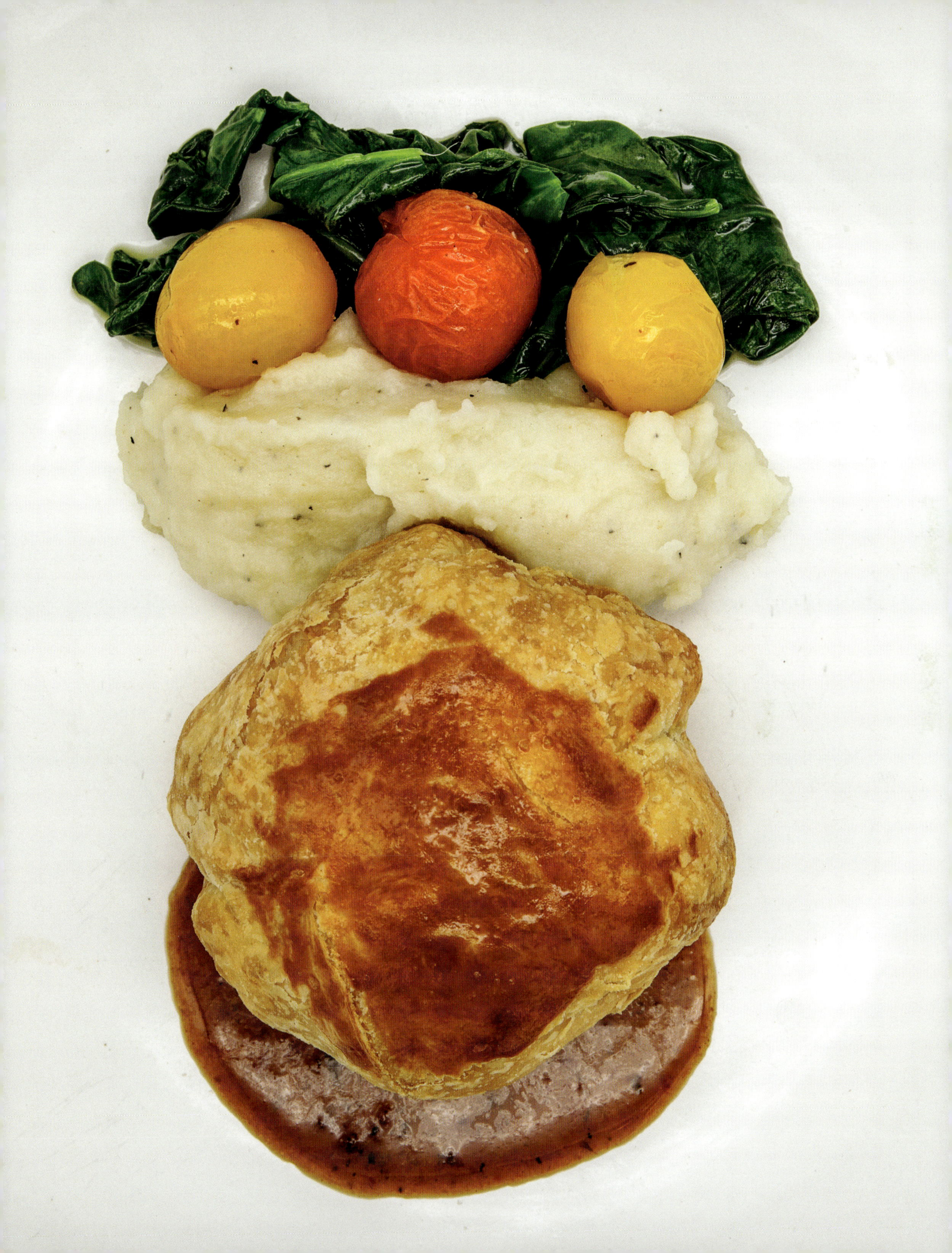

CRISPY DUCK AND MUSHROOM NAPOLEON
WITH CRUMBLED GOAT AND BLUE CHEESES, PORT WINE REDUCTION

This was a signature appetizer we served at the French Country Inn and was also featured in Bon Appétit *magazine. Using a very lean duck breast that is scored allows the fat to render out of the skin. The duck breast is then sliced and layered Napoleon style with crispy wontons, a Portobella Port wine reduction, crumbled Goat and Blue Cheeses, and finished off with frizzled leeks.*

SERVES 8

INGREDIENTS:

4 boneless duck breasts, 6 oz each

2 oz butter, unsalted

1 Tbsp garlic, chopped

¼ cup green onions, chopped

4 cups Portobella mushrooms, sliced ¼ inch

8 oz Port wine

1 cup stock, beef and chicken

1 Tbsp parsley, chopped

16 wonton wraps, fried

½ cup Frizzled Leeks (see recipe on page 202)

½ cup Goat and Blue Cheese crumbles

Chef John's Signature Seasoning, to taste

PREPARATION:

1. Score skin on duck breast and sear both sides in medium hot pan, 3-4 minutes.
2. Reserve duck breast, let rest, and remove ¾ of fat from pan.
3. Add butter, garlic, green onions, and sauté for 1 minute, then add mushrooms. Sauté an additional 4 minutes.
4. Deglaze with Port wine; add stock and chopped parsley. Let reduce in half; season with Chef John's Signature Seasoning.

PLATING:

1. Slice duck breast into six slices each and reserve. Place a few mushrooms in center of plate
2. Top with Wonton and add more mushrooms
3. Arrange 3 slices duck breast on top of mushrooms.
4. Repeat steps 2 and 3 while placing 2 slices of duck on top layer.
5. Drizzle pan sauce reduction on duck breast.
6. Garnish with crumbled cheeses and Frizzled Leeks.

CRISPY WONTON

INGREDIENTS:

Wonton wraps, 3 inches

Canola oil

PREPARATION:

1. Slice Wonton diagonally.
2. Heat oil to 335°F.
3. Fry Wontons in oil until light golden brown. Be careful as Wonton will continue to cook and get darker after removed from oil.
4. Drain on absorbent paper towel.

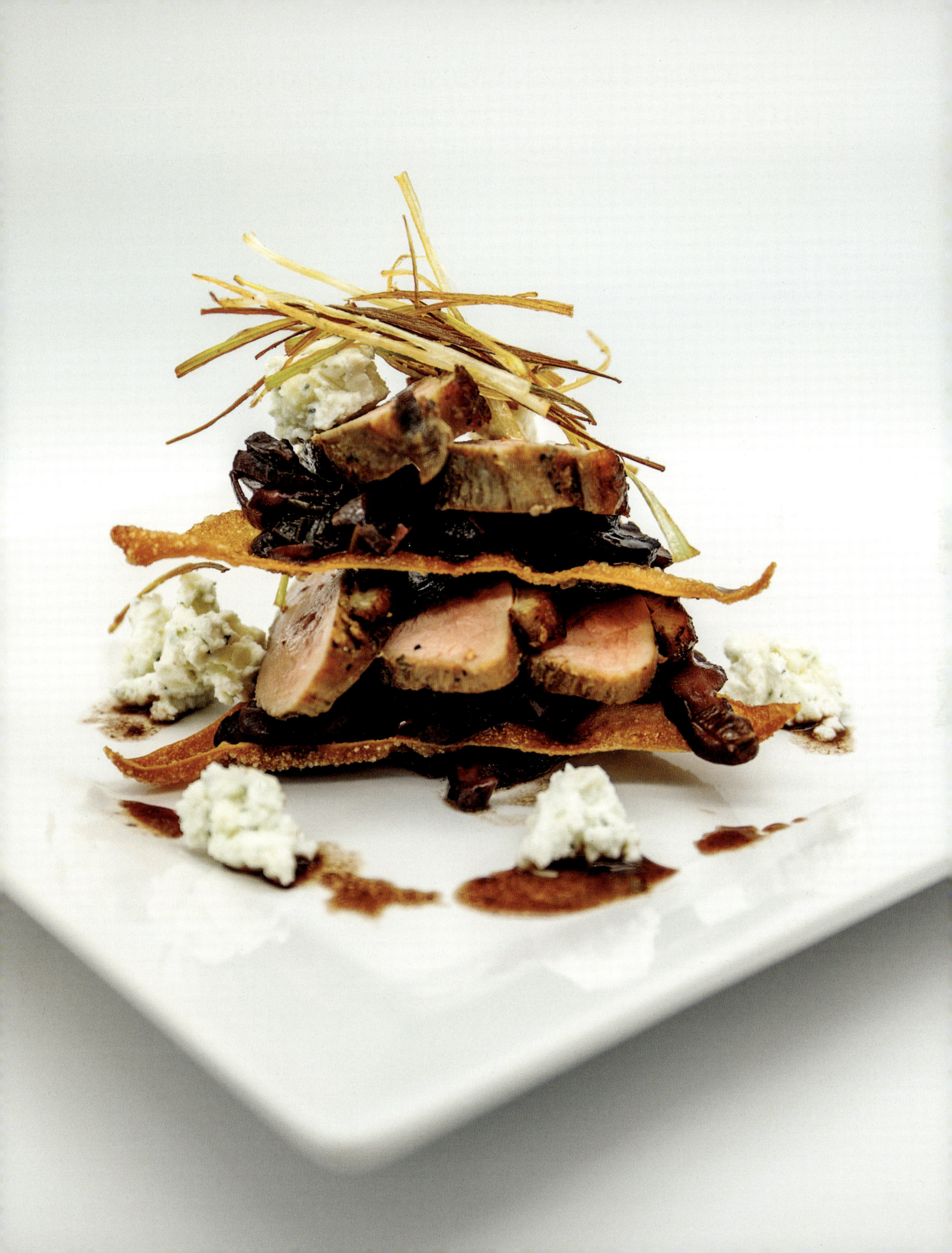

STEAK DIANE
WITH BRANDY MUSHROOM REDUCTION

This dish was ideally created to be featured tableside. The Filet Mignon would be pounded out to ½ inch thickness, and pan sautéed right in front of guests at their table. While at the table, mushrooms and shallots would be added and deglazed with brandy. The brandy ignites, so be careful, but it makes an exceptional presentation.

SERVES 10

INGREDIENTS:

10 Filet Mignon, 5 oz each

4 Tbsp butter

2 Tbsp olive oil

¼ cup shallots, chopped fine

1 tsp garlic, chopped fine

3 cups mushrooms, sliced ¼ inch

1 Tbsp Worcestershire sauce

2 Tbsp Dijon mustard

3 oz brandy

8 oz beef stock reduction

3 oz heavy cream

1 Tbsp parsley, chopped

Chef John's Signature Seasoning, to taste

PREPARATION:

1. With a meat tenderizer, pound filets to a ½-inch thickness.
2. In a large 12-inch sauté pan, heat 2 Tbsp butter and olive oil over medium heat.
3. Season steaks and sear over high heat without crowding pan (2-3 minutes each side). Remove from pan and let cool to room temperature. Discard cooked butter/olive oil mixture.
4. Add remaining 2 Tbsp of butter and sauté the shallots and garlic for 2-3 minutes in the pan over medium-high heat.
5. Add mushrooms; sauté an additional 3 minutes. Deglaze the pan with brandy. Let the flame catch the brandy's vapors and ignite it. Swirl pan slightly and let the flame burn out.
6. Add the Worcestershire, Dijon mustard, and beef stock reduction; and let reduce in half.
7. Add heavy cream, parsley, and Chef John's Signature Seasoning.
8. Reduce until desired thickness.

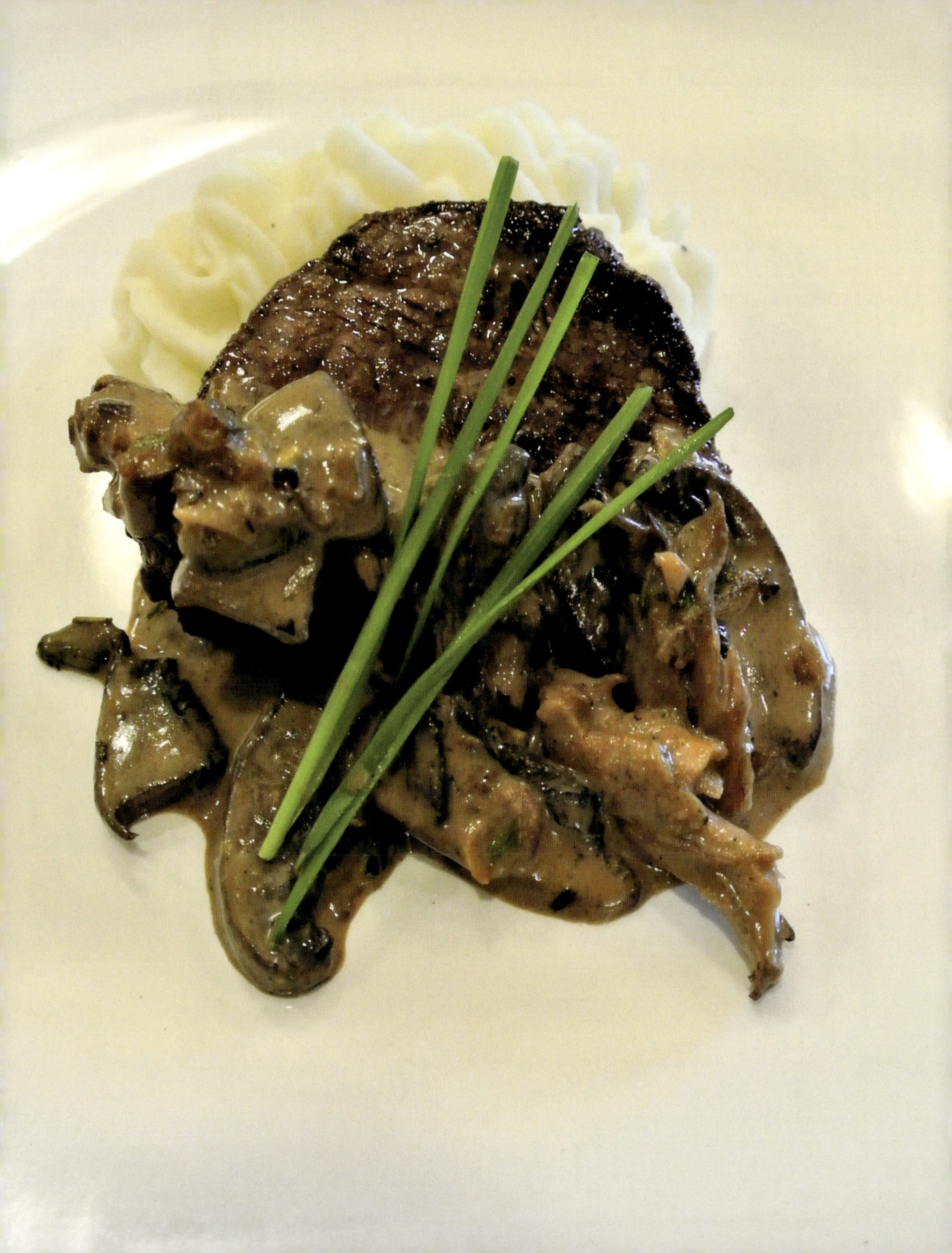

Stout Braised Prime Beef Short Ribs
With Tomatoes and Roasted Poblanos

This is a perfect entree for the Winter season. The prime beef short ribs are braised in the oven for 2-3 hours with "Mirepoix" and stout beer, such as Guinness. The collagen in the short ribs break down and becomes exceptionally tender. Served with Butter Whipped Potatoes and sautéed carrots, this is a comforting Winter dinner.

SERVES 8

INGREDIENTS:

- 2 fresh Poblano chilies, medium size
- 2 Tbsp pork fat or olive oil
- 5 lbs prime beef short ribs, boneless
- 1 large onion, medium dice
- 2 celery stalks, medium dice
- 2 carrots peeled, medium dice
- 4 cloves garlic, chopped
- 4 tomatoes, seeded and chopped
- 12 oz Stout beer
- 2 cups Beef Stock Reduction (see recipe on page 197)
- Chef John's Signature Seasoning, to taste
- 2 tsp fresh thyme, chopped
- 1 Tbsp fresh parsley, chopped

PREPARATION:

1. Preheat oven to 325°F.
2. Lay Poblano peppers directly on stove burner flame (or grill) over medium heat. Turn every minute or so until softened and charred, about 7-10 minutes. Remove from flame, place in pan, and cover with plastic wrap until cool enough to handle. Remove the skins, stems, and seeds while rinsing off. Slice into medium dice.
3. In a medium-large roasting pan, heat the pork fat or olive oil over medium-high heat. Cut the short ribs into 4-6 oz pieces. Lay the short ribs in a single, uncrowded layer, working in batches if necessary.
4. When richly browned on one side, about 5 minutes, turn them over and brown the other side, 3-5 minutes more. Remove short ribs from pan and let rest.
5. Set roasting pan back on the stove and reduce the heat to medium. Add the onions, celery, carrots to cook, stirring frequently, until golden, about 7 minutes. Add the garlic and stir for another minute, then add the tomatoes. Stir occasionally until the tomatoes have softened.
6. Add beer, beef stock reduction, and stir in the Poblano peppers.
7. Nestle the browned meat into the braising liquid, spooning some of it over the top. Cover the pan and set in the oven.
8. After 2 hours, check the meat; it should be fork-tender. If not, re-cover and braise an extra 15 minutes or so.
9. Remove the meat to a warm serving platter.
10. Strain the sauce into a smaller container and press out the vegetables from braising liquid. Spoon off fat from top of liquid.
11. Taste the sauce; season with herbs and Chef John's Signature Seasoning.
12. Ladle braising liquid over short ribs.

Note: "Mirepoix" is a blend of diced onion, carrots, and celery.

Serving Suggestion: Butter Whipped Potatoes (see recipe on page 200) with Blanched and Sautéed Carrots (see recipe on page 198).

APPENDIX

SAUCES AND CREAMS 194
Three Mustard Sauce • Hollandaise Sauce
Chantilly Cream • Crème Anglaise
Berry Coulis

STOCKS 197
Chicken Stock • Beef Stock Reduction

VEGETABLES 198
Quick Sautéed Vegetables • Blanched and Sautéed Vegetables
Roasted Whole Beets • Grilled Corn

POTATOES 200
Butter Whipped Potatoes • Black Garlic Whipped Potatoes
Dijon Whipped Potatoes • Wasabi Whipped Potatoes
Crispy Hash Browns

BASICS 201
Pasta Dough • Frizzled Leeks
Saffron Basmati Rice • Wisconsin Cheddar Baskets

CULINARY TERMS 204

CULINARY CONVERSIONS 205

Three Mustard Sauce

YIELDS: 3 CUPS
INGREDIENTS:

3 Tbsp Dijon mustard

3 Tbsp honey mustard

3 Tbsp whole grain mustard

2 Tbsp white wine

1 Tbsp white wine vinegar

12 oz half and half

6 oz heavy cream

Chef John's Signature Seasoning, to taste

PREPARATION:

1. Whisk all ingredients together in a saucepan.
2. Bring to a boil and let simmer for 20 minutes.

Hollandaise Sauce and Variations

YIELDS: 1 ¼ CUPS OR ENOUGH FOR 6-8 MAIN-COURSE SERVINGS
INGREDIENTS:

6 Tbsp water

6 egg yolks

1 lb butter, clarified (about ⅔ cup clarified)

Worcestershire sauce, to taste

Tabasco, to taste

White pepper, to taste

2 Tbsp fresh lemon juice

PREPARATION:

1. Combine the water and egg yolks in a Windsor pan or metal bowl set over a saucepan of barely simmering water.
2. Whisk slowly at first until the mixture froths up, then whisk rapidly until you see deep traces on the bottom of the pan.
3. Immediately remove the mixture from the heat. Whisk in butter 1 Tbsp at a time.
4. Season with Worcestershire, Tabasco, and white pepper.
5. Whisk fresh lemon juice into the finished sauce.

START WITH THE HOLLANDAISE SAUCE RECIPE TO CREATE THESE VARIATIONS:

BÉARNAISE SAUCE:
Combine ⅓ cup white wine vinegar; 1 shallot, minced; 5 cracked black peppercorns; 3 tarragon sprigs, chopped; and simmer until reduced to 2 Tbsp liquid. Add into the finished Hollandaise Sauce.

TOMATO BÉARNAISE SAUCE (SAUCE CHORON):
Cook ½ cup tomato paste over medium heat, reducing until very condensed (about ⅓ cup). Whisk into the Béarnaise Sauce.

ORANGE HOLLANDAISE (SAUCE MALTAISE):
This classic sauce is ideal for asparagus. Remove ¼ of the zest from an orange. Squeeze juice from the orange and strain into a saucepan and simmer until the juice is reduced to about 2 Tbsp. Whisk the reduced juice and zest into the finished Hollandaise Sauce.

HOLLANDAISE SAUCE WITH WHIPPED CREAM (SAUCE MOUSSELINE):
This luxurious sauce is delicious on seafood. Whip ½ cup heavy cream to medium peaks. Just before serving, fold the cream into the Hollandaise Sauce.

Chantilly Cream

YIELDS: 2 CUPS

INGREDIENTS:

2 cups heavy cream

1 tsp vanilla extract

3 Tbsp powdered sugar

PREPARATION:

1. Put cream in the chilled bowl of an mixer fitted with the whisk attachment and beat until soft peaks begin to form.
2. Add vanilla and sugar, continue whipping until firm peaks form.
3. Cover and refrigerate until serving.

Crème Anglaise

YIELDS: 3 CUPS

INGREDIENTS:

1 cup milk

1 cup heavy cream

½ Vanilla Bean split lengthwise

6 large egg yolks, whites reserved for another use

⅓ cup sugar

PREPARATION:

1. Prepare Vanilla Bean by using the tip of a paring knife to split the Vanilla Bean in half lengthwise, scrape the little seeds from each half of the bean pod.
2. In a saucepan, combine the milk, heavy cream, and Vanilla Bean seeds, and bring to a simmer over medium heat.
3. In a second bowl, whisk together the egg yolks and sugar for about 2 minutes, or until pale yellow.
4. Remove the milk/cream mixture from the heat and while whisking, gradually pour about ⅓ of the hot cream into the egg yolk mixture, continue to whisk the mixture.
5. Return the combined mixtures to the saucepan and stir until well mixed.
6. Return the pan to medium-low heat and cook, stirring constantly with a wooden spoon, for about 8-10 minutes, or until the ripples disappear and are replaced by smooth, silky waves.
7. Don't let the mixture come to a boil or it will curdle.
8. Remove from the heat, place in an ice bath, and continue to stir for a couple of minutes, so the heat retained in the pan doesn't cause the yolks to curdle.
9. Pass through fine mesh strainer, let cool, and refrigerate.

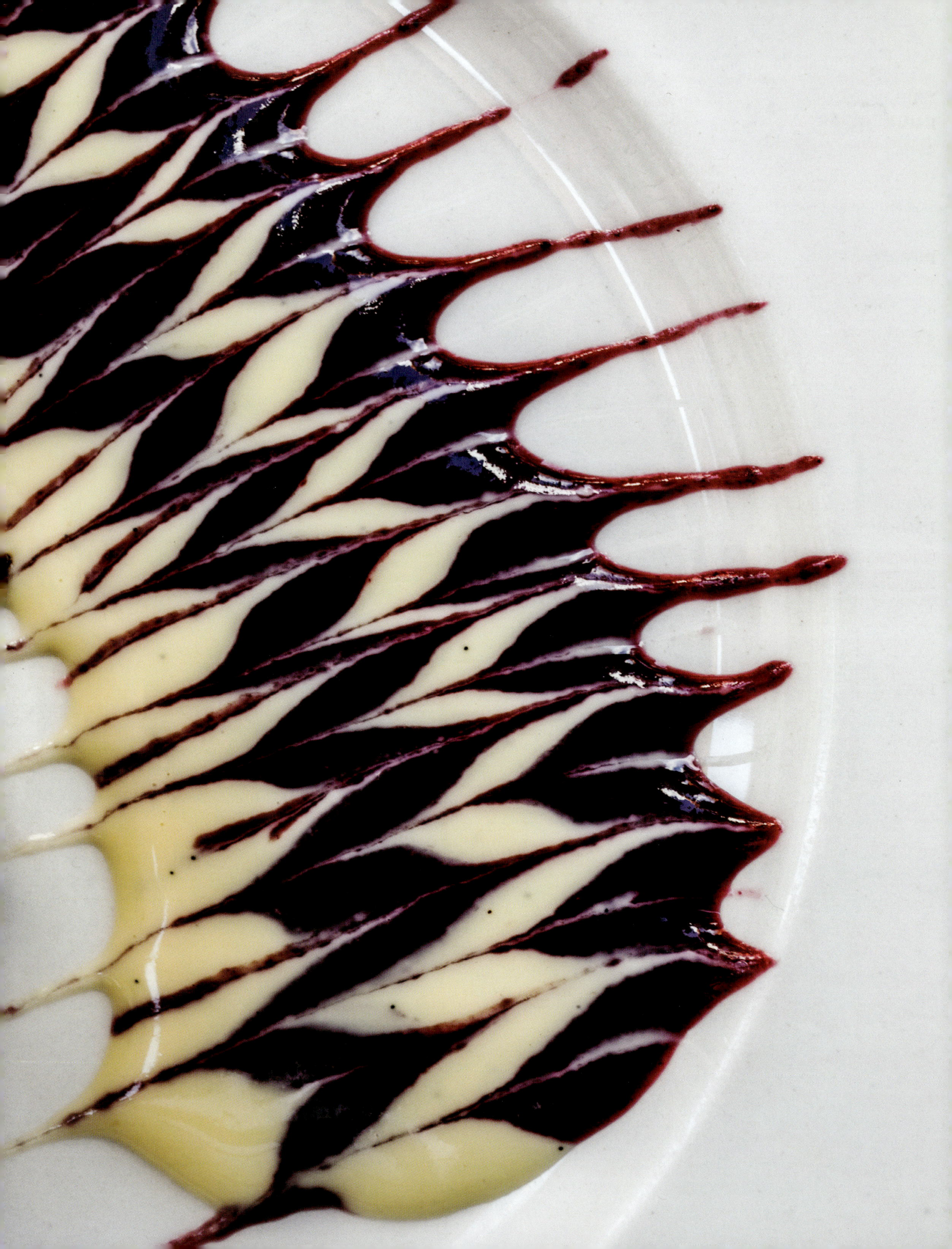

Berry Coulis

YIELDS: 3 CUPS

INGREDIENTS:

4 cups fresh or frozen mixed berries

¾ cup granulated sugar

1-2 Tbsp lemon juice

PREPARATION:

1. In a medium saucepan, add berries, granulated sugar, and 1 Tbsp of lemon juice.
2. Bring mixture to a simmer until sugar dissolves, about 10 minutes. Add more sugar or lemon juice if desired.
3. Puree berry mixture with food processor or immersion blender until smooth.
4. Strain seeds with fine sieve.
5. Cool and place in squirt bottle or container.

Chicken Stock

YIELDS: 1 GALLON

INGREDIENTS:

6 quarts water

2 chicken carcasses, bones

1 large carrot, chopped

2 large celery ribs, large chop

1 yellow onion, quartered

10 black peppercorns, whole

2 bay leaves

PREPARATION:

1. Cut up chicken carcasses (fit snuggly into pot) and cover with water.
2. Add carrot, celery, onion, bay leaves, and peppercorns.
3. Bring to a boil and reduce to low simmer, partially covered, 4-6 hours.
4. Continually scrape off the foam and fat from the top of stock.
5. Strain stock through fine mesh strainer to remove solids.
6. Cool stock before refrigerating or freezing.

Beef Stock Reduction

YIELDS: 1 GALLON

INGREDIENTS:

5-6 lbs veal and/or beef bone mixture

3 cloves garlic, whole

3 large celery ribs, large chop

3 large carrots, large chop

3 yellow onion, quartered

1 can (6 oz) tomato paste

10 black peppercorns, whole

2 bay leaves

1 bunch fresh parsley

3 cups red wine

6 quarts water

PREPARATION:

1. Preheat oven to 395°F
2. Place veal and beef bones, carrots, celery, onion, and garlic in large roasting pan and coat with tomato paste. Roast and brown bones and vegetables in oven for about 30-45 minutes. Remove bones and veggies from roasting pan. Place in a 4-5 gallon pot.
3. Deglaze the roasting pan with red wine and remove the browned roasted bits that may be on the bottom or sides of pot.
4. Add the wine and drippings to the browned beef bones and vegetables. Fill the pot with 6 quarts of water, making sure the contents are covered by 1-2 inches.
5. Add bay leaves, black peppercorns, and parsley; bring to a boil and reduce to low simmer, partially covered, 4-6 hours.
6. Continually scrape off the foam and fat from the top of stock.
7. Strain stock through fine mesh strainer to remove solids.
8. Cool stock before refrigerating or freezing.

Note: Veal bones contain more gelatin than beef bones.

Quick Sautéed Vegetables

YIELDS: 8 SERVINGS

INGREDIENTS:

24 spears fresh asparagus or 24 slices zucchini/yellow Squash

1 Tbsp Orange Extra Virgin Olive Oil

1 Tbsp White Peach Balsamic

Chef John's Signature Seasoning, to taste

PREPARATION:

1. Rinse asparagus; snap off and discard tough stem ends. Peel ends 3 inches up stalk. If using squash, slice into ¼ inch slices on the bias.
2. In 12-inch sauté pan, heat Orange EVOO to medium-hot, add vegetables, and sauté for 2-3 minutes. Deglaze with White Peach Balsamic. This will in turn steam the vegetables. Then let balsamic reduce to create a glaze to be drizzled over vegetables while serving.
3. Season with Chef John's Signature Seasoning.

Blanched and Sautéed Vegetables

YIELDS: 8 SERVINGS, PER VEGETABLE

INGREDIENTS:

24 Brussels sprouts or 8 broccoli spears or 24 carrots 5 inches long or 8 bunches cauliflower or 40 each green beans

3 quarts boiling water

1 Tbsp kosher salt

1 Tbsp Orange Extra Virgin Olive Oil

1 Tbsp White Peach Balsamic

Chef John's Signature Seasoning, to taste

PREPARATION:

1. Boil vegetables 4 minutes in salted boiling water. Remove and shock in an ice bath to stop the cooking and keep the vegetables' bright color. Drain vegetables and pat very dry.
2. In 12-inch sauté pan heat Orange EVOO to medium-hot, add vegetable, and sauté for 2-3 minutes.
3. Deglaze with White Peach Balsamic. This will in turn steam the vegetable. Then let balsamic reduce to create a glaze to be drizzled over vegetable while serving.
4. Season with Chef John's Signature Seasoning.

Roasted Whole Beets

YIELDS: 8 SERVINGS

INGREDIENTS:

4 beets, medium size

1 Tbsp extra virgin olive oil

¼ cup water

Chef John's Signature Seasoning, to taste

PREPARATION:

1. Preheat oven to 395°F.
2. Coat beets in pan with EVOO, water, and Chef John's Signature Seasoning; cover and roast for 50-60 minutes. Remove from oven and let cool. Wash skins off of beet and dice into a small dice, ¼ inch.
3. Sauté beets in EVOO for 2-3 minutes and season with Chef John's Signature Seasoning.

Grilled Corn

YIELDS: 8 SERVINGS

INGREDIENTS:

4 ears of corn, husked

1 Tbsp butter

Chef John's Signature Seasoning, to taste

PREPARATION:

1. Grill husked corn on hot grill for 2 minutes on each side, for a total of 8 minutes.
2. Let cool slightly, then cut kernels off of cob.
3. Sauté corn in pan with butter and season with Chef John's Signature Seasoning.

Butter Whipped Potatoes and Variations

YIELDS: 4 CUPS

INGREDIENTS:

3 potatoes peeled, medium dice

½ cup butter (1 stick), cut into pieces

¾ cup milk

Chef John's Signature Seasoning, to taste

1 Tbsp kosher salt

PREPARATION:

1. Add the potatoes to a large saucepan and fill with enough cold water to cover potatoes by 2 inches.
2. Add 1 Tbsp of kosher salt to the water and bring to a simmer over medium-high heat. Simmer until the potatoes are tender.
3. Drain well and using a ricer, rice back to the pan.
4. Place the pan on a very low flame for 1 minute to dry the potatoes.
5. Heat the butter and milk in saucepan.
6. Add to potatoes with Chef John's Signature Seasoning; and mix until smooth and fluffy.

START WITH THE BUTTER WHIPPED POTATOES RECIPE TO CREATE THESE VARIATIONS:

ROASTED BLACK GARLIC WHIPPED:
Mince 2 cloves of black garlic and add to the heated butter and milk. Continue by adding mixture to the potatoes and blend until smooth.

DIJON WHIPPED:
Add 2 Tbsp of finely chopped tarragon and 3 Tbsp of Dijon mustard to the heated butter and milk. Continue by adding mixture to the potatoes and blending until smooth.

WASABI WHIPPED:
Add 2 Tbsp of Wasabi powder to the heated butter and milk. Continue by adding mixture to the potatoes and blending until smooth.

Crispy Hash Browns

YIELDS: 8 ORDERS

INGREDIENTS:

1 medium leek, thinly sliced ½-inch rounds

3 medium baking potatoes, peeled

2 cloves garlic, thinly sliced

Chef John's Signature Seasoning, to taste

¼ cup olive oil

¼ cup butter

PREPARATION:

1. Preheat oven to 375°F.
2. Grate the potatoes on the large holes of a box grater.
3. Rinse well in cold water and dry thoroughly.
4. In a bowl, mix together the potatoes, garlic, and leeks. Add Chef John's Signature Seasoning, to taste.
5. Cook the potatoes in two 10-inch non-stick sauté pans. Heat the oil and butter to medium-high.
6. Add potato mixture and reduce the heat to medium. Cook about 10 minutes until golden brown.
7. Invert onto a sheet pan, place back in pan for about 5 more minutes.
8. Finish in oven for 10 minutes. Slice into 8 wedges and sprinkle with Chef John's Signature Seasoning.

Pasta Dough

YIELDS: 4 ORDERS

INGREDIENTS:

2 large eggs

2 cups flour

1 Tbsp olive oil

¼ cup water

Chef John's Signature Seasoning, to taste

PREPARATION:

1. Put eggs, olive oil, water, and Chef John's Signature Seasoning in a bowl. Add 1 cup of flour and mix with a fork until a dough is formed.
2. Place ½ cup of flour on a clean work surface. Place the dough on the floured work surface and knead approximately 6 turns, or until most of the flour is absorbed. Add more flour as needed.
3. Once finished, flour the dough and roll out with a rolling pin to approximately ¼ inch (be sure to check if rolled dough is as wide as pasta maker). Let rest for 1 hour.
4. Flour pasta maker and roll the dough through it, starting at notch 1.
5. After each pass through the pasta machine, be sure to re-flour the pasta sheet.

Serving Suggestions:

    For Linguine: Run dough through pasta maker 4 times, each time going up one notch on pasta maker.

    For Ravioli: Run dough through pasta maker 5 times, each time going up one notch on the pasta maker.

Frizzled Leeks

YIELDS: 1 CUP

INGREDIENTS:

1 leek

3 cups Canola oil

Chef John's Signature Seasoning, to taste

PREPARATION:

1. Slice white part of leek into 3-inch lengths, then into julienne match stick size. Rinse under cold water and dry thoroughly.
2. Heat Canola oil to 335°F.
3. Fry in oil until light golden brown.
4. Drain on absorbent paper and season with Chef John's Signature Seasoning.

Saffron Basmati Rice

YIELDS: 6 CUPS

INGREDIENTS:

2 cups Basmati rice

2 Tbsp butter

4 cups water

1 pinch Saffron threads

1 tsp turmeric

Chef John's Signature Seasoning, to taste

PREPARATION:

1. Preheat oven 350°F.
2. Coat rice in pan with butter, sauté until kernels turn pearl white.
3. Add Saffron; stir in. Add water and seasonings.
4. Bring to boil.
5. Cover and bake for 20 minutes.

Wisconsin Cheddar Baskets

YIELDS: 8

INGREDIENTS:

8 Tbsp Wisconsin Cheddar cheese, sharp and mild, grated

PREPARATION:

1. Preheat oven to 375°F.
2. Mix together both the grated sharp and mild cheeses.
3. Place 4 individual Tbsp of grated cheese on sheet pan or Silpat and spread out into 2-inch rounds.
4. Bake for 7 minutes.
5. Remove melted Cheddar cheese from Silpat; place hot cheese over silicon mold while pressing down on second silicon mold to form bowl.
6. Let cool.
7. Repeat.

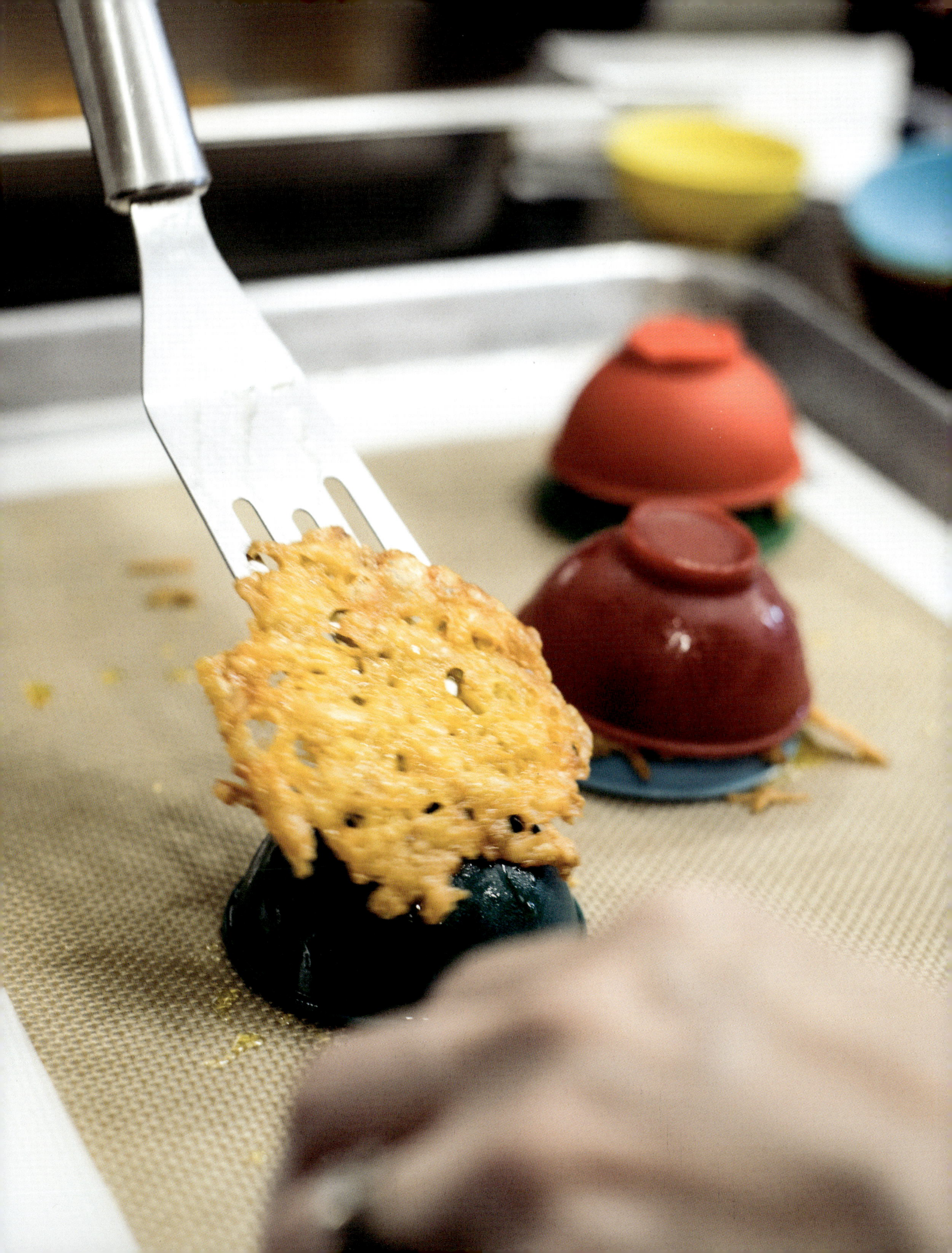

Culinary Terms

Baby Greens
A mixture of red oak leaf, arugula, frisee, and other small leafy, buttery, and spicy lettuces.

Balsamic Vinegar
A dark, sweet, mellow wine vinegar that is aged in a series of oak and hickory barrels. It is produced only in Modena, Italy. The older the vinegar, the sweeter and less acidic it will be. Aged Balsamic is available at Lake Geneva School of Cooking. Balsamic vinegar is a commercial product available at many local grocery stores.

Bisque
A soup based on crustaceans or a vegetable puree. It is classically thickened, pureed, and usually finished with cream.

Black Garlic
Heating whole bulbs of garlic over a low heat for a course of several weeks. Cloves turn dark and develop a sticky, date-like texture.

Blind Baking
The dough is topped with parchment paper then par baked with weights or dry beans to stop the dough from rising during baking. This helps the dough from rising and shrinking at the same time.

Brunoise
Very fine dice approximately 1/8-inch square.

Chiffonade
Fine strips, about 1/16-inch wide. Usually used in reference to leafy vegetables, which are rolled up and finely sliced.

Clarified Butter
Butter formed from which the milk solids and water has been removed, leaving pure butter-fat. Has a higher smoking point than whole butter.

Coddled Eggs
Eggs cooked in simmering water, in their shells, until the whites of the egg are set, approximately 2 minutes.

Coulis
Coulis is a very fine puree that is strained.

Deglaze
When foods have been sautéed or roasted, flavorful deposits and juices are left in the pan. Deglazing is the process of adding liquid (i.e., wine, brandy) to the pan and dissolving the flavorful deposits over heat.

Frenching
The act of exposing the tip of a rib bone by cutting away the fat and meat from the bone of a rib chop or protein.

Flambé
To ignite foods that have liquor or liqueur added. This is done for dramatic effect and to develop a rich flavor of the liqueur to the food without adding the alcohol.

Fortified Butter
An even mixture of butter and oil used to raise the smoking point while cooking, helping to not burn the butter.

Culinary Terms

Mirepoix
A blend of chopped or diced onions, carrots, and celery.

Mise en place
A French culinary term which means "putting in place" or "everything in it's place"

Pupu
An appetizer or hors d'oeuvres platter or presentation.

Singer
A French term that refers to the dusting of flour over ingredients that have been cooked in fat. When the flour is combined with the fat the two form a roux (fat and flour). The roux is cooked for a few minutes before adding a liquid to make a soup or sauce.

Truffles
A subterranean fungus that is highly prized for its pungent aroma and flavor. Olive oils that have been infused with the highly pungent truffle are available in gourmet shops.

Wasabi
A pungent green Japanese radish. Available in paste or powder form. The powder is mixed with water to produce a smooth sauce.

Culinary Conversions

Dash	Less than ⅛ tsp
3 tsp	1 Tbsp (½ fluid ounce)
4 Tbsp	¼ cup (2 fluid ounces)
8 Tbsp	½ cup (4 fluid ounces)
12 Tbsp	¾ cup (6 fluid ounces)
16 Tbsp	1 cup
1 cup	8 fluid ounces
2 cups	1 pint
2 pints	1 quart (approximately 1 liter)
4 quarts	1 gallon
16 ounces	1 pound (453.59 grams)
1 gallon	4 quarts
4 quarts	8 pints
8 pints	16 cups
16 cups	128 ounces

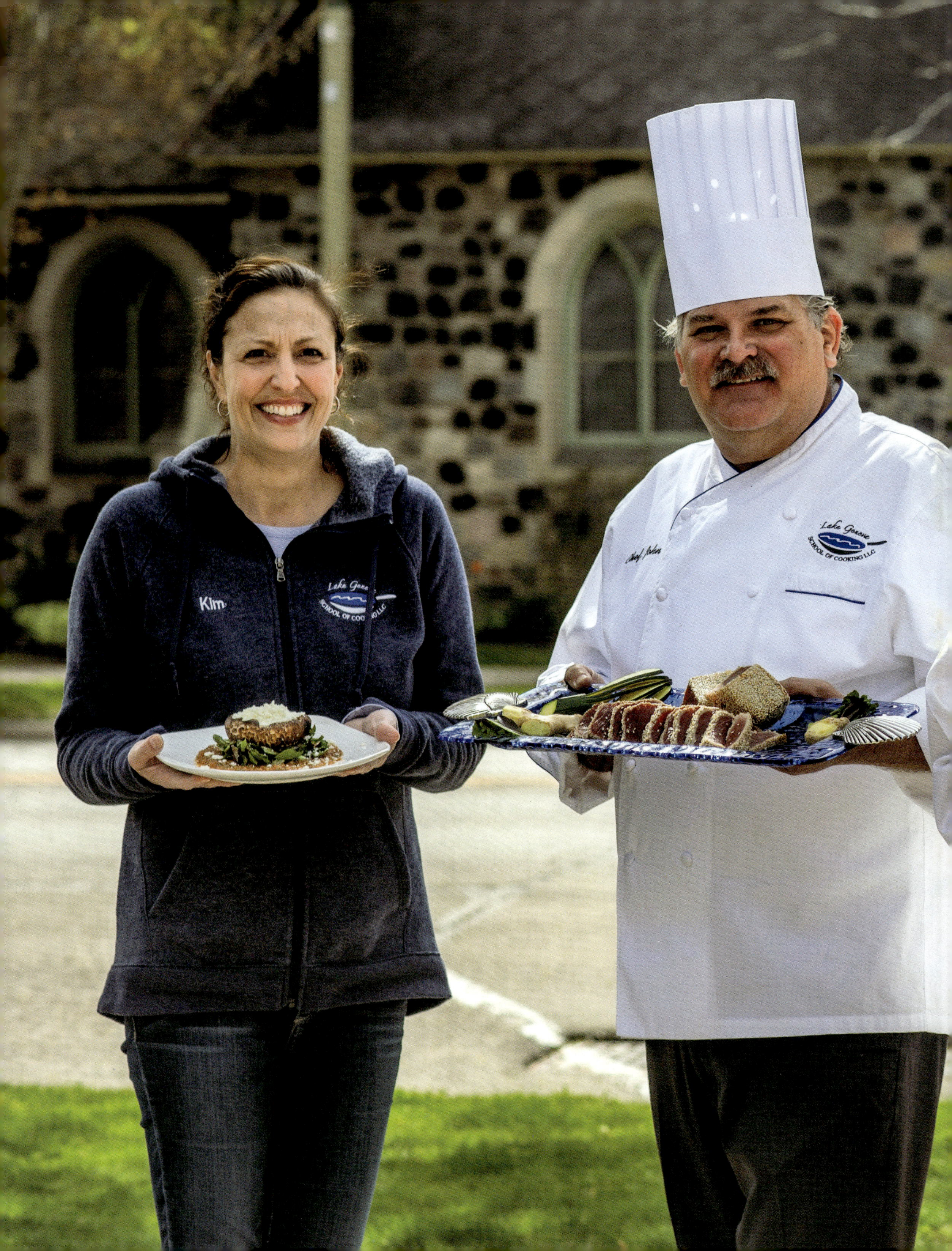
Kim
Lake Geneva
SCHOOL OF COOKING LLC

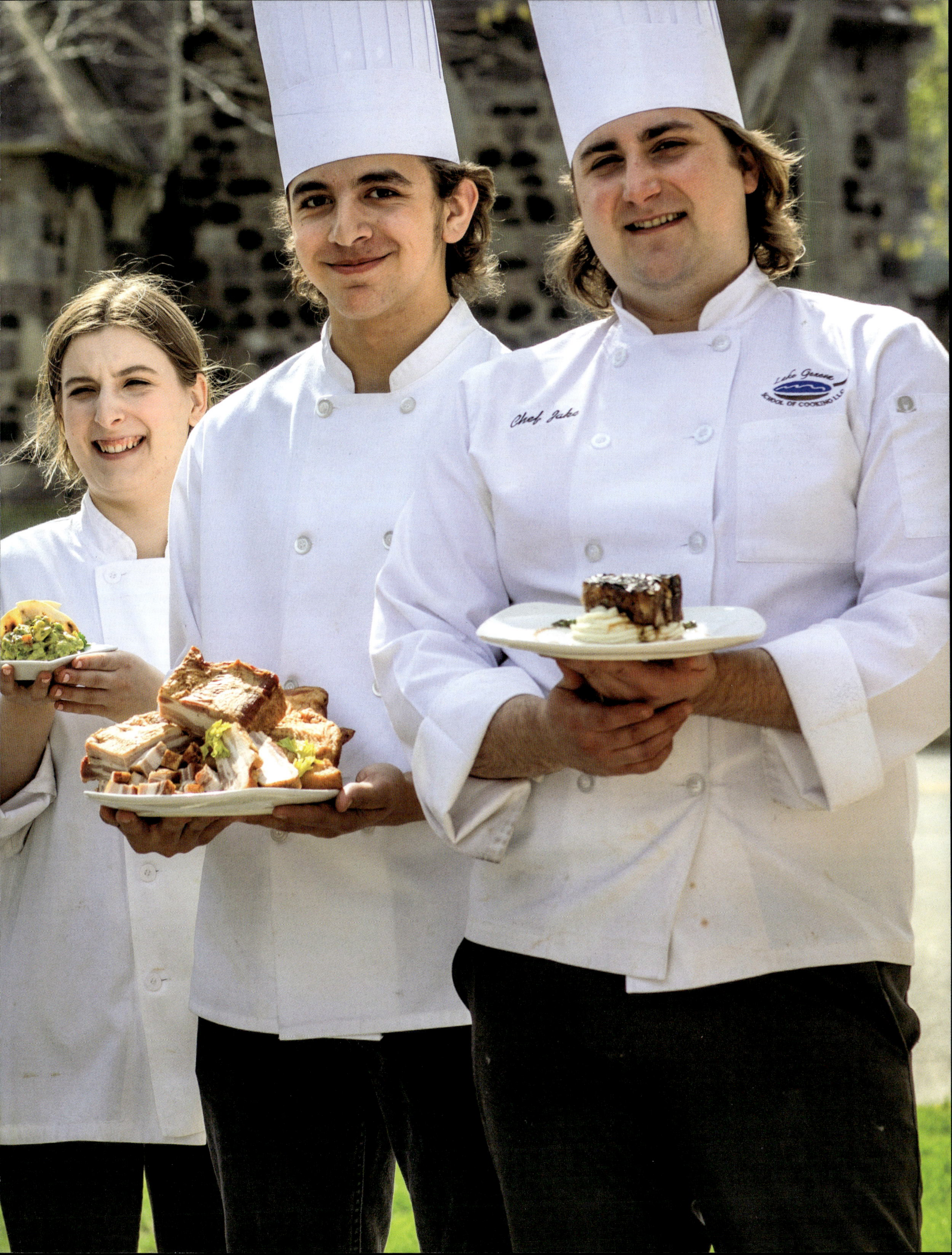
Chef Jake
Lake Geneva
SCHOOL OF COOKING LLC

INDEX

Acorn Squash and Sage Bisque 122

"Ahi" Tuna Napoleon, Mackenna Anuhea 64

Apples with Walnuts and Raisins, Baked 140

Asparagus with Mediterranean Chopped Egg, Grilled 24

Asparagus with Prosciutto, Grilled 26

Baby Greens with Pecans and Smoked Bacon 128

BACON

Baby Greens with Pecans and Smoked Bacon 128

Wisconsin Wedge Salad, Wilson Farm Bacon 106

Balsamic Vegetables, Roasted 134

Banana Muffins, Tahitian Lanai 56

Bananas Foster 144

BEEF

Beef Short Ribs, Stout Braised Prime 182

Beef Stock Reduction 197

Beef, Blackened Tenderloin Crostini with Blue Cheese 40

Chateaubriand, Jacque's Kona Crusted 60

Filet Medallions with Red Wine Sauce 42

Filet Mignon with Roasted Balsamic Onions 92

Flat Iron Steak, Chef Jake's Grilled 134

Steak Diane with Brandy Mushroom Reduction 180

Beef Stock Reduction 197

Beet and Goat Cheese En Croute Salad 126

Beets, Roasted Whole 199

Beignet, Blue Cheese 20

Beignet, Cinnamon 20

Berries, Balsamic with White Chocolate Biscotti 94

Berry Coulis 197

BISQUE

Bisque, Acorn Squash and Sage 122

Bisque, Broccoli and Brie 168

Bisque, River Valley Ranch Mushroom 110

Clam Chowder, New England 156

French Onion Soup, Classic 166

Gumbo, Mardi Gras 170

Broccoli and Brie Bisque 168

Brownie, Kahlúa Espresso 188

Caesar Salad, Grilled 154

Caesar Salad, Jerry Pawlak's 172

Calamari, Pan Fried 30

Chantilly Cream 195

Chateaubriand, Jacque's Kona Crusted 60

Cheddar Baskets, Wisconsin 202

Cherry Tomatoes and Baby Greens 82

Chloe's Italian Sausage Gravy 158

CHICKEN

Chicken au Poivre, Grilled 84

Chicken Medallions with Sage and Prosciutto 130

Chicken Milanese 82

Chicken Stock 197

Chicken au Poivre, Grilled 84

Chicken Medallions with Sage
and Prosciutto 130

Chicken Milanese 82

Chicken Stock 197

CHOCOLATE

Berries, Balsamic with White
Chocolate Biscotti 94

Brownie, Kahlúa Espresso 188

Chocolate Grand Marnier Tart 186

Chocolate Midnight Truffle Cake 184

Chocolate Mousse, Grand Marnier
Dark Chocolate 98

Chocolate Pâté, Flourless 48

Clam Chowder, New England 156

Cobbler, Rhubarb Strawberry 44

Corn, Grilled 199

Crab Cakes, Sweet 28

Crème Anglaise 195

Crème Brûlée, Vanilla Bean 46

Deviled Soy Marinade 64

DUCK

Duck and Mushroom Napoleon, Crispy 178

Filet Medallion with Red Wine Sauce 42

Filet Mignon with Roasted
Balsamic Onions 92

Flat Iron Steak, Chef Jake's Grilled 134

French Onion Soup, Classic 166

Giambotta, Lake Geneva 160

Gnocchi, Homemade Potato 34

Gougeres, Smoked Gouda 20

Gumbo, Mardi Gras 170

Hash Browns, Crispy 201

Hollandaise Sauce 194

Italian Sausage, Homemade 150

LAMB

Lamb Dijonnaise, Pinn-Oak Ridge Farms
Rack of Lamb 116

Lamb Porterhouse, Pinn-Oak Ridge Farms 114

Leeks, Frizzled 202

Macadamia Nut Pesto 62

Mango Avocado Salsa, Aina Haina 58

Mushroom and Port Wine Reduction 60

Mushroom Bisque, River Valley Ranch 110

Mushroom Caps, Spinach Stuffed 124

Mustard Sauce, Three 194

Panzanella 78

Panko Crusted Goat Cheese En Croute 126

Pasta Dough 201

Pasta Shells Stuffed with
Three Cheeses 158

Pears, Gorgonzola Stuffed 142

POPOVERS

Beignet, Blue Cheese 20

Beignet, Cinnamon 20

Gougeres, Smoked Gouda 20

Popovers, Oktoberfest 20

Popovers, Parmigiano 18

Popovers, Queso 20

Toad in the Hole 152

PORK

Pork Rib Chop, Grilled Stuffed Frenched 90

Pork Schnitzel with Spätzle, Sautéed.............. 136

Pork Tenderloin with Apple
Brandy, Grilled 138

Portobellini, River Valley Ranch...................... 112

Pound Cake with White Balsamic Peaches,
Grilled.. 96

Ratatouille... 80

Ravioli, Spinach and Four Cheese 36

Rice, Saffron Basmati 202

Risotto Cakes, Henry Kekoa's Harvest 68

Roasted Red Peppers 40

SALAD

Asparagus with Mediterranean
Chopped Egg, Grilled.. 24

Asparagus with Prosciutto, Grilled 26

Baby Greens with Pecans and
Smoked Bacon 128

Beet and Goat Cheese
En Croute Salad 126

Caesar Salad, Grilled.. 154

Caesar Salad, Jerry Pawlak's........................... 172

Panzanella.. 78

Poached Egg Salad Lyonnaise,
Yuppie Hill 108

Wisconsin Wedge Salad, Wilson
Farm Bacon 106

Salad Lyonnaise, Yuppie Hill Poached Egg 108

SEAFOOD

"Ahi" Tuna Napoleon, Mackenna Anuhea 62

Calamari, Pan Fried 30

Clam Chowder, New England 156

Crab Cakes, Sweet.. 28

Gumbo, Mardi Gras 170

Salmon Fillet, Potato Crusted 132

Sea Scallop au Gratin, Colossal 174

Shrimp and Zucchini, Sautéed 86

Shrimp Briana Kaiulani with
Macadamia Nut Pesto...................................... 62

Shrimp Scampi, Colossal 32

Swordfish, Braised Steak Neapolitan................ 88

Sea Scallop au Gratin, Colossal 174

Shrimp and Zucchini, Sautéed......................... 86

Shrimp Briana Kaiulani with
Macadamia Nut Pesto...................................... 62

Shrimp Scampi, Colossal 32

Spätzel 136

Steak Diane with Brandy
Mushroom Reduction..................................... 180

Swordfish Steak Neapolitan, Braised.................. 88

Toad in the Hole 152

Tomato Basil Reduction 36

Turkey Breast Wellington, Roasted 176

Vegetables, Blanched and Sautéed 198

Vegetables, Sautéed 198

Wedge Salad, Wilson Farm
Bacon Wisconsin 106

White Bean Puree... 40

White Chocolate Biscotti 94

Zucchini Fontinella... 76

Henry Kekoa Lee
Future Executive Chef